On Deaf Ears

GEORGE C. EDWARDS III

On Deaf Ears

THE LIMITS OF THE BULLY PULPIT

Yale University Press
New Haven
& London

Published with assistance from the foundation established in memory of Philip Hamilton McMillan of the Class of 1894, Yale College.

Set in Sabon type by Keystone Typesetting, Inc. Printed in the United States of America by Sheridan Books, Chelsea, Michigan.

The Library of Congress has cataloged the hardcover edition as follows:
Edwards, George C. III
On deaf ears : the limits of the bully pulpit / George C. Edwards III.
p. cm.
Includes bibliographical references and index.
ISBN 0-300-10009-4 (cloth : alk. paper)
1. Communication in politics—United States. 2. Rhetoric—Political aspects—United States—History—20th century. 3. Presidents—United States—Public opinion. 4. Public opinion—United States. I. Title.
JA85.2.U6E38 2003 320.973′01′4—dc21 2003009047

A catalogue record for this book is available from the British Library.

The paper in this book meets the guidelines for permanence and durability of the Committee on Production Guidelines for Book Longevity of the Council on Library Resources.

ISBN-13: 978-0-300-11581-9 (pbk. : alk. paper)
ISBN-10: 0-300-11581-4 (pbk. : alk. paper)

10 9 8 7 6 5 4 3 2 1

To George and Julie Jordan

I can no other answer make but thanks,
And thanks, and ever thanks.
— *Twelfth-Night,* Act III, Scene 3

Contents

Part IV The Audience

Part V Conclusion

Preface

Much to the surprise of many political observers, George W. Bush launched a massive public relations campaign on behalf of his priority initiatives soon after taking office. At the core of this effort was the most extensive domestic travel schedule of any new president in American history. Bush spoke in twenty-nine states by the end of May, often more than once. The president also used his Saturday radio addresses to exhort members of the public to communicate to Congress their support for his tax cut and education plans.

It is one thing to go public. It is something quite different to succeed in moving public opinion. Table P.1 shows responses to Gallup Poll questions on the president's tax cut proposal. The results show that public opinion did not change in response to the president's efforts.

In the fall of 2002, the president's agenda included a possible war with Iraq. The administration stepped up its rhetorical efforts, and the president addressed the nation, the United Nations, and a host of smaller audiences. In response, public opinion barely moved, as the results in Table P.2 show.

The president's lack of success in leading the public was not unusual for any president, and it poses an interesting conundrum. Modern presidents choose to engage in a permanent campaign for the public's support as their core strategy for governing. Yet presidents usually fail in their efforts to move the public to support them and their policies. If going public does not work,

Table P.1. Public Support for Bush Tax Cut

Poll Date	Favor	Oppose	No Opinion
February 9–11, 2001	56%	34%	10%
February 19–21, 2001	53	30	17
March 5–7, 2001	56	34	10
April 20–22, 2001	56	35	9

Note: Gallup Poll, "Based on what you have read or heard, do you favor or oppose the federal income tax cuts George W. Bush has proposed?"

are presidents both wasting their time and losing the opportunity to pursue more profitable approaches to governing? The answers to these questions have broad implications for governing. My goal is to investigate the ability of presidents to move the public and thus the utility of the permanent campaign for governing.

Not long after becoming director of the Center for Presidential Studies, I turned to a group of talented scholars at Texas A&M and asked them to begin a Program in Presidential Rhetoric. The program, headed by Martin Medhurst, one of the leading experts in this burgeoning field, sponsors an annual national conference on some aspect of how presidents articulate their views. These conferences have been quite successful, and it was the first conference, in 1995, that gave birth to this book. Somewhat to my surprise, Professor Medhurst asked me to present a paper. Because rhetoric has never been my field of study, I was reluctant to accept the invitation. Marty was pleasantly persistent, however, and eventually I agreed. Not knowing where to begin, I asked for a list of the best work on presidential rhetoric. As I read through the literature, I noticed that it contained many assertions about the effect of rhetoric but virtually never offered proof, much less systematic evidence, on behalf of these causal inferences. In response to my reading, I focused my paper on the issue of evidence, pointing out that it was missing. Equally important, I raised questions about many of the specific inferences, which I was reasonably sure were incorrect. As one can imagine, I was a big hit with the auditorium full of dedicated scholars of rhetoric.

To be fair, scholars of presidential rhetoric are sophisticated and broadly knowledgeable analysts from whom I have learned a great deal. Many of them come from the tradition of literary criticism and are unaccustomed to marshaling systematic evidence on behalf of their conclusions. Yet the problem of unsupported and possibly faulty assertions about the effect of going public remains.

Table P.2. Public Support for Invasion of Iraq

Poll Date	Favor	Oppose	No Opinion
February 19–21, 2001	52%	42%	6%
November 26–27, 2001	74	20	6
June 17–19, 2002	61	31	8
August 19–21, 2002	53	41	6
September 2–4, 2002	58	36	6
September 5–8, 2002	58	36	6
September 13–16, 2002	57	39	4
September 20–22, 2002	57	38	5
October 3–6, 2002	53	40	7
October 14–17, 2002	56	37	7
October 21–22, 2002	54	40	6
November 8–10, 2002	59	35	6
November 22–24, 2002	58	37	5
December 9–10, 2002	55	39	6
December 16–17, 2002	58	35	7
December 19–22, 2002	53	38	9
January 3–5, 2003	56	39	6
January 10–12, 2003	56	38	6
January 23–25, 2003	52	43	5

Note: Gallup Poll, "Would you favor or oppose sending American ground troops to the Persian Gulf in an attempt to remove Saddam Hussein from power in Iraq?"

The problem is not limited to the field of rhetoric, however. There is now a substantial body of literature focused on how presidents pursue popular support and an equally robust body of literature on how the public evaluates the president. What is missing is an understanding of the linkage between what the president says and does and the public's response. In the meantime, scholars and commentators routinely refer to the White House as a "bully pulpit" and assume that a skilled president can employ it to move the public and create political capital for himself. The fact that such efforts almost always fail seems to have no effect on the belief in the power of public leadership.

My next step was to seek financial support for the project. On the advice of Paul Light, I approached the Smith Richardson Foundation. I am pleased to recognize the critical support the foundation awarded me and wish to express my gratitude for its invaluable help. Program officer Mark Steinmeyer has been supportive at every step in the research process.

Yale University Press heard about the project, and John Covell asked to do a separate evaluation of my proposal. I readily agreed, and soon I signed a contract. John's successor as editor, John Kulka, has been an equally enthusiastic and encouraging editor. I am grateful to both of them. I am also indebted to Charles O. Jones and Robert Shapiro, who read the entire manuscript and offered thoughtful suggestions for improvement. Many other scholars, including Robert Erikson, Bryan Jones, Martha Joynt Kumer, Michael MacKuen, and James Stimson, have shared their thoughts on various portions of the argument. They all have my thanks. The Roper Center of Public Opinion Research was an invaluable source of data.

Finally, and most importantly, I dedicate this book to George and Julie Jordan. It is difficult to express what the Jordans have come to mean to my wife Carmella and me. At first generous financial supporters of Texas A&M University, they have become patrons of my work and, most significantly, dear friends. Their support has made it possible for me to devote time to my research and writing, engage in institution building, and travel widely to share my ideas and benefit from the feedback of audiences around the world. All the while, the Jordans have asked for nothing more in return than how they could be even more helpful. I have been blessed and am deeply honored to have their names grace the dedication page.

PART I

Moving the Public

1

The Permanent Campaign: Why Does the President Go Public?

No president ever invested more in attempting to mold public opinion than Bill Clinton. His was a presidency based on a perpetual campaign to obtain the public's support[1] — a campaign fed by public opinion polls, focus groups, and public relations memos. The White House even polled voters on where it was best for the First Family to vacation. In 1995, the White House spent an unprecedented $18 million in advertising on behalf of the president—a year *before* the presidential election.[2]

Public leadership dominated the policy-making process in the Clinton White House, serving as both the focus of the president's energies and the criterion by which it evaluated itself. In a typical year, Clinton spoke in public 550 times,[3] and he traveled around the country every fourth day.[4] Equally important, the administration repeatedly interpreted its setbacks, whether in elections or on such policies as health care reform, in terms of its failure to communicate[5] rather than in terms of the quality of its initiatives or its strategy for governing.

Although it may have been on the extreme end of the spectrum, the Clinton administration's focus on public leadership did not represent a sharp break with the past. Ronald Reagan took office oriented to using his communications skills to persuade the public and thus the Congress to do his bidding.[6] The Clinton White House was merely the latest stage in an evolution that can be traced back to Theodore Roosevelt and Woodrow Wilson.[7]

Presidents clearly believe that they need to lead the public, and they "go public" more than ever, depending on a steadily expanding White House public relations infrastructure to take their messages to the American people.[8] In 1976, pollster Patrick Caddell wrote a memo to President-elect Jimmy Carter titled, "Initial Working Paper on Political Strategy." In it Caddell argued that "governing with public approval requires a *continuing* [italics added] political campaign." He also suggested implementing a working group to begin planning the *1980* presidential campaign.[9]

Leading the public is at the core of the modern presidency. Even as they try to govern, presidents are involved in a permanent campaign. Both politics and policy revolve around presidents' attempts to garner public support, both for themselves and for their policies. The division between campaigning and governing has become obscured. Indeed, governing often seems little more than an extension of the campaign that won the president his office in the first place. Both candidate and president travel widely for political purposes, appear frequently before organized constituencies, make extensive use of television, commission an endless stream of polls, and constantly brief the press. Summing up much of the modern presidency, journalist Sidney Blumenthal declared, "For the Reagan White House, every night is election night on television."[10]

As Bill Clinton reflected on the results of the 1994 elections, he concluded that the principal cause of the Democrats' stunning defeat was neither his presidency nor his policies. Instead, the main problem was communication. He had achieved a great deal, he felt, but the public neither recognized nor appreciated his accomplishments. He had failed to communicate them, and "the role of the President of the United States is message."[11] "I got caught up in the parliamentary aspect of the presidency," he said, "and missed the leadership, bully pulpit function which is so critical."[12]

President Clinton's remark reflects three fundamental and widely shared premises about presidential leadership. The first is that public support is a crucial political resource for the president. It is difficult for others who hold power to deny the legitimate demands of a president with popular support. A president who lacks the public's support is likely to face frustration and perhaps humiliation at the hands of his opponents. As Clinton exclaimed after he was acquitted in his impeachment trial, "Thank god for public opinion."[13]

The second premise manifested in Clinton's comments is the view that the president must not only earn public support with his performance in office, but also must actively take his case to the people. Moreover, he must do it not only at reelection time but all the time. Richard Nixon was perhaps the first president to adopt the view of the need for a permanent campaign, remarking to domestic adviser John Ehrlichman that "Great ideas that are conceived and not sold are like babies that are stillborn."[14] Thus, Nixon institutionalized units devoted to public relations in the White House.

More recent presidents have taken Nixon's increased emphasis on public relations a step further. Clinton adviser Dick Morris explained the basis of their thinking: "Once upon a time, elections settled things for the term of office. Now, they are mere punctuation marks in an ongoing search for public support and a functioning majority. Each day is election day in modern America. . . . A politician needs a permanent campaign to keep a permanent majority."[15] Another Clinton communications adviser, Sidney Blumenthal, agreed: "Under the permanent campaign, governing is turned into a perpetual campaign. . . . What was once a forced march for votes becomes unceasing forays for public approval."[16]

The president's third premise, that through the permanent campaign the White House *can* successfully persuade or even mobilize the public, is the primary focus of this book. Commentators on the presidency in both the press and the academy often assume that the White House can move public opinion if the president has the skill and will to effectively exploit the "bully pulpit." In Blumenthal's words, in the permanent campaign "the citizenry is viewed as a mass of fluid voters who can be appeased by appearances, occasional drama, and clever rhetoric."[17] Even those who lament the "plebiscitary presidency" may base their analyses on the premise of the president having established a direct and persuasive relationship with the public.[18]

Equally important, those in the White House share the premise of the potential of presidential leadership of the public. David Gergen, an experienced White House communications adviser, favorably cites Winston Churchill's assertion that "of all the talents bestowed upon men, none is so precious as the gift of oratory. He who enjoys it wields a power more durable than that of a great king. He is an independent force in the world."[19] He goes on to add that Ronald Reagan turned television "into a powerful weapon to achieve his legislative goals."[20] Sidney Blumenthal agreed, declaring that Reagan had "stunning success in shaping public opinion," which in turn was central to transforming his ideas into law.[21]

Similarly, in interviews in the 1990s, Lawrence Jacobs and Robert Shapiro found among both White House and congressional staff widespread confidence in the president's ability to lead the public. Evidently President Clinton shared this view, as his aides reported that he exhibited an "unbelievable arrogance" regarding his ability to change public opinion and felt he could "create new political capital all the time" through going public—a hubris echoed by his aides.[22]

The assurance with which presidents, scholars, and journalists accept the assumption of the potential of presidential public leadership belies our lack of understanding of that leadership. As I discuss in the following chapter, we actually know very little about the effect of the president's persuasive efforts because we have focused on the stimulus rather than the response in examining presidential public leadership.

For example, there is a substantial and rapidly increasing body of literature focusing on presidential rhetoric.[23] Underlying most of this research is the premise that the president can employ rhetoric to move the public. An individual president may be ineffective and fail to move opinion, but the potential is there. The authors of these fine works concentrate on analyzing *what* the president said. In the process, they make numerous inferences regarding the effect of the president's rhetoric on public opinion. However, scholars of presidential rhetoric virtually never provide evidence for their inferences about the president's effect.[24]

Yet one of the crowning ironies of the contemporary presidency is that at the same time that presidents increasingly attempt to govern by campaigning—"going public"—public support for presidential policies is elusive, perhaps more than ever before. President Clinton was not alone in his frustration with communicating with the public. In the century since Theodore Roosevelt declared the White House a "bully pulpit," presidents have often found the public unresponsive to issues at the top of the White House's agenda and unreceptive to requests to think about, much less act on, political matters. When asked about his "biggest disappointment as president," George Bush replied, "I just wasn't a good enough communicator."[25]

In his memoirs, Ronald Reagan—the "Great Communicator"—reflected on his efforts to ignite concern among the American people regarding the threat of communism in Central America and mobilize them behind his program of support for the Contras. "For eight years the press called me the 'Great Communicator,' he wrote. "Well, one of my greatest frustrations during those eight years was my inability to communicate to the American people and to Congress the seriousness of the threat we faced in Central America."[26]

If the frustration that presidents often experience in their efforts to obtain the public's support were nothing more than an irritating cost of doing the job, then public leadership would be a topic of only passing interest to political scientists, historians, and journalists. Governing by campaigning is much more important than that, however. The way presidents attempt to govern, and their success in doing so, has profound consequences for politics and public policy.

If there is substantial potential for presidents to govern through leading the public, then it is reasonable to evaluate them on their success in public leadership. If presidents do not succeed in obtaining the public's support, it is a failure of leadership for which they should be held accountable. However, if the premise of the potential of public leadership is false, then we may be evaluating presidents and presidential candidates on the wrong criteria.

If the conventional wisdom is wrong and presidents are not able to persuade, much less mobilize, the public, then presidents may be wasting their time and adopting governing styles that are prone to failure. For example, the massive Clinton health care reform plan of 1993–1994 was based on the underlying, and unquestioned, assumption within the White House that the president could sell his plan to the public and thus solidify congressional support. Because the administration believed it could move the public, Clinton and his aides felt they could focus on developing their preferred option in health care policy in 1993. In the process they discounted centrist opinion and underestimated how opponents could criticize their plan as big government. Moreover, even as the bill's fortunes soured, the White House refused to compromise. As Jacobs and Shapiro put it, "The White House's unquestioned faith that the president could rally Americans produced a rigid insistence on comprehensive reforms."[27]

In the end, Clinton was not able to obtain even a vote in either house of Congress on what was to have been his centerpiece legislation. Not long after, the Democrats lost majorities in both the House and the Senate for the first time in four decades. The administration's health care proposal was the prime example of the Republicans' charge that the Democrats were ideological extremists who had lost touch with the wishes of Americans. Summing up the health care reform debacle, Jacobs and Shapiro conclude that the "fundamental political mistake committed by Bill Clinton and his aides was in grossly overestimating the capacity of a president to 'win' public opinion and to use public support as leverage to overcome known political obstacles — from an ideologically divided Congress to hostile interest groups."[28]

This is not the lesson that Clinton learned, however. Indeed, the premise of the power of the presidential pulpit is so strong that each downturn in the bill's progress prompted new schemes for going public rather than a reconsideration of the fundamental framework of the bill or the basic strategy for obtaining its passage.[29] Ultimately, the president concluded that health care reform failed because "I totally neglected how to get the public informed. . . . I have to get more involved in crafting my message — in getting across my core concerns."[30] In other words, his strategy was not inappropriate, only his implementation of it. The premise of the potential of presidential public leadership seems to be nonfalsifiable.

The Clinton White House was not alone in its myopia regarding the effectiveness of the permanent campaign. The Reagan administration suffered from the same malady. For example, one of the president's highest priorities was obtaining congressional support for the Contras in Nicaragua. The White House launched a full-scale public relations campaign portraying the conflict in Nicaragua as a crucial confrontation between the United States and the Soviet Union. As we will see, the public was not persuaded. Nevertheless, one White House official concluded that the problem was not in the potential of presidential leadership of the public but rather in "the packaging of the activity, in terms of policy and presentation to the public. It wasn't well staged or sequenced."[31]

It is appropriate, then, that we reevaluate presidential public leadership. Given its prominence as a governing strategy, it is necessary to investigate the utility of going public as rigorously as possible. As a start, however, it is useful to examine briefly the context of that leadership so that we understand why presidents make such extraordinary efforts to seek public support.

Public Support as a Critical Resource

Why do presidents see themselves as dependent on public support to accomplish their goals, especially in Congress, and devote so much time, energy, and resources to obtaining it? The answer is straightforward: presidents know that without the public's backing in most instances they lack the influence to persuade Congress to support their legislative proposals and to reject congressional initiatives that the president opposes. Moreover, presidents believe that Congress responds to public opinion.

Going public is the central strategy for governing, but it is not the only element of a governing strategy. For example, party leadership, the mobilization of interest groups, and the exercise of legislative skills, both strategic and tactical, may also be components of such a strategy. In theory, the president may not need to move the public if other elements of a governing strategy are successful in obtaining what the president wants. Or the president may have a sufficient level of public support to persuade members of Congress to support his initiatives.

I have written on the effectiveness of the president exploiting opportunities handed to him by the public, opportunities such as the huge and cohesive liberal majorities enjoyed by Lyndon Johnson in 1965–1966 and the perception of a clear mandate for Ronald Reagan in the 1980 presidential election.[32] Such circumstances are rare, however. When in the past generation has the president enjoyed large cohesive majorities, either partisan or ideological, in Congress? Never. In what presidential election since 1980 has there been a widespread perception of a presidential mandate? None. On what major initiative has the president concluded that he had sufficient public backing and thus did not have to go public? None. In such a strategic context, presidents feel compelled to go public.

OBSTACLES TO CONGRESSIONAL COALITION BUILDING

Some presidents want to undo the work of their predecessors while others want to break new ground in public policy. All presidents, however, wish to produce a legacy of important legislation. Table 1.1 shows that there were 287 presidential initiatives of potentially significant legislation over the period from 1953 to 1996 period. These are the proposals that have the most potential to leave a mark on public policy. It is reasonable to infer that these are also the policies about which presidents care the most.

Of these 287 presidential initiatives of potentially significant legislation, only 41 percent became law. In other words, in the majority of cases *presidents lose on their major legislative initiatives*. In addition, many of the presidential initiatives that Congress does pass are delayed or diluted by legislative opposition. In sum, presidents are typically frustrated in their efforts to bring about major policy changes.

Constitutional Structure

The president faces many obstacles to obtaining congressional support. The first barrier to success is the structure of the constitutional system. The system of checks and balances is designed to produce sound, moderate legislation through a process of negotiation and compromise that accommodates minority viewpoints. The open and deliberative nature of the process is to confer legitimacy on the legislation that it generates. At the same time, checks and balances complicate coalition building. Indeed, the necessity of congressional support forces the president to build coalitions in the first place. The bicameral structure of Congress further complicates the process by requiring the president to build not one but two coalitions from among quite different sets of representatives.[33] In addition, the requirement that the Senate ratify treaties by a two-thirds vote is a structural provision that increases the burden of coalition building because it forces the president to gain a supermajority to achieve ratification.

Checks and balances alone do not explain the president's challenges in forming supportive coalitions in Congress. Theoretically, the two branches could be in agreement. However, checks and balances provide the context within which other potentially divisive factors may become obstacles to coalition building. For example, the Senate's rules, especially those regarding

Table 1.1. Presidential Initiatives That Became Law

Years	Number of Initiatives	Number Became Law	Percent Became Law
1953–54	9	5	56
1955–56	6	2	33
1957–58	11	7	64
1959–60	4	0	0
1961–62	24	13	54
1963–64	22	9	41
1965–66	30	17	57
1967–68	19	13	68
1969–70	16	4	25
1971–72	18	4	22
1973–74	17	5	29
1975–76	19	2	11
1977–78	19	7	37
1979–80	17	9	53
1981–82	12	3	25
1983–84	10	0	0
1985–86	5	1	20
1987–88	2	1	50
1989–90	8	3	38
1991–92	4	3	75
1993–94	15	9	60
1995–96	0	0	0
Total	287	117	41
Unified	155	82	53
Divided	132	35	27

Source: George C. Edwards III and Andrew Barrett, "Presidential Agenda Setting in Congress," in *Polarized Politics,* ed. Jon R. Bond and Richard Fleisher (Washington, DC: CQ Press, 2000), p. 128.

debate, protect minority interests and force advocates of change to build coalitions of at least 61 percent of the members.

Party Support

Members of the president's party almost always form the core of the president's support in Congress. As Table 1.2 shows, since 1953, presidents have obtained support from the typical senator or representative of their party about two-thirds of the time. This is twice the rate of the support that they receive from the opposition.

*Table 1.2. Partisan Support for Presidents, 1953–2000**

	House		Senate	
	Democratic President	Republican President	Democratic President	Republican President
Democrats	71%	26%	70%	33%
Republicans	31	67	32	70
Difference†	40	41	38	37

Source: George C. Edwards III and Stephen J. Wayne, *Presidential Leadership*, 6th ed. (Boston: Wadsworth, 2003).

*On roll-call votes on which the president took a stand and on which the winning side was supported by fewer than 80 percent of those voting.

†Differences expressed as percentage points.

On one hand, the president can depend on the support of most members of his party most of the time. On the other hand, there is plenty of slippage in party support, and the opposition party opposes him most of the time. If the opposition party is in the majority, which it frequently is, the odds are against the president building a winning coalition.

In recent years, congressional parties have become more ideologically homogeneous and, as a result, more cohesive.[34] This change has not advantaged presidents, however. Presidents have a more difficult time obtaining votes from the opposition party as parties become more polarized. When their parties are in the minority in Congress (as they were for Reagan's, Bush's, and most of Clinton's tenures), polarization makes it more difficult for presidents to prevail on votes. In addition, with the exception of Ronald Reagan, winning candidates in the past three decades have positioned themselves as more moderate than their congressional parties. At the same time that winning presidential candidates have moved to the center, their congressional cohorts have become more polarized. As the number of conservative Democrats and liberal Republicans has diminished, there has been less pressure to compromise within the party caucus. The inevitable tension between centrist presidents and polarized party caucuses has meant that party support for the president has not increased in conjunction with party homogeneity.[35]

Party Opposition

The most important resource the president can have in building coalitions is like-minded members of Congress.[36] Such members are most likely to be found among those in the president's party. We have seen that the president receives twice as much support on the average from members of his party as from members of the opposition party. Presidents have had little success in exercising legislative skills and systematically changing the minds of many senators and representatives as legislation comes to the floor.[37] As a result, the president is largely dependent on the cards voters have dealt him in previous elections.

There are a number of methods of electing chief executives and members of the legislature. The most common is a parliamentary system in which the chief executive is elected from a single legislative district during the general elections for parliament. Thus, the members of the legislature and the chief executive are elected at the same time. This simultaneous election encourages voters across the nation to support the leader's party by voting for candidates of the leader's party. Since the prime minister is selected by a majority of the legislature, the prime minister's party or party coalition must have the support of a majority in the legislature.

In the United States, voters cast their votes separately for executive and legislative officials, who have terms of different lengths. Thus they may split their votes between candidates of different parties. Not supporting the president's party is even easier during midterm elections, when the president is not on the ballot. In addition, one-third of the Senate is not elected in any election during a president's four-year term. The result is often divided control of the executive and legislative branches, which has occurred nearly two-thirds of the time in the past half-century and in all but two of the national elections since 1978.

Divided government has important consequences for the president's policies. Under unified government, the president succeeds in obtaining passage of 53 percent of his significant legislative proposals.[38] Under the less sanguine conditions of divided government, however, the success rate for presidential initiatives is cut nearly in half, falling to 27 percent because of the opposition of the majority party in Congress. Divided government matters.[39] Moreover, divided government exacerbates the tendency stemming from the Senate's filibuster rules to delay or dilute bills that eventually pass.

Intraparty Diversity

The president faces a second party-related obstacle to building coalitions: the diversity of policy preferences within his own party. In a large and diverse country with a two-party system, it is not surprising that representatives of each of the two parties reflect a range of constituents' policy positions. This diversity inevitably poses a challenge to intraparty cohesion.

The system of primaries for selecting congressional candidates undermines at a minimum the ability of party leaders to control who runs under their party's label, and thus weakens their ability to discipline errant members for not supporting the president. Most members of Congress gain their party's nomination by their own efforts, not the party's. Because virtually anyone can vote in party primaries, party leaders do not have control over those who run under their parties' labels. Moreover, even though national party organizations have been active in fund-raising in recent years, candidates remain largely responsible for providing the money and organization for their own election, precluding party control over another aspect of electoral politics.

The relative independence of presidential and congressional elections is illustrated by the modest number of coattail victories, in which presidential coattail votes provide the increment of the vote necessary for a representative of the president's party to win a seat. Such victories may provide the president an extra increment of support out of a sense of gratitude for the votes that winners of congressional races perceive were received because of presidential coattails or out of a sense of responsiveness to their constituents' support for the president. However, the outcomes of very few congressional races are determined by presidential coattails.[40] For example, in 1988 George Bush won election while his party actually lost seats in both houses of Congress. Similarly, the Democrats lost ten seats in the House and gained none in the Senate when Bill Clinton won election in 1992, and they lost two seats in the Senate when he won reelection in 1996. (Clinton ran behind all but a handful of members of Congress in their states or districts in both elections.) This is nothing new: In 1792, George Washington easily won reelection, but the opposition Democrat-Republicans captured the House of Representatives. Most House seats are too safe for a party, and especially for an incumbent, to have the election outcome affected by the presidential election. Senate elections are more affected by the president's standing with the public,[41] but the president's party typically gains no seats at all in a presidential election year.

Modern presidents have tried to increase the size of their party cohort in Congress and encourage party cohesion by taking an active role in midterm congressional elections. Typically, however, they are disappointed in the results of their efforts.[42] The results of George W. Bush's relentless campaigning in 2002 stand as an interesting exception as his party increased marginally its representation in each house.

Party leaders also have few ways to enforce party discipline among those who are elected. What sanctions might be applied, such as poor committee assignments, are rarely used because legislators are very hesitant to set precedents that could be used against them. The strong centralization of party leadership in the House under Newt Gingrich soon gave way to the more collegial leadership of Dennis Hastert. The finding in Table 1.2 that the typical member of the president's party fails to support him about one-third of the time is not surprising.

The independent tenures of the president and members of Congress also diminish cohesion in the president's party. In a parliamentary system, the government falls if the prime minister loses the support of the legislature. Typically, such a loss of support leads to new elections for the entire legislature. Since facing the electorate under circumstances of party disunity is usually not in the interests of the prime minister's party, its members have an incentive to support their leader.[43] No such incentive exists in the United States, however. Members of Congress retain their jobs (at least in the short run) independently of the president's legislative success.

Institutional Assets

The most important influences on congressional voting are party, ideology, and constituency.[44] These factors are largely beyond the president's control, especially in the short run. Aside from the veto power, the president has few institutionalized legislative powers. He may call Congress into special sessions and adjourn it in the case of disputes between the two chambers. Both of these powers have fallen into disuse and give the president little leverage in an age of year-round congresses. The president also may give a State of the Union message and recommend legislation to Congress. As we have seen, the president's role in setting Congress's agenda is substantial, although it is difficult to see how the "right" to recommend legislation is at the core of it. Given the First Amendment, the right to recommend legislation is a truism. How could anyone limit it? The White House has a modest-sized institutional staff devoted to congressional relations. Although presidents have employed this staff in a variety of ways and although some operations work more effectively than others,[45] the performance of the legislative liaison office is not at the core of presidential leadership in Congress.[46]

Presidents, then, face a range of obstacles to obtaining congressional support for their policies, and the Constitution provides few assets for moving Congress. It is natural that they turn to an extraconstitutional source of political power: public opinion.

CONGRESSIONAL RESPONSIVENESS TO PUBLIC OPINION

It is not only the *need* for leverage with Congress that drives the White House to seek public support; it is also the *belief* that leading the public—changing opinions and mobilizing citizens into action—is the ultimate presidential resource. For example, Newt Gingrich declared, "If the President's popularity is at 80 percent, I think the president can do whatever he wants."[47] A senior legislative strategist on the staff of a senior Democratic senator argued, "It's an absolute rule up here: popular Presidents get what they want; unpopular ones don't."[48] Representative Lee Hamilton agreed: "when a President is riding high his influence goes up, and when a President is in the dumps . . . his influence declines."[49]

As the central figure in American politics, the president is the object of a constant stream of commentary and evaluation by all segments of society. Indeed, press coverage of the president and his policies exceeds that of all other political figures combined.[50] The poll question "Do you approve or disapprove of the way President ______ is handling his job as president?" is probably the most prominent question in the history of public opinion research. The Gallup Poll has been asking the same question since 1945.[51] Other polling organizations have followed. The visibility of the "presidential popularity" measure has made it the subject of almost constant commentary among observers and participants in national politics. Because of the high visibility and frequency of presidential approval polls, it is safe to assume that members of Congress are aware of the president's standing with the public. In addition, senators and representatives learn of the public's opinion of the president and his policies from other political elites, political activists, leaders of interest groups, the press, attentive publics, and constituents. Some of what they hear may be echoes of their own actions in government. It is easy to understand, then, why the White House believes that members of Congress might respond to public opinion regarding the president.

The View from the White House

Presidents and their aides firmly share the view that public support for the president is an important asset for obtaining votes in Congress and that it is difficult for others who hold power to deny the legitimate demands of a president with popular support.[52] A president who lacks the public's support, on the other hand, is likely to face frustration and perhaps humiliation at the hands of his opponents.

Dwight Eisenhower, one of our most popular post–World War II presidents, went to considerable lengths to nurture his public support. According to Fred Greenstein, Ike "was fully aware that his popularity was essential to his ability to exercise influence over other leaders. As he once noted, 'one man can do a lot . . . at any particular given moment, if at that moment he happens to be ranking high in public estimation.' "[53] Eisenhower's congressional liaison chief, Bryce Harlow, reports that Democrats in Congress saw that openly opposing Eisenhower was unpopular and thus became more cooperative.[54]

Other observers have concluded that his popularity helped him to preempt challenges from congressional Democrats[55] and to bring around Republicans like Everett Dirksen.[56]

Lyndon Johnson understood well the advantage that public support afforded him. In his memoirs he declared that "presidential popularity is a major source of strength in gaining cooperation from Congress."[57] Johnson's aide Harry McPherson agrees, remembering that members of Congress "listened hard for evidence of how the President stood in their states in order that they might know how to treat him."[58]

Richard Nixon agreed with his predecessor about the importance of the president's standing in the public, arguing that a strong incentive for members of Congress to support the president was "the fear that a popular president may oppose them in the next election."[59] His chief of staff, H. R. Haldeman, wrote after the 1972 election that he felt things would be easier in Congress because of the Nixon landslide.[60] On the evening of his second inauguration, Nixon recorded in his diary his concern over the drop he expected in his approval levels in response to the extensive Christmas bombing of North Vietnam. The polls could affect his ability to lead, "since politicians do pay attention to them."[61] Earlier, Nixon also expressed his concern at his dependence on his general support from the public when he wrote: "No leader survives simply by doing well. A leader survives when people have confidence in him when he's not doing well."[62]

In 1969, Nixon celebrated the landing on the moon by personally observing the splashdown of Apollo XI in the Pacific Ocean. When he returned home, he cashed in on the increased approval the publicity had brought him. He had the Gallup Poll results sent to those members of Congress "who might have thought that it will now be safe to give in to their deepest desires and kick us in the teeth."[63] But, of course, this is just what would eventually happen. And his aides recognized that it was easier for members of Congress to vote against the president as his approval dropped.[64] Legislative liaison chief William Timmons wrote to Nixon at the end of 1973 that when the president's approval is low, "Its advantageous and even fun to kick him around."[65]

President Carter's aides were quite explicit about the importance of the president's public approval in their efforts to influence Congress. One stated that the "only way to keep those guys [Congress] honest is to keep our popularity high."[66] The president's legislative liaison officials generally agreed that their effectiveness with Congress ultimately depended on the president's ability to influence public opinion. As one of them said: "When you go up to the Hill and the latest polls show Carter isn't doing well, there isn't much reason for a member to go along with him. There's little we can do if the member isn't persuaded on the issue."[67] Another aide at the White House was even more explicit: "No president whose popularity is as low as this President's has much clout on the Hill."[68]

President Reagan's administration was especially sensitive to the president's public approval levels. According to David Gergen, the head of the White House Office of Communication during Reagan's first term, "Everything here is built on the idea that the president's success depends on grassroots support."[69]

In a televised discussion in 1994, Fred McClure, the chief congressional liaison aide to President Bush, and Tony Coelho, the former House Democratic whip, agreed that the higher the president was in the polls, the easier it was for him to obtain congressional support.

In early 1993, President Clinton's pollster, Stanley Greenberg, argued that at the beginning of Clinton's tenure "popular support is the key to congressional support."[70] Four years later a presidential aide found that "Clinton has come to believe that if he keeps his approval ratings up and sells his message as he did during the campaign, there will be greater acceptability for his program."[71] The president's aides found that when Clinton's ratings were up, interest groups feared him and were ready to deal; when his ratings were down, the same groups were less willing to deal. Public support gave the White House clout with Congress.[72]

Presidential strategist Dick Morris agreed. Noting that when Clinton was down in the polls, members of Congress began to desert him, Morris concluded: "A President doesn't just need a majority on Election Day. The President needs a majority every day of the week behind every bill that he has."[73] "Politicians and the media ignore titular power and focus only on an elected official's actual ability to command a following. . . . they understand that a president without popularity is without power as well. When he dips below 50 percent, he is functionally out of office."[74] It is not surprising that the president was convinced that he could not govern unless his poll numbers were high.

Congressional Responsiveness

Congressional behavior lends support to the view that public support is a critical resource for the president. Members of Congress appear to anticipate the public's reaction to their decisions to support or oppose the president and his policies. Depending on the president's public standing, they may choose to be close to him or independent from him to increase their chances of reelection. Polls find that a significant percentage of voters see their votes for candidates for Congress as support for the president or opposition to him.[75]

Members of Congress spend more time in their constituencies when the president's approval ratings are low, explaining how they differ from him.[76] Similarly, members of the president's party try to distance themselves from him during election periods if he is low in the polls.

This anticipation of the voter's reaction to their support for the president is quite sensible. As analyst William Schneider put it: "popularity is power. Members of Congress are all in business for themselves. If a President is popular, they'll support him because they want to be with a winner. If he starts losing popularity, they'll abandon him. Even members of his own party don't want to be associated with a loser."[77]

Members of Congress defeated in the election of 1974 had supported Richard Nixon more than their colleagues had who won reelection.[78] Regardless of party, the voters do not punish representatives who do not support the president's programs if the president's policies are perceived as unsuccessful, but strong supporters of the president are less fortunate.[79] In districts where Bill Clinton was weak in 1994, Democratic candidates were more likely to be defeated.[80]

Scholars have found that the president's popularity strongly influences the vote in individual Senate races.[81] It appears that voters in Senate elections express their support for or dissatisfaction with the president by respectively rewarding or punishing candidates of his party—a national referendum effect.

The White House encourages members of Congress to infer from the president's approval levels the public's support for his policies. Ultimately, the effectiveness of this strategy is tied to the potential for making the support of a senator or representative a campaign issue. Presidents who are high in the polls are in a position to make such threats. According to an aide to Reagan, for example, the president's contacts with members of Congress before the tax vote of 1981 were "merely a device to keep the congressmen thinking about what could happen next year. I'm sure Mr. Reagan is charming as hell, but that isn't what is important. It's his reminding these people that they could lose their jobs next year."[82]

Members of Congress may also use the president's standing in the polls as an indicator of his ability to mobilize public opinion against his opponents. Senators and representatives are especially likely to be sensitive to this possibility after a successful demonstration of the president's ability to mobilize the public, as appears to have occurred in response to the efforts of Reagan's White House in 1981.[83] As Richard Neustadt put it, "Washingtonians . . . are vulnerable to any breeze from home that presidential words and sighs can stir. If he is deemed effective on the tube, they will anticipate."[84]

Looking at the matter from another perspective, low presidential approval ratings free members of Congress from supporting the president if they are otherwise inclined to oppose him. A senior political aide to President Carter noted: "When the President is low in public opinion polls, the Members of Congress see little hazard in bucking him. . . . After all, very few Congressmen examine an issue solely on its merits; they are politicians and they think politically. I'm not saying they make only politically expedient choices. But they read the polls and from that they feel secure in turning their back on the President with political impunity. Unquestionably, the success of the President's policies bears a tremendous relationship to his popularity in the polls."[85]

A president with strong public support provides a cover for members of Congress to cast votes to which their constituents might otherwise object. They can defend their votes as having been made in support of the president rather than on substantive policy grounds alone. Of course, a president without public support loses this advantage and may find himself avoided by members of Congress who will certainly not articulate their decisions as having been made in support of the president if the president is caught in the depths of the polls. Lyndon Johnson, for example, found fewer members of Congress eager to attend White House receptions or discuss matters of policy with him when his standing in the polls declined.[86]

In addition, low ratings in the polls may create incentives to attack the president, further eroding his already weakened position. For example, after the arms sales to Iran and the diversion of funds to the Contras became a cause célèbre in late 1986, it became more acceptable in Congress and in the press to raise questions about Ronald Reagan's capacities as president. Disillusionment is a dangerous force for the White House.

Constraints on the Effect of Public Support

We have focused on explaining why presidents expend so much effort seeking to influence public opinion. We have seen that the White House has reason to believe that public support can be a critical resource in its efforts to influence public policy and that it is unlikely to succeed in these efforts in the absence of the public's backing. In the chapters that follow, I explore the ability of the president to influence public opinion.

Before moving to this discussion, however, it is important that we briefly address a related question that is central to the issue of attempting to govern by campaigning. This question is the degree to which presidents actually benefit from public support—as opposed to their perceptions of the extent of that benefit. If public support affects congressional behavior less than the conventional wisdom suggests, we should be even more skeptical about the utility of the permanent campaign.

In 1998, Bill Clinton averaged well over 60 percent job approval, and about two-thirds of the public consistently opposed his impeachment. In addition, the Democrats gained seats in the midterm elections — the first time the president's party had gained seats in sixty-four years! Yet in the face of overwhelming public opposition, Republicans impeached and tried the president.

Many commentators were mystified at how congressional Republicans could act in defiance of public support for the president. They should not have been. Senators and representatives do not pay equal heed to all the voters they represent. Instead, they are most responsive to their reelection constituencies, those who compose their electoral coalitions. In addition, members of Congress receive communications from their electoral supporters more frequently than from other constituents.[87] Not surprisingly, these communications are likely to support the views of the senator or representative.

In the 1998 congressional elections, the typical Republican House incumbent who faced a Democratic challenger *gained* 3 percent of the vote over his or her performance in the 1996 elections. Fifty-five other Republican incumbents faced no opposition at all. Thus, 74 percent of the Republicans voting on the question of impeaching the president had just won reelection unopposed or saw their share of the two-party vote increase. In addition, Republicans did *not* suffer losses in districts in which Bill Clinton had done well in 1996.[88]

So it was reasonable for Republican lawmakers to interpret the results in their districts as indicating that Clinton's national popularity did not affect their own elections and was not indicative of *their* constituents' views. In the end, the House impeached the president, who then was acquitted in the Senate. The votes in both houses were heavily partisan. Despite his widespread and sustained public support, the president was not able to change the minds of hardly any members of Congress who were predisposed to oppose him.

In an entirely different context, George W. Bush learned of the limited effect of public support. Even as the country displayed great solidarity in the face of the terrorist attacks of September 11, 2001, and even when he enjoyed record levels of personal approval, Bush could not win on the issue of keeping airport security guards in the private sector. Nor could he pass his economic stimulus package, a bill to make the 2001 income tax cut permanent, or a host of other core initiatives.

Scholars, including the author, have raised questions about the actual responsiveness of Congress to the president's public support.[89] At the most, we should expect this responsiveness to be modest. We know, for example, that no matter how low a president's standing with the public or how small the margin of his election, he still receives support from a substantial number of senators and representatives. Similarly, no matter how high his approval levels climb or how large his winning percentage of the vote, a significant portion of the Congress still opposes his policies.

The president's public support must compete for influence with other, more stable factors that affect voting in Congress, including ideology, party, personal views, commitments on specific policies, and constituency interests. Although constituency interests may seem to overlap with presidential approval, they should be viewed as distinct. It is quite possible for constituents to approve of the president but oppose him on particular policies, and it is opinions on these policies that will ring most loudly in congressional ears. Members of Congress are unlikely to vote against the clear interests of their constituents or the firm tenets of their ideology solely in deference to a widely supported chief executive. And, as we have seen, the electoral constituencies of senators and representatives may not reflect general opinion in the nation.

Both Neustadt and Edwards argue that presidential approval (or "prestige") should be viewed as a strategic influence, a factor that may affect the outcome in every case, but that will not necessarily determine the outcome in a specific case.[90] As Neustadt makes clear, public approval is a "factor operating mostly in the background as a conditioner, not the determinant, of what Washingtonians will do about a President's request." It "tends to set a tone and to define the limits of what Washingtonians do for him or do to him." However, "rarely is there any one-to-one relationship between appraisals of his popularity in general and responses to his wishes in particular."[91]

Widespread support should give the president leeway and weaken resistance to his policies. Thus, public support gives a president, at best, leverage, but not control. On the other hand, when the president lacks popular support, this strengthens the resolve of those inclined to oppose him and narrows the range in which he receives the benefit of the doubt. The president's options are reduced, his opportunities diminished, and his room for maneuver checked; he loses crucial "leeway."[92]

THE PARADOX OF THE PERMANENT CAMPAIGN

The permanent campaign presents us with an intriguing paradox. Presidents see themselves as dependent on public support to accomplish their goals, especially in Congress, and invest deeply in governing by campaigning. Yet even if presidents succeed in obtaining support for themselves and their policies, the potential of such a strategy is limited. Nevertheless, the White House persists in seeking any advantage it can obtain in the struggle to govern. Clearly, governing by campaigning deserves further investigation.

Investigating Presidential Public Leadership

To guide our investigation of the president's ability to move the public, we employ a model that identifies the critical elements in presidential public leadership and specifies the relationships among these elements. Figure 1.1 presents a simple graphic presentation of the model. The major elements in the model are the messenger (the president), the president's message, the audience (the public), and the public's response. Understanding what it takes for the president to succeed in moving public opinion will make it easier to ask useful questions about presidential public leadership.

Under normal circumstances, we would begin at the left side of the model (the stimulus) and investigate each relationship as we moved to the right (the response). To study presidential public leadership, however, I adopt a slightly different approach. The specific questions we are likely to ask about the relationships on the left side of the model will differ, depending on whether or not we find that the president is able to move public opinion with some regularity. If at least some chief executives are successful much of the time, then we will want to explain why some presidents are more successful than others in leading the public. Our questions will focus on the nature of the president's appeals, his presentation of himself, the public's perceptions of him, and the conditions under which the public pays attention to, understands, and responds positively to the president.

Conversely, if presidents—all presidents—are rarely able to move the public, our questions will focus on explaining why presidential leadership of the public is not more effective. If even the most rhetorically skilled presidents find it difficult to move the public, then studying variations in those skills among presidents will not reveal explanations for the president's difficulties. If all kinds of messages fail to resonate with the people, then the question is broader than the nature of the messages themselves. Our questions will focus instead on investigating and explaining the *absence* of relationships in the model. For example, why don't the messenger's characteristics matter, why doesn't the

Fig. 1.1. A Simple Model of Presidential Public Leadership

president focus his messages more tightly, and why doesn't the public hear the president's messages?

Thus, the next two chapters focus on the most basic question: does the public response to the president's leadership? The remaining chapters address various relationships posited in the model in an attempt to explain the findings in Chapters 2 and 3.

Conclusion

The premise of the potential of presidential public leadership is so widespread and so central to our understanding of politics that we rarely focus on it explicitly. We should not assume, however, that presidents, even skilled presidents, will be able to lead the public (or that Congress will follow the public if the president succeeds). Instead, we need to reconsider our thinking about public leadership and broaden our focus to include the nature of public opinion formation and the president's likely influence on it.

After we reach a better understanding of public leadership, we may conclude with confidence that at least skilled presidents have the potential to lead the public. If this is the case, we can narrow our focus in studying the public presidency to the personal and organizational skills necessary for leadership. We can devote our attention to examining the quality of the president's presentations, the substance of his messages, and the nature of the White House public relations operation.

On the other hand, if we conclude that there is little potential for public leadership, we must ask whether we are looking in the right direction as we seek solutions to the problems of governing. If presidents cannot transform public opinion and through such changes alter the political landscape, then it follows that we should invest less in evaluating their public leadership skills and in attributing their failure to lead the public to their rhetorical or public relations deficiencies. Instead, we should focus more on presidents' abilities to evaluate the possibilities for change and effectively exploit the opportunities presented by the broad configuration of political forces in American society.

The place to start in our investigation is with the record of presidential success in leading public opinion.

2

Presidential Persuasion: Does the Public Respond? Part I

The premise that the president has considerable potential to move the public is so widespread and so central to our understanding of politics that we rarely focus on it explicitly. However, it is questionable that we should *assume* that presidents, even skilled presidents, will be able to lead the public. John F. Kennedy once suggested an exchange from *King Henry IV, Part I* as an epigraph for Clinton Rossiter's classic work, *The American Presidency:*

> GLENDOWER: "I can call spirits from the vasty deep."
> HOTSPUR: "Why, so can I, or so can any man.
> But will they come when you do call them?"[1]

Kennedy's sardonic proposal reflected both his own frustrations in leading the public and his skepticism about the potential of public leadership.

What is the nature of presidential public leadership? In an earlier work, I outlined two contrasting views of presidential leadership. In the first the president is the *director* of change, establishing goals and leading others where they otherwise would not go. A second perspective is less heroic. Here the president is primarily a *facilitator* of change, reflecting and perhaps intensifying widely held views and exploiting opportunities to help others go where they want to go anyway.[2]

The director creates a constituency to follow his lead, whereas the facilitator endows his constituency's views with shape and purpose by interpreting them and translating them into legislation. The director restructures the contours of the political landscape to pave the way for change, whereas the facilitator exploits opportunities presented by a favorable configuration of political forces.

In this chapter we take a first cut at the complex relationship between the president and the public. Before we investigate further the president's leadership of the public, we need to know if the president can be a director, whether the public actually moves in the president's direction. If it does, at least some of the time, then perhaps the assumption of many journalists and scholars that the White House *can* persuade or even mobilize the public if the president is simply skilled enough at using the bully pulpit is justified. If this is the case, we can narrow our focus in studying presidential leadership of the public to the personal and organizational skills necessary for leadership and the conditions in which presidents are most successful in influencing the public. We can examine the quality of the president's presentations, the substance of his messages, the nature of the White House public relations operation, and the situations in which the public seems most responsive to leadership.

On the other hand, if the public rarely moves in the direction the president is trying to lead it, then Kennedy's skepticism about the potential of public leadership might be the more appropriate response. If presidents cannot transform public opinion, if they are facilitators rather than directors of change, then it follows that we should devote less attention to evaluating presidents' public leadership skills. Similarly, if presidents do not have the potential to move the public, we should not attribute the failure of presidents to lead the public to their rhetorical or public relations deficiencies. Our analytical task becomes explaining why presidents are not more successful. Such a focus leads us to consider broader forces in American society that may influence leadership of public opinion.

Most importantly, if the potential of the bully pulpit is less than the conventional wisdom suggests, we must ask whether the White House is looking in the right direction as it seeks solutions to the problems of governing. If the pulpit is less than bully, it seems reasonable to focus more on presidents' abilities to evaluate the possibilities for change and effectively exploit the opportunities presented by the broad configuration of political forces in American society.

To help us determine whether presidential leadership of the public allows presidents to be directors or facilitators of change, it is useful to examine briefly previous work on presidential public leadership.

The Little We Know

As a society, we devote extraordinary attention to what the president says and how he says it. Political commentators in both the press and the academy routinely evaluate presidents in terms of their public leadership and their ability to articulate a vision, rouse a crowd, or even stick to a speech. Yet we know very little about the effect of the permanent campaign. Despite the prominence of going public in scholarly commentary on the presidency, very few studies focus directly on the effect of presidential leadership of opinion, and no full-length studies do so.

A few experimental studies provide suggestive findings. Lee Sigelman ascertained public opinion on six potential responses to the 1979–1980 hostage crisis in Iran. He then asked those who opposed each option whether they would change their view "if President Carter considered this action necessary."[3] In each case a substantial percentage of respondents changed their opinions in deference to the supposed opinion of the president. In another experiment during the Reagan presidency, Dan Thomas and Lee Sigelman posed policy proposals to sample subjects. When informed that the president was the source of the proposals, enthusiastic supporters of Reagan evaluated them in favorable terms, but when the source was withheld, Reagan supporters evaluated these same proposals unfavorably.[4]

Not all results are as positive, however. In another study, Lee and Carol Sigelman asked sample groups whether they supported two proposals, a domestic policy proposal dealing with welfare and a proposal dealing with foreign aid. One of the groups was told that President Carter supported the proposals, while the president was not mentioned to the other group. The authors found that attaching the president's name to either proposal not only failed to increase support for it, but actually had a negative effect because those who disapproved of Carter reacted very strongly against proposals they thought were his.[5] Jeffrey Mondak found that reference to the president in issue surveys affects results only when other information is scarce and that the president needs a high level of support (more than 57 percent) before his policy endorsement constitutes a positive cue. Thus, he concludes, the president's credibility mediates his effect as a cue giver.[6]

Roberta Glaros and Bruce Miroff evaluated the reactions of some people watching Ronald Reagan address the nation. Their conclusion was that the principal effect of the speeches was to reinforce the audience's predispositions. They found little evidence of persuasion occurring.[7]

Scholars have devoted substantial attention to what some years ago I termed "the public presidency."[8] Another stream of literature focuses on the efforts of presidents to "go public" and attempt to influence public opinion,[9] including managing the news.[10] As in the literature on presidential rhetoric discussed in Chapter 1, this literature emphasizes what the president and his staff do rather than the effect of their activity on public opinion. Other studies have examined public evaluations of the president, but not the president's influence on those evaluations.[11]

A few studies have examined aggregate responses to the president's communications. Lyn Ragsdale found a short-term increase of about 3 percentage points in presidential approval following a televised presidential address,[12] and Paul Brace and Barbara Hinckley concluded that a major presidential address added 6 percentage points to the president's approval ratings.[13] There is reason to be skeptical about the effect of presidential speeches, however, as we will see later in this chapter.

A few studies have concluded that presidents could influence public opinion a small amount on issues, but only when they themselves have high approval ratings.[14] Others have found that people who approved of the president's performance were more supportive of policy stances of the president than those who disapproved.[15] Dennis Simon and Charles Ostrom concluded that presidential televised speeches typically did not affect the president's approval at all.[16]

Jeffrey Cohen has done the most extensive work on aggregate opinion.[17] He finds that presidents can influence the public's agenda through symbolic speech in State of the Union messages, at least in the short run. He also finds, however, that presidents are able to affect the public's agenda over time only on foreign policy and that substantive policy rhetoric has no effect on the public's policy agenda. His work on agenda setting has received support from Kim Hill.[18] In general, Cohen finds the president to be able to affect public opinion only modestly.

Samuel Kernell's work is the most prominent work on the president going public but provides only a few case studies of actual opinion leadership.[19] Since his focus is on describing and analyzing the strategy of going public, he does not provide a systematic study of the response of public opinion to the president. We will examine Kernell's case studies in more detail later.

People can usually relate domestic policy issues more easily and directly to their own experience. Foreign policy matters, in contrast, are typically more distant from the lives of most Americans than domestic policy, and it is easy for members of the public to view foreign policy as more complex and based on more specialized knowledge. There is some evidence that people tend to defer more to the president on foreign issues than on domestic problems. Studies have shown public opinion to have undergone changes in line with presidents' policies on the liberation of Kuwait, the invasion of Grenada, the testing of nuclear weapons, relations with the People's Republic of China, isolationism, and both the escalation and the deescalation of the Vietnam War.[20]

In sum, very little work has focused on systematically examining the president's ability to influence the public. The studies that we have, although innovative and suggestive, offer mixed results and do not provide the basis for firm conclusions about the effect of the president's public leadership. We lack models of opinion leadership, including a sense of how people receive, understand, accept, and retain the president's messages. We have frequent references to the contribution of charisma and other personal characteristics of presidents in eliciting public support, but virtually no evidence that such characteristics play any role in public leadership. Similarly, despite innumerable assertions to the contrary, we do not know how presidents can change public opinion on issues, mobilize the public to political action, or rally it to support themselves and their policies.

The Elusiveness of Public Approval

Certainly one of the highest priorities of presidents is to obtain the public's support for themselves. As we saw in the previous chapter, presidents believe that public approval increases the probabilities of obtaining the passage of legislation in Congress, positive coverage in the press, and even responsiveness in the bureaucracy. As a result of their belief in the importance of public approval, they devote an impressive amount of time, energy, and money to securing it.

How well have they done? Table 2.1 shows the average approval levels of presidents over the past three decades. Presidents Nixon, Ford, and Carter did not receive approval from even 50 percent of the public on the average. Even Ronald Reagan, often considered the most popular of recent presidents, averaged only 52 percent approval—a bare majority. George Bush achieved the highest average approval, at 60 percent. Yet when he needed the public's support the most, during his campaign for reelection, the public abandoned him. He received only 38 percent of the popular vote in the 1992 presidential election.

The fact that Bill Clinton enjoyed strong public support during his impeachment trial should not mask the fact that he struggled to obtain even 50 percent approval during his first term and did not exceed such an average for a year until his fourth year in office. Clinton's failure was not from lack of trying. The president operated on an explicit strategy of raising his approval ratings in

Table 2.1. Average Levels of Presidential Approval

President	Years in Office	Average Approval
Nixon	1969–1974	48%
Ford	1974–1977	47
Carter	1977–1981	47
Reagan	1981–1989	52
Bush	1989–1993	60
Clinton	1993–2001	55

Source: George C. Edwards III, with Alec M. Gallup, *Presidential Approval* (Baltimore, MD: Johns Hopkins University Press, 1990); updated by the author.

order to create public support for his specific proposals. According to Mandy Grunwald, one of his closest political advisers: "The President's popularity first had to be improved, then Congress could be moved by a popular president." "It's a bank shot, what you say to the American people bounces back to Congress."[21]

The president was an indefatigable traveler on behalf of his efforts to move the public. Charles O. Jones reports that Clinton traveled to 194 places and made 268 appearances in the United States between his inauguration in January 1993 and the midterm election in November 1994, mostly to sell himself and his policy proposals. Yet, as Jones concludes, the president's efforts were "a colossal failure"—his approval ratings did not rise.[22]

We mentioned earlier that some authors have concluded that the president can reliably increase his support by delivering an address to the American people. Table 2.2 shows the difference in presidential approval in the Gallup polls taken most closely before and after each live presidential televised address to the nation since January 1981. In comparing survey results of two samples such as those used by Gallup, differences between the results must be about 6 percentage points before we can be reasonably sure that the results reflect a real difference.

The figures in the third column of the table show that statistically significant changes in approval rarely follow a televised presidential address. Typically, the president's ratings hardly move at all. Most changes are well within the margin of error—and many of them show a *loss* of approval. In most cases we can readily explain the exceptions by the actions the president was announcing or the context of the announcement rather than by the power of the bully pulpit. The only change of 6 percentage points or more in Ronald Reagan's tenure followed his speech on April 14, 1986, announcing an air strike against

Table 2.2. Approval Change After Nationally Televised Addresses (1981–2001)

Date	Principal Subject	Opinion Change (percentage points)
Reagan		
January 20, 1981	Inaugural	NA
February 5, 1981	Economy	4
February 18, 1981	Economy	5
April 28, 1981	Economy	1
July 27, 1981	Tax reduction	4
September 24, 1981	Deficit reduction	4
December 23, 1981	Christmas; Poland	0
January 26, 1982	State of the Union	0
April 29, 1982	Budget	1
August 16, 1982	Budget	1
September 1, 1982	Middle East	0
September 20, 1982	U.S. troops to Lebanon	0
October 13, 1982	Economy	0
November 22, 1982	Arms control; nuclear deterrence	−2
January 25, 1983	State of the Union	−2
March 23, 1983	Defense spending	0
April 27, 1983	Central America	4
September 5, 1983	Soviet attack on Korean civilian airliner	4
October 27, 1983	Lebanon; Grenada	4
January 16, 1984	U.S.–Soviet relations (morning)	3
January 25, 1984	State of the Union	3
May 9, 1984	Central America	2
January 21, 1985	Inaugural	2
February 6, 1985	State of the Union	−4
April 24, 1985	Budget	3
May 28, 1985	Tax reform	3
November 14, 1985	U.S.–Soviet Summit	3
November 21, 1985	U.S.–Soviet Summit	2
January 28, 1986	*Challenger* explosion	−1
February 4, 1986	State of the Union	−1
February 26, 1986	National security	−1
March 16, 1986	Nicaragua	−1
April 14, 1986	Air strike against Libya	6
June 14, 1986	Nicaraguan Contras	3
July 4, 1986	Statue of Liberty centennial	−1
September 14, 1986	Campaign against drug abuse	2
October 13, 1986	U.S.–Soviet Summit	0

Table 2.2. Continued

Date	Principal Subject	Opinion Change (percentage points)
November 13, 1986	Iran-Contra	−16
December 2, 1986	Iran-Contra	−16
January 27, 1987	State of the Union	−6
March 4, 1987	Iran-Contra	−6
June 15, 1987	Economic summit; budget	−4
August 12, 1987	Iran-Contra	4
December 10, 1987	U.S.–Soviet Summit; INF treaty	1
January 25, 1988	State of the Union	1
January 11, 1989	Farewell address	No data
G. H. W. Bush		
January 20, 1989	Inaugural	NA
February 9, 1989	Administration goals	6
September 5, 1989	National drug control strategy	6
November 22, 1989	Thanksgiving address	1
December 20, 1989	Panama (morning)	9
January 31, 1990	State of the Union	−7
August 8, 1990	Desert Shield	0
September 11, 1990	Persian Gulf; Budget deficit	−4
October 2, 1990	Budget agreement	−2
January 16, 1991	Desert Storm	19
January 29, 1991	State of the Union	−1
February 23, 1991	Desert Storm, ground attack	0
February 26, 1991	Iraqi withdrawal (morning)	−2
February 27, 1991	Suspension of combat in Gulf War	−2
March 6, 1991	End of Gulf War	−2
December 25, 1991	Breakup of USSR	−4
January 28, 1992	State of the Union	1
May 1, 1992	Los Angeles riots	0
September 1, 1992	Hurricane Andrew	−1
December 4, 1992	Somalia (afternoon)	0
Clinton		
January 20, 1993	Inaugural	2
February 15, 1993	Economic program	8
February 17, 1993	Economic program	8
June 26, 1993	Air strike against Iraq	7
August 3, 1993	Budget	2
September 22, 1993	Health care reform	10

Table 2.2. Continued

Date	Principal Subject	Opinion Change (percentage points)
October 7, 1993	Somalia	−6
January 25, 1994	State of the Union	4
September 15, 1994	Troops to Haiti	4
September 18, 1994	Troops to Haiti	4
October 10, 1994	Iraq	−2
December 15, 1994	Middle class Bill of Rights	1
January 24, 1995	State of the Union	2
June 13, 1995	Budget	1
November 27, 1995	Bosnia	−2
January 23, 1996	State of the Union	7
January 20, 1997	Inaugural	−5
February 4, 1997	State of the Union	−5
January 27, 1998	State of the Union	5
August 17, 1998	Grand jury testimony	4
August 20, 1998	Air strike against Afghanistan and the Sudan	1
December 16, 1998	Air strikes against Iraq	10
December 19, 1998	Air strikes against Iraq	10
January 19, 1999	State of the Union	0
February 12, 1999	Impeachment	3
March 24, 1999	Air strikes in Kosovo	0
June 10, 1999	End of air strikes in Kosovo	0
January 27, 2000	State of the Union	−1
January 18, 2001	Farewell address	No data
G. W. Bush		
January 20, 2001	Inaugural	NA
February 27, 2001	Administration goals	1
August 9, 2001	Stem cell research	2
September 11, 2001	Terrorist attack	35
September 20, 2001	Terrorist attack	4
October 7, 2001	War in Afghanistan (afternoon)	2
November 8, 2001	War on terrorism*	0
January 29, 2002	State of the Union	−2
June 6, 2002	Department of Homeland Security	4
September 11, 2002	Anniversary of terrorist attacks	4
October 7, 2002	War with Iraq†	−5
January 28, 2003	State of the Union	1

Source: Gallup Poll.

*Broadcast by only one network.

†Broadcast by only Fox, not ABC, NBC, CBS, or PBS.

Libya, a highly consensual policy against what was widely viewed as an outlaw state.

Similarly, two of the four times that George H. W. Bush obtained at least a 6 percentage point increase in approval occurred following announcements of important military actions against unpopular foes: the December 20, 1989, morning speech announcing invasion of Panama and the effort to arrest Manuel Noriega and the January 16, 1991, address announcing the launching of Operation Desert Storm against Iraq. The huge increase in Bush's approval can easily be understood as a rally behind a successful war effort rather than as a response to the president's speech. Another of Bush's statistically significant increases in approval occurred following his February 9, 1989, speech outlining his administration's goals. The increase in this instance (like the slightly smaller increases for Reagan) was the product of the unusually low initial approval level (51 percent) Bush experienced in the first Gallup Poll of his tenure when a large segment of the public withheld judgment on the president's performance. Finally, the president's September 5, 1989, speech on national drug control strategy was once again focused on a highly consensual policy.

Over his eight years in office, Bill Clinton obtained increases in approval of 6 percentage points or more following five of his speeches. The first instance occurred after he delivered two addresses two days apart on his administration's goals and economic program on February 15 and 17, 1993. I count these speeches as one effort although they are listed separately in Table 2.1. The changes in approval reflect the same change in opinion in the same polls. As in the case of Reagan and Bush, there is more potential for increases in approval at the beginning of a term when people are undecided about the new chief executive. Clinton gained 7 percentage points in approval following his announcement on June 26, 1993, of an air strike against Iraq after U.S. intelligence determined that Saddam Hussein had planned to assassinate former President George Bush while Bush was on a trip to Kuwait. Once again, the attack on Iraq was a highly consensual policy and did not generate criticism by political elites.

Perhaps Clinton's greatest success in using a speech to increase support for himself was his address on health care reform on September 22, 1993. The speech was well received by the public, although support for his reform program soon dissipated, as we will see later in this chapter. On January 23, 1996, the president delivered his State of the Union message following the resolution of two government shutdowns and a year of bitter fighting over the Republican Contract with America. After the speech, the president's approval rose 7 percentage points. Finally, the president gained 10 percentage points in his approval ratings following his short addresses on December 16 and 19, 1998, regarding air strikes against Iraq. It does not strain logic to argue that the public was reacting more to the House's impeachment of the president on December 19, which it overwhelmingly opposed, than to the president's comments on Iraq.

George W. Bush enjoyed the most dramatic increase shown in Table 2.2: 35 percentage points after the terrorist attack on September 11, 2001. Few would attribute the public's rallying around the commander in chief to the president's brief comments that evening.

The limited effect of presidential addresses on their public approval is nothing new. Matthew Baum and Samuel Kernell found that Franklin D. Roosevelt's radio appeals had less than a 1 percentage point increase on his approval.[23]

Bill Clinton and Opinion on Policy

Presidents typically are as interested in obtaining public support for their policies as they are for themselves. To determine whether there is a prima facie case for successful presidential leadership of public opinion, I focus on two recent presidents, Ronald Reagan and Bill Clinton. Republican Reagan and Democrat Clinton are best-test cases for presidential leadership of the public. Each president displayed formidable rhetorical skills, and both supporters and detractors frequently commented on their unusual rapport with the public. Each president overwhelmingly won a second term in office and became the only presidents since Eisenhower's tenure in the 1950s to win and complete two terms. If we cannot find successful public leadership during the tenures of Reagan and Clinton, we are unlikely to find it anywhere.

Because of Ronald Reagan's reputation as a successful leader of public opinion, represented by his sobriquet of "The Great Communicator," and his role as leader of a conservative "revolution," I devote the entire following chapter to public responsiveness to his policy stances. I also focus on public responses to some of Reagan's individual speeches in the chapter on charisma and personality.

An articulate and energetic speaker, Bill Clinton displayed an impressive mastery of public policy as well as a unique ability to empathize with his audience. The president's political resurrection following the dramatic Democratic losses in the 1994 midterm elections and his *rise* in public esteem in the face of clear evidence of lying to the public and engaging in what most people saw as immoral behavior in the Oval Office left an indelible imprint on pundits and politicians alike.

The best evidence, as we will see, is that Clinton typically was frustrated in his efforts to move public opinion in his direction. In a discussion of his problems in governing, President Clinton declared that he needed to do a better job of communicating: "it's always frustrating to feel that you're misunderstood . . . and you can't quite get through."[24] A basic problem for the president was his overestimation of the extent to which the public was susceptible to his appeals for support.

ECONOMIC PROGRAM

Bill Clinton's 1992 presidential election campaign kept a clear focus on the economy. On February 15, 1993, the new president addressed the nation on his economic program. Two days later he delivered a much more detailed address to the Congress on his policy plans. His economic proposals included spending for job creation, a tax increase on the wealthy, investment incentives, and aid to displaced workers. In the same month he introduced his first major legislative proposal, a plan to spend more than $16 billion to stimulate the economy. It immediately ran into strong Republican opposition. During the April 1993 congressional recess, Clinton stepped up his rhetoric on his bill, counting on a groundswell of public opinion to pressure moderate Republicans into ending the filibuster on the bill. (Republicans, meanwhile, kept up a steady flow of sound bites linking the president's package with wasteful spending and Clinton's proposed tax increase.) The groundswell never materialized, and the Republicans found little support for any new spending in their home states. Instead, they found their constituents railing against new taxes and spending.[25] The bill never came to a vote in the Senate.

The figures in Table 2.3 show that public support for the president's economic plan peaked immediately following his speech on February 17 and then dropped dramatically a few days later. (Clinton's chief speechwriter reports that the speech was viewed in Washington as a failure.[26]) During the period when the president needed support the most and when he worked hardest to obtain it, it diminished to the point that by May a plurality of the public *opposed* his plan.

HEALTH CARE REFORM

Health care reform was to be the centerpiece of the Clinton administration. In September 1993, the president delivered a well-received national address on the need for reform. Yet the president was not able to sustain the support of the public for health care reform. The White House held out against compromise with the Republicans and conservative Democrats, hoping for a groundswell of public support for reform. But it never came.[27] In the meantime, opponents of the president's proposal launched an aggressive

Table 2.3. Public Support for Clinton's Economic Plan

Date	Support	Oppose	Mixed	No Opinion
2/17/93*	79%	16%	2%	5%
2/26–28/93	59	29	6	6
3/22–24/93	54	34	6	6
4/22–24/93	55	39	2	4
5/21–23/93	44	45	5	5
6/29–30/93	44	49	2	5

Note: Gallup/CNN/*USA Today* Poll question: "Do you generally support or oppose Bill Clinton's economic plan?"

*"Do you generally support or oppose the economic plan that President (Bill) Clinton outlined tonight (in his speech February 17, 1993)?"

counterattack, including running negative television advertisements. Clinton's tendency to carry the campaign mode to governance by demonizing opponents such as the medical profession and the drug and insurance industries probably exacerbated his problems in obtaining public support. As the figures in Table 2.4 show, by mid-July 1994, only 40 percent of the public favored the president's health care reform proposals, and 56 percent opposed them.

THE 1993 BUDGET

The Clinton administration faced a series of budget battles during its two terms in office, but none was more important or more difficult than the fight over the reconciliation bill for the fiscal year 1994 budget in 1993. The president took a considerable political risk by focusing on deficit reduction by raising taxes and limiting expenditures. On August 3, 1993, he spoke on national television on behalf of his budget proposal, and Senate Republican leader Robert Dole spoke against the plan. A CNN overnight poll following the president's speech found that support for his budget plan *dropped*.[28] A CBS News/*New York Times* Poll with before-and-after samples on August 2 and 3 found that support for the president's budget remained unchanged even in the immediate aftermath of the speech (although opposition weakened). Several million calls were made to Congress in response to Clinton and Dole, with the callers overwhelmingly opposed to the president's plan.[29] In the end, the president prevailed, but not a single Republican supported his budget. The absence of public support made it easier for Republicans to label him in the 1994 midterm elections as a supporter of tax increases.

Table 2.4. Public Support for Clinton's Health Care Reform

Date	Favor	Oppose	Don't know
9/24–26/93	59%	33%	8%
10/28–30/93	45	45	10
11/2–4/93	52	40	8
11/19–21/93	52	41	7
1/15–17/94	56	39	6
1/28–30/94	57	38	5
2/26–28/94	46	48	5
3/28–30/94	44	47	9
5/20–22/94	46	49	5
6/11–12/94	42	50	8
6/25–28/94	44	49	8
7/15–17/94	40	56	5

Note: Gallup Poll question, "From everything you heard or read about the plan so far . . . do you favor or oppose President Clinton's plan to reform health care?"

GOVERNMENT SPENDING

The president engaged in a perennial series of battles with Republicans over the extent of government services and spending. In 1995–1996, this conflict led to two government shutdowns. Although the president was an active and articulate spokesperson for doing and spending more, the public did not move much in his direction. The figures in Table 2.5 show that public support for government spending in general was the same in 1998 as it was in 1992, even with declining budget deficits. After eight years in office as Clinton was leaving the White House in 2000, opinion had moved only 3 percentage points in his direction.

Table 2.6 shows that support for spending on food stamps decreased during the president's first term and support for increased spending was the same in 2000 as in 1992 (the National Election Studies did not ask questions about spending on specific policies in 1998). The increase in support in the second term, as Greg Shaw and Robert Shapiro argue, was probably due to the passage of welfare reform in 1996 and the general prosperity in the late 1990s.[30] These two factors combined to drastically decrease the number of people on welfare, decreasing the resentment associated with the issue in the process.

Support for federal spending on child care (Table 2.7) did not increase in line with the president's stance in his first term, although it did increase

Table 2.5. Public Support for Government Spending

Date	Fewer	Same	More
1992	27%	30%	43%
1994	43	28	31
1996	37	31	31
1998	30	28	42
2000	24	29	46

Notes: National Election Studies (NES) question, "Some people think that government should provide fewer services, even in areas such as health and education, in order to reduce spending. Other people feel that it is important for the government to provide many more services even if it means an increase in spending. Where would you place yourself on this scale?"

Fewer services = 1–3; Same = 4; More services = 5–7 on NES seven-point scale.

Table 2.6. Public Support for Food Stamp Spending, 1992–2000

Date	Increased	Kept About the Same	Decreased
1992	16%	60%	24%
1994	10	48	42
1996	11	42	46
2000	16	51	31

Note: National Election Studies question, "Should federal spending on food stamps be increased, decreased, or kept about the same?"

substantially in his second term. The explanation for this change is not clear. It seems unlikely, however, that it was the result of the president's persuasion, as he did not make child care a central issue of his second term. Changes in society and a dramatic increase in available budgetary resources are more reasonable explanations. Support for spending on the environment fell slightly during Clinton's tenure (Table 2.8).

Perhaps no policy interested the president as much as education. Yet the figures in Table 2.9 show that public support for increased federal spending for education remained stable during his first term. As in the case of child care, support for federal aid to public schools did increase substantially in the second Clinton administration. The president regularly spoke out on behalf of more federal spending, but not more so than in his first term (as Table 6.2

Table 2.7. Public Support for Child Care Spending, 1992–2000

Date	Increased	Kept About the Same	Decreased
1992	52%	39%	9%
1994	54	33	9
1996	51	37	11
2000	63	29	7

Note: National Election Studies question, "Should federal spending on child care be increased, decreased, or kept about the same?"

Table 2.8. Public Support for Environmental Spending, 1992–2000

Date	Increased	Kept About the Same	Decreased
1992	55%	40%	5%
1994	40	49	11
1996	41	51	8
2000	52	39	9

Note: National Election Studies question, "Should federal spending on the environment be increased, decreased, or kept about the same?"

Table 2.9. Public Support for Federal Public School Spending, 1992–2000

Date	Increased	Kept About the Same	Decreased
1992	67%	30%	4%
1994	68	25	7
1996	67	26	6
2000	77	19	4

Note: National Election Studies question, "Should federal spending on public schools be increased, decreased, or kept about the same?"

shows). Again, the budget surplus may have encouraged support for more aid, and support for education funding is always strong.

CRIME

Central to Bill Clinton's basic political strategy was co-opting Republican issues. One such issue was crime. When the crucial rule regarding debate on the 1994 crime bill was voted down in the House, the president immediately went public. Speaking to police officers with American flags in the background, he blamed special interests (such as the National Rifle Association) and Republicans for a "procedural trick," but his appeal failed to catch fire. Meanwhile, Republicans were tapping public resentment by talking about pork barrel spending. Clinton's public push yielded only the votes of three members of the Black Caucus. So he had to go to moderate Republicans and cut private deals.

HAITI

It is more difficult to characterize Clinton's foreign policy than it is to articulate a focus for Reagan's. One hallmark of foreign policy during the Clinton administration was a series of military interventions. One of these interventions occurred in Haiti in September 1994. On September 15, the president addressed the nation on military buildup for a possible intervention in Haiti, explaining U.S. involvement. Three days later on September 18, Clinton addressed the nation again, this time on the resolution of the Haitian conflict. The figures in Table 2.10 show that the president received a short-term increase in support for his handling of the situation in Haiti following his speech to the nation on September 15, 1994,[31] but this support quickly deteri-

Table 2.10. Public Approval of Clinton's Handling of Haiti

Date	Approve	Disapprove	Don't Know
7/15–17/94*	28%	56%	16%
9/6–7/94	27	58	15
9/14/94	35	49	15
9/15/94†	53	43	4
9/23–25/94*	48	48	4
10/11/94	43	49	9

Note: Gallup Poll question, "Do you approve or disapprove of the way (President) Bill Clinton is handling . . . the situation in Haiti?"

*Same question, different lead in: "Now thinking of some issues, . . ."

†Reinterview of four hundred respondents from the previous day after the president's speech.

orated into plurality disapproval less than a month later. Indeed, Clinton faced near-majority disapproval only five days after his September 18 speech announcing a peaceful resolution of the crisis.

BOSNIA

Conflict within the former Yugoslavia posed a problem throughout Clinton's tenure in office. On November 27, 1995, the president gave a nationally televised address seeking the public's support for deploying U.S. peacekeeping troops to Bosnia. As the figures in Table 2.11 show, the president's plea met with little success. In fact, public support for sending U.S. troops to Bosnia dropped steadily as the president implemented this policy. It was not until two years later that a plurality of the public supported the deployment of U.S. troops in Bosnia.

KOSOVO

On March 24, 1999, Clinton gave a nationally televised address informing the public that he was ordering bombing on Serbia to stop the ethnic cleansing of ethnic Albanians in Kosovo province. From the beginning, the

Table 2.11. Public Support of Troops in Bosnia

Date	Approve	Disapprove	Don't Know
9/19–22/95*	50%	44%	6%
11/6–8/95*	47	49	4
11/27/95†	46	40	14
12/15–18/95	41	54	5
1/5–7/96	36	58	6
5/28–29/96	42	51	7
6/26–29/97	39	53	8
12/18–21/97	49	43	8
1/16–18/98	53	43	5

Note: Gallup Poll question, "Do you approve or disapprove of the presence of U.S. (United States) troops in Bosnia?"

*Gallup/CNN/*USA Today* Poll question, "There is a chance a peace agreement could be reached by all the groups currently fighting in Bosnia. If so, the Clinton Administration is considering contributing U.S. (United States) troops to an international peacekeeping force. Would you favor or oppose that?"

†Gallup/CNN/*USA Today* Poll question, "Now that a peace agreement has been reached by all the groups currently fighting in Bosnia, the Clinton Administration plans to contribute U.S. (United States) troops to an international peacekeeping force. Do you favor or oppose that?" Six hundred thirty-two respondents were interviewed after the president's speech.

Table 2.12. Clinton's Handling of Kosovo

Date	Approve	Disapprove	No Opinion
3/25/99	58%	32%	10%
4/6–9/99	58	35	7
4/13–14/99	61	34	5
4/26–27/99	54	41	5
4/30–5/2/99	54	41	5
5/7–9/99	55	35	10
6/4–5/99	56	39	5
6/10/99	55	35	10
6/11–13/99	57	38	5

Note: Gallup Poll question, "Do you approve or disapprove of the way President Clinton is handling the situation in Kosovo?"

Table 2.13. Clinton's Kosovo Policy

Date	Clear and Well-Thought-Out Policy	Disapprove	No Opinion
3/30–31/99	46%	47%	7%
4/6–7/99	39	50	11
4/13–14/99	41	51	8
4/26–27/99	38	54	8
6/11–13/99	43	52	5

Note: Gallup Poll question, "From what you have heard or read, do you think the Clinton administration has a clear and well-thought-out policy on the Kosovo situation, or don't you think so?"

public supported the president's handling of Kosovo, with little variation in public opinion over the entire period of the bombing (see Table 2.12). The public appears more willing to support bombing than the use of troops on the ground. At the same time, at no time did the public agree that the president had a clear and well-thought-out policy on the Kosovo situation (see Table 12.13). Indeed, for most of the period of the bombing, a majority of the public thought that he did *not* have such a policy.

NAFTA

Free trade was another hallmark of Clinton's foreign policy. The first major free trade agreement to reach Congress during the Clinton administration was the North American Free Trade Agreement (NAFTA). The White

Table 2.14. Public Support for NAFTA

Date	Favor	Oppose	Don't Know
6/21–24/93	43%	45%	12%
8/2–3/93	35	46	19
8/8–10/93*	41	44	15
9/10–12/93*	35	40	25
9/16–19/93†	33	40	27
11/2–4/93†	38	46	16
11/8–9/93†	34	38	29
11/11–14/93‡	37	41	22
11/15–16/93*	38	41	21

Note: Gallup/CNN/*USA Today* Poll, CBS News/*New York Times* Poll, and NBC/*Wall Street Journal* Poll question, "Do you favor or oppose the proposed North American Free Trade Agreement—called NAFTA—with Mexico and Canada that eliminates nearly all restrictions on imports, exports, and business investment between the United States, Mexico, and Canada?"

*Gallup/CNN/*USA Today* Poll question: "Do you favor or oppose the proposed free trade agreement between the United States and Mexico?"
†Gallup/CNN/*USA Today* Poll, "Do you favor or oppose the North American Free Trade Agreement between the United States and Mexico and Canada, sometimes known as N.A.F.T.A.?"
‡CBS News/*New York Times* Poll question, "Would you say you (Favor/Oppose) N.A.F.T.A. (North American Free Trade Agreement) strongly or not so strongly?" (*strongly* and *not strongly* responses combined in the table).

House fought hard for the agreement, but the figures in Table 2.14 show that the White House never achieved plurality support for NAFTA before Congress's decision to pass it.

The White House made a shrewd gamble when it agreed to have Vice President Al Gore debate NAFTA opponent Ross Perot on the *Larry King Live* television show. The show had the highest rating for any regularly scheduled program in the history of cable TV. In addition, it was also carried on broadcast stations, so perhaps twenty million people watched the show. Among the 357 adults who Gallup found had watched the debate, support for NAFTA increased from 34 percent to 56 percent and opposition decreased from 38 percent to 36 percent. The vice president succeeded in convincing many undecided voters, and Perot's negatives rose from 39 percent to 51 percent after the debate.[32] Thus, Gore provided political cover for members of Congress who feared a Perot-led backlash against their support for NAFTA and weakened the threat of Perot at the polls.

The small percentage of Americans who watched the debate limited the White House's ability to move public opinion, however. Gallup polls taken on November 2–4 and on November 15–16 (right before the House vote on November 17) both showed only 38 percent of the entire public in favor of the trade agreement. (Opposition diminished from 46 to 41 percent, however.) Thus, claims that the White House turned the public around on NAFTA are considerably exaggerated.[33] The president simply was not successful in obtaining the public's support.

ON THE DEFENSE

The presidency of Bill Clinton was a tumultuous one. Congress was highly polarized, and the Republican majorities he faced for six of his eight years in office were eager to bring about change to which the president was opposed. Under such conditions, Clinton frequently had to defend both himself and his policies. The burden of moving public opinion in such cases was on his opponents, who had to build support to change the status quo. The White House's task was to *maintain* existing support. Under these circumstances, we would expect the White House to have more success than when it wished to change opinion. In other words, we would expect the president to do better on defense than on offense.

Blame for Government Shutdowns

A prime example of Clinton fighting for public opinion on the defense is the government shutdowns of November 14–20, 1995, and December 16, 1995–January 6, 1996. These shutdowns were part of the president's larger battle with Republicans, especially in the House, over the policies represented in their Contract with America. The Republicans sought major changes in public policy, and Clinton fought to thwart their efforts.

The figures in Table 2.15 show whom the public blamed for the two shutdowns of the federal government. For purposes of analysis, I have separated the poll taken more than two weeks before the first shutdown and the poll taken nine months after the second shutdown. The results are unequivocal: each poll found the public more likely to blame the Republicans for the shutdown than they were to blame the president. The results of polls taken during the shutdowns show essentially no change in public opinion during that period. The beginning and ending percentages for both the Republicans and Clinton are within 1 percentage point of each other.

Although we may conclude that Clinton won the battle for public opinion, it is more difficult to infer that this victory resulted from Clinton's leadership of public opinion. At the height of the pitched public relations battle, when

Table 2.15. Responsibility for Government Shutdowns

			Responsibility			
Poll	*N*	Dates of Poll	Republicans	Clinton	Both	No Opinion
NBC[1]	1,465	10/27–31/95	43%	32%	18%	7%
Gallup[2]	652	11/14/95	49	26	19	6
Gallup[3]	615	11/17–18/95	47	25	21	7
CBS[4]	819	11/19/95	51	28	15	6
NBC[5]	805	11/19/95	47	27	20	6
ABC[6]	852	1/6–7/96	50	27	20	3
CBS[7]	1,479	10/17–20/96	53	28	11	8

[1]"If President (Bill) Clinton and the Republican Congress do not reach a budget agreement in time to avoid a major shutdown of the federal government, who do you think will be more to blame—President Clinton or the Republican Congress?"

[2]"Overall, who do you blame more for the recent shutdown of the federal government—President (Bill) Clinton or the Republican leaders in Congress?"

[3]"(As you may know, the Republicans in Congress and President [Bill] Clinton have not reached an agreement on the federal budget. As a result, the federal government has shut down all nonessential services.) Overall, who do you blame more for the recent shutdown of the federal government . . . President (Bill) Clinton, or the Republican leaders in Congress?"

[4]"Monday night, the federal government was partially shut down when President (Bill) Clinton and the Republican leaders in Congress could not agree on a resolution to keep the government running while they debated the federal budget. Who do you blame more for the partial government shutdown—the Republicans in Congress or Bill Clinton?"

[5]"As you know, President (Bill) Clinton and the Republican Congress have not reached a budget agreement, and this has led to a shutdown of the federal government. Who do you think is more to blame for this shutdown—President Clinton or the Republican Congress?"

[6]"As you may know, the Clinton Administration and the Republicans have agreed to temporarily reopen the government offices that were closed for nearly three weeks while they worked on a new budget. Whose fault do you think this partial government shutdown mainly was—(President Bill) Clinton's or the Republicans' in Congress?"

[7]"Who do you think was more responsible for the government shutdowns (last winter because of disagreements between Congress and the President over the budget), the Republicans in Congress or President (Bill) Clinton?"

both the president and the public were focused on actual events, the shutdowns, public opinion was remarkably stable. Perhaps the president's leadership was effective in assigning the Republicans culpability *before* the shutdowns, and we lack measures of the movement of public opinion at that time. Or perhaps opinions simply reflected views about the highly visible reform efforts of the Republicans and their leader, Speaker of the House Newt

Table 2.16. Support for Clinton's Impeachment and Conviction

Poll Date	Remove from Office	Not Remove from Office	No Opinion
6/5–7/98	19%	77%	4%
8/7–8/98	23	75	2
8/10–12/98	20	76	4
8/17/98	25	69	6
8/18/98	26	70	4
8/21–23/98	29	67	4
9/10/98	31	63	6
9/11–12/98	30	64	6
9/13/98	31	66	3
9/20/98	35	60	5
9/21/98	32	66	2
9/23–24/98	29	68	3
10/6–7/98	32	65	3

Note: Gallup Poll, "Based on what you know at this point, do you think that Bill Clinton should or should not be impeached and removed from office?"

Poll Date	Vote in Favor of Impeaching	Vote Against Impeaching	No Opinion
10/9–12/98	31%	63%	6%
10/23–25/98	30	63	7
11/13–15/98	30	68	2
11/20–22/98	33	64	3
12/4–6/98	33	65	2
12/12–13/98	35	61	4
12/15–16/98	34	63	3

Note: Gallup Poll, "As you may know, removing a president from office involves two major steps in Congress. First, the House of Representatives must vote on whether there is enough evidence to bring a president to trial before the Senate. This step is called impeachment. Next the Senate must vote on whether to remove the president from office, or not. What would you want your member of the House of Representatives to do?

1. Vote in favor of impeaching Clinton and sending the case to the Senate for trial.
2. Vote against impeachment of Clinton.
3. Don't know/refused answer.

Table 2.16. Continued

Poll Date	Vote in Favor of Convicting	Vote Against Convicting	No Opinion
12/19–20/98	29%	68%	3%
1/6/99	33	63	4
1/8–10/99	32	63	5
1/18/99	33	63	4
1/22–24/99	33	64	3
2/4–7/99	36	62	4
2/9/99	31	66	3

Note: Gallup Poll, "As you may know, the House has now impeached (Bill) Clinton and the case has been sent to the Senate for trial. What do you want your Senators to do — vote in favor of convicting Clinton and removing him from office, or vote against convicting Clinton so he will remain in office?"

Gingrich. It is reasonable to conclude that opinions were shaped before the issue of blame came to a head. Although it is possible that these opinions were responses to Clinton's focused assertions about the cause of a potential shutdown, it is more likely that the public was reacting to the much more salient policies and personalities of the time.

Impeachment

Certainly the most dramatic issue of the Clinton administration was its successful effort to fight the president's removal from office following the Monica Lewinsky scandal. The media attention devoted to the impeachment controversy and thus the issue's visibility make it unique.

The results in Table 2.16 show that the public did not support the impeachment and conviction of the president. In a brief nationally televised speech on August 17, 1998, the president admitted lying to the public about his relationship with Monica Lewinsky. Over the five and one-half months between the poll on August 21–23, 1998, and the final poll on February 9, 1999, public opinion barely changed at all. Despite, or because of, the enormous volume of commentary from advocates on both sides of the issue, the public did not budge from opinions it had reached *before* the issue came to a head. As in the case of the government shutdowns, opinions were shaped before the issue was joined and before the president and his spokespeople took to the airways to combat the Republican impeachment effort. The president's task was to maintain the strong support he enjoyed on the issue, and he seems to have done an effective job. It is difficult to determine whether Clinton's success was the result of his leadership of the public or the result of public reaction against what it saw as the overreaching of the Republicans.

At the same time that the president was fighting to win or maintain public support in opposition to impeachment, Clinton was frustrated on other issues. His efforts to spark national dialogues on race and to forge a consensus on reforming the financing of Social Security died on the vine.[34] Perhaps it was the highly charged, polarized atmosphere of 1998–1999, but the bottom line was that he could not generate much less sustain interest in the public or the media in his priority concerns.

Clinton in Perspective

As we have seen, Bill Clinton based his strategy of governing on moving the public to support his policy initiatives. Despite his impressive political and communications skills, the evidence is clear that the president typically failed to obtain public support. He did succeed in defending the status quo against radical departures proposed by his Republican opponents, but he could not rally the public behind his own initiatives. Given his experience with attempting to lead the public, it is no wonder that at the middle of his first term Clinton lamented that "I've got to . . . spend more time communicating with the American people about what we've done and where we're going."[35] Although he often declared that he needed to do a better job of *communicating,* it seems never to have occurred to him or his staff that his basic strategy may have been inherently flawed.

3

Presidential Persuasion: Does the Public Respond? Part II—Ronald Reagan

In contrast to his immediate predecessors, the public viewed Ronald Reagan as a strong leader, and his staff was unsurpassed in its skill at portraying the president and his views in the most positive light. This seeming love affair with the public generated commentary in both academia and the media about the persuasiveness of "The Great Communicator." Reagan's views were notable for their clarity and there is little doubt that the public knew where the president stood on matters of public policy. The question for us is the degree to which the public moved in Reagan's direction.

Reagan's Coming to Power

In his farewell address on January 11, 1989, Reagan reflected on his tenure in office: "They called it the Reagan Revolution, and I'll accept that, but for me it always seemed more like the Great Rediscovery: a rediscovery of our values and our common sense."[1] Reflecting on the public on inauguration day, Haynes Johnson declared, "In believing in him they were reaffirming a belief in their nation and in themselves."[2] The question for us is whether Ronald Reagan moved the public to support his clearly identifiable political views. Or was he the agent around whom already existing conservative thought coalesced?

The evidence suggests that Ronald Reagan, like presidents before him, was a facilitator rather than a director. The basic themes Reagan espoused in 1980 were ones he had been articulating for many years: government was too big; the nation's defenses were too weak, leaving it vulnerable to intimidation by the Soviet Union; pride in country was an end in itself; and public morals had slipped too far. In 1976 conditions were not yet ripe for his message. It took the Carter years, with their gas lines, raging inflation, high interest rates, Soviet aggression in Afghanistan, and hostages in Iran, to create the opportunity for victory. By 1980 the country was ready to listen.

Martin Anderson, Reagan's first chief domestic policy adviser, agrees: "What has been called the Reagan revolution is not completely, or even mostly, due to Ronald Reagan. He was an extremely important contributor to the intellectual and political movement that swept him to the presidency in 1980. He gave that movement focus and leadership. But Reagan did not give it life."[3]

Anderson goes on to argue that "neither Goldwater nor Nixon nor Reagan caused or created the revolutionary movement that often carries their name, especially Reagan's. It was the other way around. They were part of the movement, they contributed mightily to the movement, but the movement gave them political life, not the reverse."[4]

As journalist Haynes Johnson put it, Reagan "was the vehicle around which conservative forces could and did rally, the magnet that attracted a coterie of conservative journalists and writers and ambitious young economic theorists who proclaimed sacred dogma and argued theoretically pure positions."[5]

William Niskanen, one of the members of Reagan's Council of Economic Advisers, agrees with Anderson, writing that several developments in the generation before Reagan's election set the stage for substantial change in economic policy. As he saw it,

> Lower economic growth, rising inflation, and increasing tax rates led to a popular demand for some change in economic policy. . . . reduced popular confidence in the government increased the appeal of policy changes that would reduce the role of government in the American economy. Several complementary changes in the perspectives of economists and an increasing number of empirical studies shaped the choice of policies to meet these concerns. . . . [Thus,] there was broad bipartisan agreement in Congress by the late 1970s for the direction of change in each of the major dimensions of federal economic policy.
>
> All that was missing was a president who could shape a coherent economic program and articulate the rationale for this program to Congress, the press, and the American public. For most voters Ronald Reagan was the logical

> candidate and the logical president for the time. For over fifteen years he had articulated a quite consistent set of views that appealed to an increasing share of the electorate. . . . There are few periods in American history for which a president so closely matched the current demands on this role. Few presidents have had a greater opportunity to guide and shape federal economic policy.[6]

More systematic data support the view that Reagan had a receptive audience. James Stimson concluded that "movements uniformly precede the popular eras." The conservative winds of the 1980s were "fully in place before the election of Ronald Reagan" (just as the liberal winds of the 1960s were blowing in the late 1950s). He was the beneficiary of a conservative mood, but he did not create it.[7] Similarly, Benjamin Page and Robert Shapiro found that the right turn on social welfare policy occurred before Reagan took office and ended shortly thereafter.[8] James Davis also found that prodefense and antiwelfare conservative trends had occurred by the late-1970s — before Reagan's nomination.[9] William Mayer produced similar findings,[10] while Tom Smith found that liberalism had plateaued by the mid-1970s.[11]

There is another aspect of Reagan's coming to power that is of direct interest to us. Although he was the preferred candidate of the American people in 1980 and 1984, Reagan was also the least popular candidate to win the presidency in the period from 1952 to 1988. His supporters displayed an unusual degree of doubt about him, and those who opposed him disliked him with unprecedented intensity.[12]

Reagan Governing

Reagan arrived at the White House on the crest of a preexisting tide of conservatism that he helped to articulate but not to create. What happened after he took office? Was he able to use the bully pulpit to move the public to support his policies if it was not already inclined to do so? Reagan knew better.

AID TO THE CONTRAS

In his memoirs, Reagan reflects on his efforts to ignite concern among the American people regarding one of his principal preoccupations: the threat of communism in Central America. At the core of his policy response to this threat was an effort to undermine the "Sandinista" government of Nicaragua through support of the opposition Contras. Reagan required congressional support to obtain aid for the Contras, and he made substantial efforts to mobilize the public behind his program of support for the Contras. Yet he consistently failed.[13] As he lamented in his memoirs,

Table 3.1. Public Support for Aid to the Contras, 1985–1986

Date	Support Aid	Oppose Aid	Don't Know
6/85[1]	34%	59%	6%
7/85[1]	28	64	7
3/86[2]	34	59	8
3/86[2]	30	54	16
3/86[3]	35	60	4
3/86[4]	42	53	5
3/86[5]	37	44	19
4/86[7]	33	62	5
4/86[8]	39	54	7
4/86[6]	28	65	7

[1]Harris Poll question: "Recently, President Reagan has had some serious disagreements with Congress. Now who do you think was more right—Reagan or Congress—in their differences over sending military aid to the Contra rebels in Nicaragua, which is favored by Reagan and opposed by Congress?"

[2]ABC News Poll question: "President Reagan is asking Congress for new military aid for the Nicaraguan rebels know as the 'Contras.' Do you agree or disagree with Reagan that Congress should approve that money?"

[3]ABC News Poll question: "The House of Representatives has refused Reagan's request for $100 million in military and other aid to the contra rebels in Nicaragua. Do you approve or disapprove of that action by the House?" (Because the question asks respondents whether they approve of the House's negative action, a response of "approve" means opposing aid to the Contras. Thus, we have reversed the results to make them consistent with the portrayal of the results from the other questions.)

[4]ABC News Poll question: "As you may know, President Reagan has asked Congress for new military aid for the Nicaraguan rebels known as the 'contras.' Do you agree or disagree with Reagan that Congress should approve that money?"

[5]*USA Today* Poll question: "Do you favor or oppose military aid to the Contras fighting the Sandinista government in Nicaragua?"

[6]ABC News/*Washington Post* Poll question: "Do you generally favor or oppose the U.S. granting $100 million in military and other aid to the Nicaraguan rebels known as the 'contras'?"

[7]Harris Poll question: "Do you favor or oppose the U.S. sending $100 million in military and nonmilitary aid to the Contra rebels in Nicaragua?"

[8]Harris Poll question: "Do you favor or oppose the U.S. sending just $30 million in nonmilitary aid to the Contra rebels in Nicaragua?"

Table 3.2. Public Support for Aid to the Contras, 1987

Date	Approve	Disapprove	Don't Know
1/87	22%	70%	7%
7/87	43	46	12
7/87	35	54	14
7/87	41	49	11
8/87	36	59	5
8/87	40	56	4
9/87	33	61	5
10/87	33	63	4

Note: ABC News/*Washington Post* Poll question: "Do you generally favor or oppose the U.S. Congress granting military aid to the Nicaraguan rebels known as the 'Contras'?"

> Time and again, I would speak on television, to a joint session of Congress, or to other audiences about the problems in Central America, and I would hope that the outcome would be an outpouring of support from Americans who would apply the same kind of heat on Congress that helped pass the economic recovery package.
>
> But the polls usually found that large numbers of Americans cared little or not at all about what happened in Central America—in fact, a surprisingly large proportion didn't even know where Nicaragua and El Salvador were located—and, among those who did care, too few cared enough about a Communist penetration of the Americas to apply the kind of pressure I needed on Congress.[14]

The problem of which Reagan spoke is reflected in Tables 3.1–3.3, which show the responses to questions inquiring about support for aiding the Contras during Reagan's second term. No matter how the question was worded, at no time did even a plurality of Americans support the president's policy of aiding the Contras. Because the questions represented in the three tables have somewhat different wording, we must be cautious about inferring trends in opinion. Nevertheless, it is difficult to conclude that Reagan's rhetorical efforts moved opinion in his direction. (The unusually low level of support in January 1987 polls is undoubtedly the result of the Iran-Contra scandal that had just broken.)

Richard Wirthlin provides additional evidence of the limits of Reagan's persuasive powers on aid to the Contras. In a memo to the president on April 20, 1985—at the height of Reagan's popularity—Wirthlin advised against Reagan taking his case directly to the people through major speeches. The

Table 3.3. Public Support for Aid to the Contras, 1987–1988

Date	Approve	Disapprove	Don't Know
1/87	28%	60%	12%
7/87	33	51	16
7/87	40	49	12
8/87	33	49	18
10/87	35	53	12
1/88	30	58	12
3/88	39	48	14

Note: CBS News/*New York Times* Poll question: "Do you approve or disapprove of the United States government giving military and other aid to the Contras who are fighting against the government of Nicaragua?"

Table 3.4. Public Support for Involvement in Central America

Date	More Involved	Middle of the Road	Less Involved
1984	25%	20%	55%
1986	24	22	54

Notes: National Election Studies (NES) question: "Some people think that the United States should become much more involved in the internal affairs of Central American countries. Others believe that the US should become much less involved in this area. Where would you place yourself on this scale . . . ?"

Help = 1–3; Middle of the road = 4; Not help = 5–7 on NES seven-point scale.

president's pollster told him that doing so was likely to lower his approval and generate more public and congressional opposition than support.[15]

Table 3.4 provides the results from National Election Studies on the broader question of the level of U.S. involvement in Central America, and Table 3.5 provides a time series of public evaluations of the president's handling of foreign policy in Central America. In every case, a majority of the public opposed Reagan's policy of greater U.S. involvement and of his handling of the issue of Central America. Moreover, there is no trend toward greater support for the president on his high-priority policy.

DEFENSE SPENDING

One of Ronald Reagan's highest priorities was increasing defense spending. Indeed, during his first term, he oversaw the greatest peacetime increase in defense spending in U.S. history. In Tables 3.6 and 3.7, we find that public

Table 3.5. Public Approval of Reagan's Handling of Central America

Date	Positive	Negative	Unsure
10/83	33%	58%	9%
11/83	40	52	8
12/83	34	59	7
1/84	30	64	6
2/84	30	61	9
3/84	29	61	10
5/84	31	62	7
6/84	33	63	4
7/84	31	66	3
9/84	41	57	2
10/84	42	53	5
12/84	37	59	4
3/85	34	59	7
5/85	32	63	5
5/85	32	63	5
6/85	39	55	6
7/85	36	59	5
9/85	32	64	4
11/85	38	57	5
1/86	39	58	3
4/86	40	54	6
8/86	33	59	8
1/87	27	66	7
8/87	31	67	2
10/87	33	63	4
12/87	26	68	6
6/88	33	63	4

Notes: Harris Poll question: "Now let me ask you about some specific things President Reagan has done. How would you rate him on . . . Handling the situation in Central America—excellent, pretty good, only fair, or poor?"

Positive = excellent/pretty good; Negative = only fair/poor.

support for defense expenditures was decidedly *lower* at the end of his administration than when he took office.[16]

Upon closer examination, the data are even more interesting. Support for increased defense spending was unusually high *before* Reagan took office. The Reagan defense buildup represented an acceleration of change initiated late in the Carter administration. A number of conditions led to broad partisan

Table 3.6. Public Support for Defense Spending, 1980–1987

Date	Too Little	About Right	Too Much	Don't Know
1/80	49%	24%	14%	13%
1/81	51	22	15	12
3/82	19	36	36	9
3/83	14	33	45	8
1/85	11	36	46	7
3/86	13	36	47	4
4/87	14	36	44	6

Note: Gallup Poll question: "There is much discussion as to the amount of money the government in Washington should spend for national defense and military purposes. How do you feel about this: do you think we are spending too little, too much, or about the right amount?"

Table 3.7. Public Support for Defense Spending, 1980–1988

Date	Decrease	About the Same	Increase
1980	11%	18%	71%
1982	34	33	33
1984	32	32	36
1986	39	29	32
1988	35	32	33

Notes: National Election Studies (NES) question: "Some people believe that we should be spending much less on money for defense. Others feel that spending should be greatly increased. Where would you place yourself on this scale?"

Decrease = 1–3; About the same = 4; Increase = 5–7 on NES seven-point scale.

support of the defense buildup in both the Carter and Reagan administrations, including the massive Soviet increase in their strategic nuclear forces; a series of communist coups in Third World countries, followed by revolutions in Nicaragua and Iran; and the Soviet invasion of Afghanistan. American hostages held in Iran, Soviet troops controlling a small neighbor, and communists in power in the Western Hemisphere created powerful scenes on television and implied that American military power had become too weak.

Nevertheless, public support for increased defense expenditures dissipated by 1982, only a year after Reagan took office. Indeed, in his second term, a plurality of the public thought the United States was spending *too much* on defense. It is possible that the decline in support for defense spending may have been the unintended consequence of the military buildup that did occur.[17] Opinion changed by 1982, long before increased defense spending could have influenced the nation's military security, however. In addition, pressures inevitably increase to spend on butter after periods of spending on guns. The point remains, however, that while Reagan wanted to continue to increase defense spending, the public was unresponsive to his wishes. As a result, Reagan suffered another disappointment, as Congress did not increase defense spending in real dollars during his entire second term.

Interestingly, when Reagan's chief public relations adviser, Michael Deaver, wrote his memoir of the Reagan years, he presented quite a different picture of the president's leadership of the public on defense spending. According to Deaver, distressed about the lack of public support for defense spending, "Reagan pulled me aside one day; 'Mike,' he said, 'these numbers show you're not doing your job. This is your fault; you gotta get me out of Washington more so I can talk to people about how important this policy is.' I did, and he would systematically add his rationale for more military spending to nearly every speech, and eventually his message would get through to the American people."[18] One does not have to challenge the sincerity of the author's memory to conclude that such commentary contributes to the misunderstanding of the potential of the permanent campaign.

STRATEGIC DEFENSE INITIATIVE

One of Ronald Reagan's most notable proposals in national security policy was the Strategic Defense Initiative (SDI), often referred to as simply "Star Wars." Reagan first broached SDI in a national address on national security in March 1983. This distinctive proposal, designed to protect the United States against nuclear attack, was also unique in that it is an issue on which public opinion appears to have changed in the president's direction. The figures in Table 3.8 show that public support for SDI increased 12 percentage points over a two-year period from 1984 to 1986.

It is possible that SDI was distinctive because public opinion had not crystallized on the issue, providing more potential for presidential leadership. We must be cautious in our interpretations of these findings, however. The results in Table 3.9 are from Reagan's own pollster, Richard Wirthlin, and tell a somewhat different story from the results in the previous table. The results of Wirthlin's surveys show that support for SDI actually *fell* during the president's second term. The president still had majority support for his initiative, which was important for the White House, but we cannot

Table 3.8. Public Support for the Strategic Defense Initiative, 1984–1987

Date	Favor	Oppose	Unsure
10/84	40%	47%	12%
8/85	45	47	8
1/86	47	44	9
12/86	52	40	8
4/87	52	36	12

Note: Gallup Poll question: "Some people feel the U.S. should try to develop a space-based 'Star-Wars' system to protect the U.S. from nuclear attack. Others oppose such an effort because they say it would be too costly and further escalate the arms race. Which view comes closer to your own?"

Table 3.9. Public Support for the Strategic Defense Initiative, 1986–1988

Date	Good Idea	Bad Idea	No Opinion
9/19/86	62%	36%	2%
10/12/86	73	25	2
11/15/86	68	29	2
12/15/86	64	33	3
3/7/87	69	29	2
10/25/87	60	34	5
4/4/88	65	31	4
7/28/88	63	31	7
8/27/88	56	39	5

Note: Wirthlin Poll question, "Some people say that research on a defense against nuclear-armed missiles, such as SDI, is a good idea because it will help deter a Soviet attack, increase the chance of reaching another, more comprehensive, arms control agreement, and reduce the risk of war. Other people say that research on a defense against nuclear-armed missiles, such as SDI, is a bad idea because it will upset the balance of power between the U.S. and the USSR, accelerate the arms race, and increase the risk of war. Which statement is closer to your own opinion . . . that research on a defense against nuclear-armed missiles is a good idea or a bad idea?"

conclude that Reagan was effectively building a supportive coalition for his defensive shield.

GRENADA

On the evening of October 24, 1983, President Reagan ordered U.S. troops to invade the island nation of Grenada. His goals were to prevent a communist takeover of the island and to rescue U.S. medical students studying there. Initial media coverage and congressional response was, in the words of Secretary of State George Shultz, "snide, scathing, and condemnatory."[19] The first public responses to the invasion were split, as Table 3.10 shows.

On October 27, Reagan made a nationally televised address on Grenada. Following the address, public support increased. The CBS News/*New York Times* Poll is especially interesting, as part of it occurred before and part of it immediately after the president's speech. We must be cautious in concluding that it was the president's speech that was responsible for changing public

Table 3.10. Public Support for the Invasion of Grenada

Date	Poll	Approve	Disapprove	Don't Know
10/25/83	ABC/*Washington Post*	53%	33%	14%
10/26/83	Gallup	53	34	13
10/26/83	ABC/*Washington Post*	53	37	10
10/26/83	CBS/*NY Times*	46	42	12
10/27/83	Reagan's National Address			
10/27/83	CBS/*NY Times*	55	31	14
10/28/83	ABC/*Washington Post*	63	31	6
10/28/83	Harris	60	36	4
11/3/83	ABC/*Washington Post*	69	24	7
11/9/83	Harris	63	32	5
11/18/83	*NY Times*	63	27	10

Notes: ABC News/*Washington Post* Poll question: "Do you approve or disapprove of the way Reagan is handling the situation in Grenada?"

Gallup Poll question: "Do you approve or disapprove of the participation of U.S. military forces—along with those of several Caribbean nations—in the invasion of Grenada?"

CBS News/*New York Times* Poll question: "U.S. troops have been sent to Grenada. Do you approve or disapprove of sending U.S. troops there?"

Harris Poll question: "Now let me ask you about some specific things President Reagan has done. How would you rate him on ordering the invasion of Grenada—excellent, pretty good, only fair, or poor?" Approve = "excellent" and "pretty good."

New York Times Poll question: "U.S. troops have been sent to Grenada. Do you approve or disapprove of sending the troops there?"

opinion, however. In a memorable scene, the first American student to descend the steps of the transport plane at Charleston Air Force Base spontaneously fell to his knees and kissed American soil. All three major television networks carried live this act of gratitude. The emotional scene was replayed repeatedly on the news before the president's speech.

Thus, it is difficult to determine whether it was the apparent success of the operation, the joy of the rescued students, or the president's speech that increased support for the invasion. It is reasonable to speculate that the television coverage alone would have increased public support, especially when we note that most of the increase in support appears to have come from those who initially withheld judgment rather than from those who initially disapproved of the president's actions.

Members of Reagan's own staff concur with this view. According to press secretary Larry Speakes: "My staff and I were watching when the first students arrived in Charleston, and when we saw how happy they were to be home, we started cheering and pounding the Table. 'That's it! We won!' I shouted."[20] Edwin Meese adds that it was lucky having one of the students kneel down to kiss the ground after getting off the plane in Charleston: "With that simple gesture, the debate about Grenada was effectively over."[21]

OTHER NATIONAL SECURITY ISSUES

We have examined in detail five national security issues that were central to the Reagan administration. There are many other foreign and defense policy issues, of course. Most of these issues are less clear-cut than spending on offensive or defensive weapons or aid to a specific group and thus do not lend themselves readily to measuring public opinion over time. Nevertheless, capable scholars have studied both the trends and the nuances of public opinion in the 1980s. They have found that whether the issue was arms control, military aid and arms sales, or cooperation with the Soviet Union, by the early 1980s public opinion had turned to the left—and *ahead of* Reagan.[22]

DOMESTIC POLICY SPENDING

Limiting spending on domestic policy was at the core of Reagan's domestic policy. For many programs, spending *is* policy. The amount of money spent on a program determines how many people are served, how well they are served, or how much of something (land, employees, vaccines, and so on) the government can purchase. Reagan was eager to limit government spending because, as he often declared, "government is the problem." Table 3.11 provides responses to a question on spending for government services that specifies by way of example health and education policy. As the data in the

Table 3.11. Public Support for Government Spending

Date	Reduce Spending	Spend the Same	Increase Spending
1980	34%	20%	47%
1982	41	29	33
1984	34	36	30
1986	26	28	46
1988	32	29	39

Notes: National Election Studies (NES) question: "Some people think that government should provide fewer services, even in areas such as health and education, in order to reduce spending. Other people feel that it is important for the government to provide many more services even if it means an increase in spending. Where would you place yourself on this scale?"

Reduce spending = 1–3; Keep the same = 4; Increase spending = 5–7 on NES seven-point scale.

table show, Reagan never obtained majority support for reducing spending. Only in 1982 did a plurality of the public favor reducing spending (despite the recession of that year). Indeed, support for Reagan's preference for reducing spending declined during his tenure, and in his second term pluralities actually favored *increasing* spending.

Numerous national surveys of public opinion have found that support for regulatory programs and spending on health care, welfare, urban problems, education, environmental protection, and aid to minorities increased, rather than decreased, during Reagan's tenure.[23] In each case, the public was moving in the *opposite* direction to that of the president. Tables 3.12–3.15 show that increasing majorities of the public wanted the federal government to spend more on health care, education, and environmental protection, and substantial pluralities supported spending more on food stamps.

Conservative orthodoxy demands a balanced budget. Balancing the budget was also attractive to Reagan because it would constrain government spending. As Table 3.16 shows, support for a balanced budget amendment declined during Reagan's tenure—even as deficits spiraled upward.

TAXES

Few issues were as important to Ronald Reagan as taxes. Taxes extracted resources from private individuals and they provided the government with resources to spend on policies of which he was skeptical. Thus, he consistently argued that taxes were too high, even after the 25 percent tax cut passed in 1981. As the data in Table 3.17 show, few people ever think that their taxes

Table 3.12. Public Support for Health Care Spending

Date	Reduce Spending	Spend the Same	Increase Spending	No Opinion
8/1/80*	12%	37%	47%	5%
1/12/82†	10	34	52	4
1/30/84	5	28	63	3
1/29/86	5	27	64	3
4/25/87‡	3	23	72	2
6/24/88	4	24	67	5

Note: Gallup Poll question: "Now I am going to ask you a question about government spending. In answering, please bear in mind that sooner or later all government spending has to be taken care of from the money you and other Americans pay in taxes. As I read each program, tell me if the amount of money being spent for that purpose should be increased, kept at the present level, reduced, or ended altogether. . . . Improving medical and health care for Americans generally."

*"Here are some of the things the federal government spends money on. For each one, would you please tell me whether you think the government should be spending more money than it is now, less money than it is now, or should the government continue spending about the same amount as now? Health."

†"Do you think federal spending in the following areas should be cut further, increased, or remain the same? . . . Medical and health care."

‡"If you had a say in making up the federal budget this year, for which of the following programs would you like to see spending increased, for which would you like to see spending decreased, or for which should spending be kept the same? . . . Improving the nation's health care."

are too low. The real debate is between those viewing taxes as too high and those who feel that they are paying about the right amount of taxes. Ironically, public support for the view that income taxes were too high peaked just after the first stage of the 1981 tax cut took effect at the beginning of 1982. From that point, the view that taxes were too high lost support throughout the remainder of Reagan's tenure.

ENVIRONMENTAL PROTECTION

A hallmark of Reagan's domestic policy was his administration's antagonism to environmental protection legislation.[24] One of the first scandals of the administration focused on the director of the Environmental Protection Agency and her close relationship with regulated interests. The data in Table 3.18, which covers only Reagan's first term, show that the public did not

Table 3.13. Public Support for Spending on Food Stamps

Date	Reduce Spending	Spend the Same	Increase Spending	No Opinion
8/1/80*	58%	25%	13%	4%
1/12/82†	40	36	17	7
1/30/84	12	37	48	3
1/29/86	11	35	46	5
6/24/88	15	35	44	6

Note: Gallup Poll question: "Now I am going to ask you a question about government spending. In answering, please bear in mind that sooner or later all government spending has to be taken care of from the money you and other Americans pay in taxes. As I read each program, tell me if the amount of money being spent for that purpose should be increased, kept at the present level, reduced, or ended altogether. . . . Providing food programs for low-income families."

*"Here are some of the things the federal government spends money on. For each one, would you please tell me whether you think the government should be spending more money than it is now, less money than it is now, or should the government continue spending about the same amount as now? Welfare."
†"Do you think federal spending in the following areas should be cut further, increased, or remain the same? . . . Food stamps."

Table 3.14. Public Support for Federal Spending for Education

Date	Reduce Spending	Keep the Same	Increase Spending	No Opinion
8/1/80*	15%	32%	49%	5%
1/12/82†	17	32	47	4
1/30/84	5	27	65	2
1/29/86	7	26	63	3
6/24/88	7	22	66	5

Note: Gallup Poll question: "Now I am going to ask you a question about government spending. In answering, please bear in mind that sooner or later all government spending has to be taken care of from the money you and other Americans pay in taxes. As I read each program, tell me if the amount of money being spent for that purpose should be increased, kept at the present level, reduced, or ended altogether. . . . Federal money to improve the quality of public education."

*"Here are some of the things the federal government spends money on. For each one, would you please tell me whether you think the government should be spending more money than it is now, less money than it is now, or should the government continue spending about the same amount as now? Education and training."
†"Do you think federal spending in the following areas should be cut further, increased, or remain the same?" . . . Aid to education/college loans."

Table 3.15. Public Support for Environmental Spending

Date	Decrease Spending	Keep about the Same	Increase Spending
1982*	12%	41%	47%
1984	8	55	36
1986	4	45	51
1988	3	34	63

Note: National Election Studies (NES) question: "Should federal spending on improving and protecting the environment be increased, decreased, or kept about the same?"

*In 1982 the categories were "too little, about right, or too much."

Table 3.16. Public Support for a Balanced Budget Amendment

Date	Favor	Against	No Opinion
4/81	65%	21%	14%
9/81	67	19	14
9/82*	75	25	—
8/85†	49	27	24
7/87	62	21	17
1/89	59	24	17

Note: Gallup Poll question: "A proposed amendment to the Constitution would require Congress to approve a balanced federal budget each year. Government spending would have to be limited to no more than expected revenues, unless a three-fifths' majority of Congress voted to spend more than expected revenues. Would you favor or oppose this amendment to the Constitution?"

*Gallup did not offer respondents the "no opinion" option, inflating support for the remaining options.

†"Under this proposed (balanced budget) amendment, any Federal budget passed by Congress would have projected tax REVENUES that are equal to projected government SPENDING, unless a three-fifths' majority of Congress voted not to do so. Would you favor or oppose this amendment to the Constitution?"

Table 3.17. Public Opinion on Federal Taxes

Date	Too High	About Right	Too Low	Don't Know
2/80	68%	27%	0%	5%
2/82	69	26	0	5
2/84	63	33	1	4
2/85	60	32	0	7
2/87	59	35	1	6
2/88	55	39	1	5

Note: General Social Survey question: "Do you consider the amount of federal income tax that you have to pay as too high, about right, or too low?"

Table 3.18. Public Support for Environmental Protection

Date	Favor	Oppose	Unsure
3/11/82	83%	14%	3%
7/9/82	85	10	5
12/27/83	84	13	3
3/8/84	88	9	3
5/16/84	84	10	6
7/2/84	85	9	6
7/20/84	84	10	6

Note: Harris Poll question, "Do you favor or oppose . . . strict enforcement of air and water pollution controls as now required by the Clean Air and Water Acts?"

follow Reagan's lead on environmental protection. Instead, the public never wavered from its strong support for strictly enforcing laws designed to protect the environment.

HELPING MINORITIES

Civil rights and a special concern for minorities have been core issues in American politics for decades. The Reagan administration came to office largely opposed to according special attention to aiding minorities, whether through civil rights laws or social welfare legislation. As Table 3.19 shows, there was a modest change in public opinion regarding helping minorities during Reagan's tenure, and that change was in the more liberal direction of aiding minorities.

Table 3.19. Public Support for Aiding Minorities

Date	Should Not Aid	Middle	Should Aid
1980	49%	29%	22%
1982	45	30	25
1984	37	31	32
1986	40	31	29

Notes: National Election Studies (NES) question: "Some people feel that the government in Washington should make every effort to improve the social and economic position of blacks and other minority groups. Others feel that the government should not make any special effort to help minorities because they should help themselves. Where would you place yourself on this scale?"

Should aid = 1–3; Middle = 4; Should not aid = 5–7 on NES seven-point scale.

IDEOLOGY

Presidents are also interested in influencing people's general ideological preferences. Success in affecting ideological preferences may translate into changing the premises on which citizens evaluate policies and politicians and thus be especially significant. Ideological self-identification may also influence the kinds of political appeals to which one is attuned.

Reagan did no better in moving citizens' general ideological preferences to the right than he did in influencing their views of specific policies.[25] The data in Table 3.20 represent how individuals characterized their own ideology and how they viewed liberals and conservatives more generally. The readings of public opinion were taken at the time of Reagan's first election in 1980, his reelection in 1984, and at the end of his term in 1988. It is clear that there was very little change in either dimension between 1980 and 1988.

One prominent study concluded that rather than conservative support swelling once Reagan was in the White House, there was a movement away from conservative views almost as soon as he took office.[26] According to another scholar, "Whatever Ronald Reagan's skills as a communicator, one ability he clearly did not possess was the capacity to induce lasting changes in American policy preferences."[27]

DEFENSIVE EFFORTS

Like Bill Clinton, sometimes Ronald Reagan's public relations focus was defensive. Was The Great Communicator more successful in resisting criticism than he was in creating positive support?

Table 3.20. Trends in Political Ideology

	1980	1982	1984	1986	1988
Self-Placement Scale					
Conservative	23.1%	22.5%	20.8%	19.3%	23.6%
Slightly conservative	21.0	19.8	20.1	20.1	21.7
Moderate	30.6	34.9	33.4	36.9	31.3
Slightly liberal	13.5	11.7	12.9	14.2	13.1
Liberal	11.8	11.1	12.7	9.5	10.3
Mean Feeling Thermometer Ratings of					
Conservatives	62.7	53.3	59.9	58.6	61.1
Liberals	51.7	45.7	55.9	53.3	51.7

Notes: National Election Studies (NES) ideological self-placement question: "We hear a lot of talk these days about liberals and conservatives. Here is a seven-point scale on which the political views that people might hold are arranged from extremely liberal to extremely conservative. Where would you place yourself on this scale, or haven't you thought much about this?"

The NES "feeling thermometer" question: "I'd like to get your feelings toward some of our political leaders and other people who are in the news these days. I'll read the name of a person and I'd like you to rate that person using this feeling thermometer. You may use any number from 0 to 100 for rating. Ratings between 50 degrees and 100 degrees mean that you feel favorable and warm toward the person. Ratings between 0 and 50 mean that you don't feel too favorable toward the person. If we come to a person whose name you don't recognize, you don't need to rate that person. Just tell me and we'll move on to the next one. If you do recognize the name, but don't feel particularly warm or cold toward that person, you would rate that person at the 50-degree mark."

In order to reduce the NES ideology scale from seven to five points, Liberal combines those who selected themselves to be either "extremely liberal" or "liberal"; Conservative combines those who indicated they were either "extremely conservative" or "conservative."

Lebanon

One of the low points of the Reagan administration occurred on October 23, 1983, when 241 Marines were killed while they slept in their barracks at the Beirut airport. The president addressed the nation about the tragedy and America's peacekeeping role in Lebanon during the same address in which he discussed the invasion of Grenada, which took place the next day. The goal of the Lebanon portion of the speech clearly was damage control.

David Gergen, who served in the Reagan White House, has argued that Reagan's speech was "an immense success," buying the president time to work things out. He cites polls by Richard Wirthlin that found a 20-percentage-

Table 3.21. Public Approval of Reagan's Handling of Lebanon

Date	Approve	Disapprove	No Opinion
10/7–10/83	28%	53%	19%
11/18–21/83	34	52	14
1/13–16/84	28	59	14
2/10–13/84	28	60	12

Note: Gallup Poll question: "Now, let me ask you about some specific foreign problems. As I read off each problem, would you tell me whether you approve or disapprove of the way President Reagan is handling that problem? . . . The situation in Lebanon."

Date	Strongly Approve	Somewhat Approve	Somewhat Disapprove	Strongly Disapprove	No Opinion
9/23-27/82	16%	23%	16%	24%	21%
11/25–29/83	20	24	17	29	10
12/14–17/83	19	24	17	33	7
2/2–4/84	14	19	19	43	5
3/7–11/84	12	20	18	40	10

Note: Wirthlin Poll question: "I am going to read you a list of issues. For each, I would like you to tell me whether you strongly approve, somewhat approve, somewhat disapprove, or strongly disapprove of the way Ronald Reagan is handling each of these issues. . . . The situation in Lebanon."

point swing in public opinion on Lebanon.[28] Our data do not support such a positive picture, however. The figures in the top half of Table 3.21 show responses to Gallup Poll questions regarding the president's handling of Lebanon. Although there was a modest boost in public approval of the president's handling of Lebanon in the weeks following the speech, the effect was small and, more importantly, short-lived. (The small increase may have been the result of the invasion of Grenada.) Before long, public opinion reverted to the same level of approval as before the speech. Moreover, the level of disapproval increased. At no time did more than a third of the public support the president.

The bottom half of Table 3.21 presents results from a similar question asked by Richard Wirthlin. There appears to be no significant change in opinion, and at no time did a plurality of the public support the president. By December 1983, Wirthlin found that 50 percent of the public disapproved.

The Bitburg Cemetery Visit

On May 5, 1985, President Reagan visited a German war cemetery at Bitburg. The visit caused a storm of protest, especially among Jews, because some Nazi Waffen SS soldiers were buried in the cemetery. Reagan had given his word to Chancellor Helmut Kohl, however, and would not change his visit. He did add a visit to a concentration camp the same day, however. Richard Wirthlin told the president that his words and actions during the visit had turned public opinion in his favor.[29] In Wirthlin's poll of April 25–27, he found that 49 percent of the public supported the president's visit while 47 percent opposed it. He reinterviewed 75 percent of that sample on May 6–8 and found that while 39 percent of the public opposed the visit, 60 percent felt the president should have visited the cemetery to show the postwar friendship between the United States and Germany.[30] An increase of 11 percentage points is indeed an impressive change in public opinion.

These results are somewhat suspect as an indicator of public opinion, however, because only 4 percent of the public failed to register an opinion in the first poll, and only 1 percent failed to do so in the reinterviews. Conversely a CBS News/*New York Times* Poll taken the day after the visit found that the public was evenly split at 41 percent each on whether or not the president should have visited the military cemetery at Bitburg. In a poll taken May 29–June 2, those supporting the visit fell to 36 percent and those opposing it rose to 47 percent. In each case a substantial percentage of the public was undecided on the issue.[31]

Iran-Contra Scandal

The greatest crisis of the Reagan administration began in November 1986 when it was revealed that the president had decided to sell weapons to Iran secretly in return for its aid in freeing American hostages. Many saw this move as foolish (it did not work) and contrary to long-standing U.S. policy of not negotiating with terrorists. Soon, officials also learned that National Security Council staffer Oliver North led an illegal effort to divert some of the money from the sale of missiles to funding the Contras in Nicaragua. The president's approval rating in the Gallup Poll dropped 16 percentage points after the scandal was unearthed and did not rise to his pre–Iran-Contra heights until two years later, after the election of his successor.

Clearly, the White House had some explaining to do. How convincing was it to the public? In the post-Watergate period, it is not surprising that two important questions regarding the Iran-Contra scandal were whether the president

Table 3.22. Reagan's Truthfulness on Iran-Contra Affair

Date	Yes	No	Don't Know
11/25/86	40%	56%	4%
12/2/86	47	49	4
1/11–13/87*	42	53	5
1/18–20/87*	33	60	7
7/15/87	34	60	6
8/12/87	39	58	4
8/16–17/87*	42	55	3
9/19–22/87*	37	60	3

Note: ABC News/*Washington Post* Poll question: "Generally speaking, do you think Reagan has been telling the public the truth about the Iran/Contra situation or not?"

*Wirthlin Poll question, "As you may know, Ronald Reagan said he knew nothing about funding the Contra effort with money from the Iranian arms deal. From what you have heard and read, do you believe he is telling the truth?"

Table 3.23. Reagan's Covering Up the Iran-Contra Affair

Date	Yes	No	No Opinion
2/26/87	38%	57%	5%
3/5–9/87	48	48	4
5/28–6/1/87	51	47	2
6/25–29/87	50	48	2
7/11–12/87	45	49	6
7/15/87	45	49	6
8/3–5/87	43	52	5

Note: ABC News/*Washington Post* Poll question: "Do you think Ronald Reagan himself participated in an organized attempt to cover up the facts about the Iran/Contra arms affair or not?"

was telling the truth and whether he was involved in a cover-up of the scandal. The White House protested its innocence during four nationally televised addresses on November 13, 1986, December 2, 1986, March 4, 1987, and August 12, 1987.

Table 3.22 shows public responses to questions about Reagan's truthfulness. Over the period of the heart of the scandal, public opinion changed little, and the percentage of the public who felt the president was telling the truth did not increase. Similarly, Table 3.23 shows that the president did not make much

Table 3.24. Reagan's Handling of the Iran-Contra Affair

Date	Approve	Disapprove	No Opinion
12/15–18/86	36%	61%	3%
1/11–13/87	33	63	4
1/18–20/87	32	64	3
11/28–30/87	34	63	3

Note: Wirthlin Poll question, "Do you approve or disapprove of the way Ronald Reagan is handling the Iranian situation?"

Table 3.25. Iran-Contra Affair and Reagan's Ability to Govern

Date	Serious	Not Serious	Don't Know
12/27/86–1/4/87	42%	53%	5%
1/28–29/87	43	49	9
2/27/87	47	43	10
3/5–6/87	40	55	6
3/14–18/87	38	53	9
6/8–14/87	42	53	5

Note: Gallup Poll question: "Do you think the Iran-Contra affair is so serious that it makes you doubt Ronald Reagan's ability to run the country or is it not serious enough to make you question Reagan's ability to do his job?"

headway in convincing the public that he had not engaged in a cover-up. Over the same period covered in the table, Gallup found that 75 percent of the public felt that Reagan was withholding information on the Iran-Contra affair.[32]

A second issue related to the Iran-Contra scandal was how it affected the way the public viewed Reagan as a president. Table 3.24 displays public evaluations of Reagan's handling of the scandal. The approval rates of the president's performance during the entire period changed very little, despite the four nationally televised presidential addresses on the subject. Only a third of the public approved of his handling of the crisis. Potentially more serious were questions raised about Reagan being up to his job. The figures in Table 3.25 show that only a bare majority of the public did not see the scandal as evidence for doubting that the president could handle the presidency. Moreover, the White House's public relations efforts were not successful in increasing this percentage.

Comparing Reagan with Margaret Thatcher

The conclusion that Ronald Reagan was not successful in moving public opinion is likely to take most readers by surprise. This is especially likely to be true for his admirers. It is important that readers understand that our concern is empirical, not ideological. The findings are in no way a criticism of Reagan. We began by noting that we were using Reagan as a best-test case. The point is not that he was poor at leadership. Instead, it is that even the most skilled leaders face insurmountable obstacles in moving the public.

We can increase our confidence in the validity of these findings by briefly examining the experience of another strong conservative leader in office at about the same time as Reagan: Margaret Thatcher. We find that the British prime minister's experience was similar to Reagan's. In a series of studies, Ivor Crewe has analyzed the support for Thatcherite values, policy beliefs, and leadership style, using opinion polls by MORI, Gallup, and the British Election Surveys (1970 to 1983). He concluded that with the exception of privatization, there was no evidence that Prime Minister Thatcher converted the electorate on the central values of strong government, discipline, and free enterprise during her first term.[33] In addition, there was no increase in the Conservative vote, partisanship, or party members during the 1980s.[34] John Rentoul,[35] John Curtice, [36] and Robert Shapiro and John Young[37] report similar findings.

Reagan in Perspective

Ronald Reagan was less a public relations phenomenon than the conventional wisdom indicates. He had the good fortune to take office on the crest of a compatible wave of public opinion, and he effectively exploited the opportunity the voters had handed him. Yet when it came time to change public opinion or mobilize it on his behalf, he typically met with failure. As press secretary Marlin Fitzwater put it, "Reagan would go out on the stump, draw huge throngs and convert no one at all."[38]

Interestingly, in the same memo that Richard Wirthlin wrote to the president discouraging him from going public on aid to the Contras, he listed the conditions under which Reagan had been successful in marshaling public support for programs:[39]

1. When the public was misinformed about an issue (air traffic controllers' strike).
2. When the policy stakes were raised on an issue (budget and tax in 1981).
3. When increased press coverage raised the saliency of the issue to the public.
4. When the president could ask people to write their senators and representatives, amplifying the public's voice.

Table 3.26. Reagan's Handling of Air Traffic Controllers' Strike

Date	Approve	Disapprove	Don't Know
8/6–8/7/81[1]	57%	30%	13%
8/10–11/81[2]	64	27	9
8/14–17/81[3]	59	30	11
11/16–17/81[2]	66	26	8
12/14–15/81[2]	64	28	8
1/22–30/82[4]	53	42	5

[1]Gallup/*Newsweek* Poll question: "Do you approve or disapprove of the way President Reagan is handling the strike (by air-traffic controllers)?"
[2]NBC News/Associated Press Poll question: "Do approve or disapprove of the way President Reagan is handling/handled the (air traffic controllers) strike?"
[3]Gallup Poll question: "Do you approve or disapprove of the way Reagan is dealing with the air traffic controllers strike?"
[4]ABC News/*Washington Post* Poll question: "As you know, Reagan fired all the air traffic controllers who went on strike last summer (1981). Did you approve or disapprove of his firing them?"

What is especially interesting here is that the president's pollster did not list conditions when the president had increased support for his policies. Except for the first condition (when people were confused and did not have crystallized opinions), Wirthlin listed conditions that presumed that the public had already made up its mind. On the second point, Wirthlin added that raising the stakes of an issue was helpful *only* (his emphasis) when the issue already had strong grassroots support. Similarly, on the third condition, he added that increasing the saliency of an issue could bring popular pressure on Congress if the issue *already* had broad support. The clear implication of the fourth condition is that the public *already* had its voice.

In addition, Reagan's performance regarding the air traffic controllers' strike was not universally lauded. Despite a well-known predisposition among the public to oppose strikes by public employees, Table 3.26 shows that the president attained the support of a bare majority of the public approximately six months after the strike.

Clearly, there was a disjunction between what the polls said and what the press and Washington insiders believed about Reagan's relationship with the public. Perhaps those inside the beltway had such a strong belief in the power of a person of Reagan's skill and charm on television and were so impressed with Reagan's communications skills that they took it for granted that he was able to move the American people. These premises made it easy to attribute the president's early legislative victories to his skill as a communicator. On closer examination, the insiders appear to have been wrong. Once the themes had been established, however, they were difficult to adjust to the reality of years of stalemate and budgets declared "Dead on Arrival." In retrospect, Reagan's image as The Great Communicator appears to owe more to his early success with Congress than to his ability to move the public in a reliable fashion.

Reconsidering Presidential Leadership of the Public

We began Chapter 2 by inquiring whether there was evidence that the president could move public opinion to support him or his policies. We have found that even able communicators like Ronald Reagan and Bill Clinton could not move the public much on their own. This finding poses a direct challenge to the faith that many have in the broad premise of the potential of presidential leadership of the public. At the very least, it is appropriate to rethink the theory of governing based on the principle of presidential success in exploiting the bully pulpit to achieve changes in public policy.

Chief executives are not directors who lead the public where it otherwise refuses to go, thus reshaping the contours of the political landscape. Instead, presidents are facilitators who reflect, and may intensify, widely held views. In the process, they may endow the views of their supporters with structure and purpose and exploit opportunities in their environments to accomplish their joint goals. Ronald Reagan did this brilliantly in 1981.

The focus in Chapters 2 and 3 has been on the president moving public opinion in his direction. The data are all the aggregate results of national polls. In addition to national totals, the president may be especially interested in moving opinion in certain states or congressional districts, those in which he has the best chance of influencing a member of Congress. It is possible that the absence of aggregate national change may mask significant change in only a few, but critical, geographic areas.

Systematic data on opinion on policies within a state or congressional district are not available, so it is not possible to provide a definitive answer to the question of targeted impact. We can say that there is simply no evidence for this kind of effect. Moreover, even the White House lacks a mechanism for attempting to influence directly public opinion in delineated areas. How could it? In the electronic age, the bully pulpit is not a precision tool. When the president speaks, anyone can listen. In addition, even a presidential visit is unlikely to be repeated often, especially to a House district. If the White House wants to focus on a particular congressional constituency, it is much more likely to attempt quietly to mobilize campaign contributors, local elites, and interest groups than it is to employ the bully pulpit.

It is possible that despite the limitations of targeting his message, the president's rhetoric could have a disproportionate effect in certain constituencies. This is unlikely, however, as public opinion tends to swing in national trends. For example, Robert Erikson, Michael MacKuen, and James Stimson found that public opinion tends to move similarly across a broad range of groups within the country.[40] Page and Shapiro reached the same conclusion. They found that although demographic groups may start from different levels of support, the direction and extent of opinion change within them is similar.[41] Moreover, if there is movement in some constituencies that is not captured by the national totals, and these totals typically do not move in the president's direction, then there must be an even greater countermovement elsewhere. It is much more likely that the national totals have captured whatever opinion change occurs.

An alternative view is that the president primarily seeks to influence those segments of the population that may be most attuned to his appeals. Of course, there is no way for the president to segment his appeals so that only a select, but sizable, audience hears them. It is possible, however, that the president is more successful in influencing some groups than others and that the aggregate national data mask movement that occurs among subgroups of the population, such as those most predisposed to support him. In Chapter 9, I present a detailed analysis of disaggregated opinion on a selection of issues from the Reagan and Clinton years and find results similar to those for national totals.

This book focuses on the president's efforts to use the bully pulpit to influence public opinion regarding themselves, their performance (including answering charges of misconduct), and their policies—ranging from legislative initiatives to military interventions. The president speaks out for other purposes as well, such as trying to influence the national agenda, satisfy a constituency with symbolic benefits, or prepare the public for a policy shift. It is possible that the White House enjoys more success in these endeavors.

At this point, we have described the movement of public opinion in relation to the president's policy positions. Our next step is to explain why the public is not more responsive to the president. To explore the obstacles to presidential leadership of the public, we must examine both the stimulus and the response in the communications chain. We begin by focusing on the president as the messenger and then move to examining voters as receivers of communications.

PART II

The Messenger

4

Charisma and Personality: Does the Messenger Matter?

Presidents are rarely able to move the public to support their policies. Nor is the bully pulpit much help to chief executives in increasing their own approval ratings. Findings so contrary to the conventional wisdom and to presidents' core strategies for governing require an explanation. Why is presidential leadership of the public not more effective?

Any causal chain between the White House and public opinion begins with the president. Every president is a unique individual, and there is perhaps no subject that receives more space in the press than the personal characteristics of the president. In addition, voters frequently focus on the personal characteristics of candidates rather than on their issue stands when deciding whom to support. Political commentators are quick to credit to presidents' personal qualities for both their successes and failures in achieving public support.

The attention that journalists, voters, and others devote to personal qualities is based on the implicit assumption that these traits matter to presidential leadership, especially to public leadership. Like other premises that we examine in this book, the strength with which the assumption of the importance of personal qualities is held seems to be in inverse proportion to the evidence in support of it.

Presidents vary in their communications skills, their personal characteristics, and their personal histories. Chapters 2 and 3 focused on two of the most skilled communicators to occupy the presidency in recent decades, Ronald Reagan and Bill Clinton. We saw that even these gifted communicators typically failed in their efforts to move the public. Communications skills, then, do not seem to be a critical factor in leadership of public opinion.

In this chapter, I examine the effect of the president's personal qualities on his ability to obtain public support. I begin with what could be the most powerful, and is certainly the most elusive, of personal qualities: charisma. It is common to hear successful figures described as "charismatic"—or lacking in charisma. Indeed, charisma is one of the most commonly used concepts in Western culture.[1] It is offered as an explanation for the "magnetic" attractiveness of presidents, preachers, and movie stars in particular and the emotionally charged aspects of social interaction in general. Its use has been extended to labeling perfume, shirts, songs, and even sheets and towels. But is the concept of charisma useful in explaining the president's public leadership? Do presidents to whom we attribute charisma evoke unique responses from the public, making their leadership more effective?

Similarly, political observers commonly associate both approval and persuasiveness with personality. In common usage the term "personality" refers to personal characteristics such as warmth, charm, and humor that may influence responses to an individual. It is not unusual for observers to conclude that the public's responses to presidents are based more on style than substance, especially during an era in which the media and sophisticated public relations campaigns play such a prominent role in presidential politics. Yet, is it true that the public evaluates presidents on their personalities rather than their policies? Are the most likable presidents more able to obtain public support? Does the public refuse to support presidents it does not particularly like?

The Concept of Charisma

The concept of charisma is taken from the idiom of early Christianity. It is a Greek word meaning gift of grace, used in two letters of St. Paul to describe the Holy Spirit.[2] Rudolf Sohm first employed the term in social science literature in his 1892 analysis of the transformation of the primitive Christian community into the Roman Catholic Church, emphasizing the "charismatic institution" and referring to the gift of grace, the possession of *pneuma,* or spirit, by a religiously inspired individual.[3] Of course, a large number of contemporary fundamentalist Christians are termed charismatic, as are the leaders of religious movements, ranging from Jim Jones to Oral Roberts.

It is with the use of the concept to understand politics, however, that is of interest to us in our efforts to understand the public leadership of presidents, and it was Max Weber who gave the term political relevance. He argued that the phenomenon of charisma was universal, although most common in the religious realm, and that it, along with the rational-legal and the traditional, was one of three pure types of legitimate authority.[4] Weber attached great importance to charisma, and he saw it as "the great revolutionary force," especially in traditionalist periods.[5]

In general, Weber is ambiguous on just what charismatic qualities are. He did not make clear whether charisma was a quality possessed by leaders independent of society or a quality dependent upon its recognition by followers. On one hand, he argues that "what is alone important is how the individual is actually regarded by those subject to charismatic authority."[6] The perceptions of followers are ultimately based on performance, and if success eludes the leader for long, his or her charismatic authority will disappear. Charismatic leaders must continually prove themselves, making their authority naturally unstable.[7]

Conversely, Weber also asserts that "as a rule, charisma is a highly individual quality."[8] He defined it as a "certain quality of an individual personality by virtue of which he is considered extraordinary and treated as endowed with supernatural, superhuman, or at least specifically exceptional powers or qualities. These are such as are not accessible to the ordinary person, but are regarded as of divine origin or as exemplary, and on the basis of them the individual concerned is treated as a leader."[9] He refers to those "truly endowed with charisma,"[10] and discusses at length the transformation of "pure" charisma.[11] Thus, Weber ends up emphasizing personality despite his earlier disclaimer.

Weber is not alone in his contradictions regarding the basis of charisma. Ann Ruth Willner, for example, maintains at one point that charisma is more perception than personality: "It is not what the leader is but what people see the leader as that counts in generating the charismatic relationship."[12] A few pages later, however, she argues that "the prime precipitant of political charisma must be the element of the leader himself or his leadership. Some attributes or actions of the leader, some combination of attributes and actions, and/or some mode of presenting these to the public serves to catalyze charismatic perceptions."[13]

Scholars since Weber have equated the charismatic in politics with a variety of phenomena. According to James MacGregor Burns, the term charisma has a "number of different but overlapping meanings: leaders' magical qualities; an emotional bond between leader and led; dependence on a father figure by the masses; popular assumption that a leader is powerful, omniscient, and virtuous; imputation of enormous supernatural power to leaders (or secular power, or both); and simply popular support for a leader that verges on love." Indeed, the term has been used in such a varied manner that Burns concludes that "it is impossible to restore the word to analytic duty."[14]

Yet, there is a need to deal with the nature of the relationship between popular leaders and their followers. Thus, reliance on the concept is widespread. Burns, for example, uses "heroic leadership" to mean "belief in leaders because of their personage alone, aside from tested capacities, experience, or stand on issues; faith in the leaders' capacity to overcome obstacles and crises; readiness to grant leaders the powers to handle crises; mass support for such leaders expressed directly."[15] Another author might well have used "charisma" in place of "heroic leadership."

The circularity of defining charisma as being perceived as charismatic diminishes its utility and reduces the concept of charisma to public relations campaigns. It certainly begs the question of whether there is such a characteristic as charisma and whether it affects others.

For our purposes, charisma refers to a personal quality or qualities of leaders that induces large segments of the public to support them. (Our focus is on relations with the mass public and not with a small entourage of personal aides or a small sect or cult of devoted followers.) These qualities may best be described as a form of personal magnetism. Charles Lindholm, for example, argues that "magnetic quality" "is the essence of charisma,"[16] and David Aberbach declares that charismatic leaders possess "magnetic power."[17]

The Search for Charismatic Leadership

Do some presidents succeed in leading the public because they possess or are perceived as possessing charisma? For us to conclude that a president has benefited from charisma, we must find evidence of a charismatic response by the public. If we find such evidence, we may pursue the nature of charismatic leadership by inquiring what is it in the leader that makes people willing to follow and under what conditions are leaders most likely to evoke charismatic responses?

Interestingly, scholars have focused on these last two questions while ignoring the prior and most important question of whether the support some leaders have enjoyed was the result of their charisma. Weber did not explicitly deal with it. For the most part, he takes for granted the nature of the appeal of the charismatic[18] and does not consider alternative explanations for what he views as public responses to charisma.[19] This assumption is even more common in subsequent analyses.

It is not unusual for authors to explain the historical significance of notable political figures entirely in terms of their charismatic qualities or to explain the success of movements such as Nazism and Bolshevism with the personal appeal of charismatic leaders. These explanations often substitute for more comprehensive analyses and preempt the search for alternative explanations.[20]

There are many possible explanations for the rise of leaders, and manifestations of popularity cannot be taken at face value as evidence of special qualities of leaders. Many factors may be more important than personality: the issues with which a leader is associated and the grievances a leader seeks to right; the manner in which a leader proposes to deal with issues; the time a leader chooses for making these issues and grievances the passionate concern of those whom he thinks will be his followers; the way a leader exploits a political environment; the use of propaganda techniques; and so on.[21]

Authors often present the importance of charismatic leadership in nonfalsifiable terms. For example, Arthur Schweitzer argues that John F. Kennedy was charismatic although most people did not recognize it. Adolf Hitler was yet another charismatic leader whom followers managed to miss, at least at first.[22]

Other authors find that charismatic leadership waxes and wanes. David Apter argues that Kwame Nkrumah had it for certain years and then lost it.[23] Richard Fagen, after examining the charisma of Fidel Castro, argues that an individual may be capable of generating a charismatic response in one context but may not succeed in doing so in another.[24] Aberbach agrees, contending that a wide range of leaders, including Napoleon, Vladimir Lenin, Abraham Lincoln, Churchill, Hitler, and Mohandas Gandhi, lacked charisma and then suddenly acquired it.[25]

Taking a somewhat different approach, Robert Tucker argues for a "situational charisma," in which a leader of "non-messianic tendency" evokes a charismatic response simply because of being in position in a time of acute distress. For example, both Churchill and Franklin D. Roosevelt, he argues, evoked charismatic responses from their publics during the dark hours of World War II. However, both lost this response in better times.[26] Similarly, Douglas Madsen and Peter Snow argue that a particular leader receives a charismatic response mostly as a result of being in the right place at right time and being able to project a dramatic and positive impression of the capacity to lead.[27] Aberbach agrees, declaring that "crisis creates charisma." Churchill, for example, was only charismatic when his personality and the needs of the people were in harmony during World War II.[28]

How are we to determine charismatic leadership if we ignore alternative explanations for mass response to leadership, or if it may go unrecognized, vary across time for the same person, or be so situational as to be independent of the person doing the leading? There is a substantial potential for charisma to be a post hoc type of attribution, a residual category of explanation that is very difficult to evaluate objectively. Moreover, we are in danger of circular reasoning if we assert that leaders are charismatic when they are supported and noncharismatic when they are not. How are we to test for charisma if it is impossible to see its results?

Numerous authors begin their analyses by simply assuming the presence of charisma. In perhaps the most widely cited work on charisma, Willner relies on anecdotal material for identifying charismatic political leaders.[29] On such a basis she is able to identify seven "unambiguous" charismatics for further study: Hitler, Gandhi, Franklin D. Roosevelt, Sukarno, Benito Mussolini, Castro, and Ruhollah Khomeini.

This certainty regarding charismatic leadership is especially impressive because of the author's demanding definition of charisma: a leader must be perceived by his or her followers as somehow superhuman, and followers must blindly believe the leader's statements, unconditionally comply with the leader's directives for action, and give the leader unqualified emotional commitment.[30] This is formidable leadership indeed, and one might expect some equally impressive supporting evidence on behalf of its existence. Willner, however, does not provide such evidence.

A recent volume on Jesse Jackson asserts that everyone agrees that he has charisma, which is "clearly manifested" because his followers see him as superhuman, and they blindly believe him, unconditionally comply with his directives, and give unqualified emotional commitment. No systematic evidence is offered to support these claims. The author later concedes that Jackson's charisma does not work with whites and that Jackson was not able to achieve the success he sought with PUSH/Excel.[31] Jackson's lack of leadership success does not seem to raise any questions for the author about the utility of the concept of charisma.

The *Handbook of Leadership* devotes 4 percent of the volume to the discussion of "Charismatic, Charismaticlike, and Inspirational Leadership." It simply asserts that a wide range of leaders, including Charles de Gaulle, Muammar al-Qaddafi, Khomeini, Lenin, Gandhi, Caesar, Franklin D. Roosevelt, and John F. Kennedy, were charismatic and goes on to discuss the characteristics of leaders and followers.[32]

Similarly, an area of research focused in industrial psychology finds charisma everywhere in complex organizations, ranging from business executives in corporations to officers in the armed forces. Analysts then provide lists of the personal attributes and behavioral components of charismatic leaders and focus on how to produce more such leaders.[33]

Lindholm simply accepts the reality of charisma and turns his attention to what involvement in it means emotionally and psychologically for leaders and followers.[34] Edward Portis premises his discussion of charisma on the "ever-present possibility of charismatic leadership" and argues that "charismatic leaders are a recurring phenomenon in any society characterized by voluntary social movements."[35]

Schweitzer finds charisma everywhere, including in both Roosevelts, Mao Tse-tung, Lenin, Mussolini, Hitler, David Lloyd George, Churchill, de Gaulle, Gandhi, Jawaharlal Nehru, Indira Gandhi, Robert Kennedy, Martin Luther King, George Wallace, and Joseph McCarthy. In general, he asserts that these leaders possessed charisma but does not critically evaluate this assumption.[36]

Edward Shils sees a charismatic element in all societies, because people in all societies confront the exigencies of life that demand a comprehensive solution. Thus, there is a universal need for order, and charisma attaches itself to those who satisfy that need or promise to do so. The generator of order arouses a charismatic response as awe and reverence are evoked. The exercise of power on a large scale evokes a legitimating attitude, so *all* [italics added] rulers possess charismatic qualities, that is, have them attributed to them. In addition, charisma need not be limited to individuals; institutions may be repositories of charisma as well.[37]

Clifford Geertz agrees with Shils, adding that charisma is ever present and stems from the "inherent sacredness of central authority,"[38] a view apparently shared also by Amitai Etzioni,[39] who argues that leaders can become charismatic *after* achieving their positions of authority. Many other scholars, including Barbara Kellerman,[40] Peter Bathory,[41] Aberbach,[42] and James Hunt,[43] assume charismatic leadership. Peter Drucker, for example, asserts that "no century has seen more leaders with more charisma than our twentieth century."[44] Yet, these authors provide little justification for such assertions.

The primary exception to the lack of rigorous examination of the existence of charismatic responses by followers is a thoughtful study by Madsen and Snow on the leadership of Juan Peron in Argentina.[45] After presenting a theory of why the country was ready for a charismatic leader, they examine election data and conclude that Peron did receive a charismatic response, although one limited to the working class.[46]

The authors examine estimates of the size of crowds at demonstrations for Peron several months before the election and conclude that one of four voters for Peron in 1946 were true believers.[47] Their confidence in their conclusions is buttressed by the fact that Peron received his strongest support in urban areas (where the authors conclude misery was the greatest) and some crucial support from migrants (who they believe were most likely to have lost the perception of coping with their problems). These voters are the ones that their theory predicts were most likely to have charismatic responses to a "savior."[48]

Such an analysis has several limitations, despite the care that the authors have taken with it. Using voting as proxy for devotion to Peron and relying on estimates of crowd size and participation in demonstrations as indicators of charismatic response are very weak bases for inferring charisma, especially when Peron received only 52.4 percent of the vote (in 1951; in 1973 he received 62 percent). How are we to differentiate this behavior from commonly occurring political behavior?

In another chapter the authors present survey data on a small segment of the population, and they argue that it displays evidence of strong emotional ties to Peron. Unfortunately, this survey data was gathered a decade after Peron had been sent into exile.[49]

In the end, scholarship on charismatic leadership provides numerous descriptions of the leaders to whom authors attribute charismatic leadership and countless assertions about charismatic responses to these leaders. We also find in the literature many discussions of the conditions favoring the appearance and disappearance of charismatic leadership and of the characteristics that charismatic leaders share.[50] As rich as these discussions often are, they circumvent the question of whether the leadership was in fact of the charismatic variety. We still lack systematic evidence that leaders to whom authors attribute charisma evoke a different response from the public than noncharismatic leaders. We must investigate charismatic leadership more rigorously before we can employ the concept usefully in explaining presidential leadership of the public.

Do People Perceive Charisma?

Robert C. Tucker argues that "to be a charismatic leader is essentially to be perceived as such."[51] If leaders are going to evoke charismatic reactions, there should be evidence that people perceive them as having charismatic qualities. If leaders are not perceived as charismatic, it will be difficult to conclude that they have evoked a charismatic response.

Systematic data on the perceptions of people about historical figures is not easy to obtain, but we do have one important resource on which to draw: the National Election Studies. This invaluable data source allows us to examine survey data on presidents over the past half century.

RECENT PRESIDENTS

When we examine recent American leaders, we find the voters' perceptions of charisma in short supply. Arthur Miller, Martin Wattenberg, and Oksana Malanchuk examined the National Election Studies during the 1952–1984 period and created a scale of "charisma" based on the perceptions of the

Table 4.1. Public's Evaluations of the Charisma of Selected Presidential Candidates

President	Year	Charisma Scale
Eisenhower	1952	+18
Eisenhower	1956	+17
Kennedy	1960	+1
Nixon	1960	+5
Johnson	1964	+8
Nixon	1968	−3
Nixon	1972	+1
Carter	1976	0
Ford	1976	−1
Reagan	1980	0
Carter	1980	−1
Reagan	1984	+6
Bush	1988	−2
Bush	1992	+1
Clinton	1992	−2
Clinton	1996	+3

Source: Adapted from Martin P. Wattenberg, "Why Clinton Won and Dukakis Lost," *Party Politics* 1 (No. 2, 1995): 245–260. Updated by Wattenberg.

public. They defined charisma in terms of responses regarding leadership abilities; the ability to communicate, inspire, and get along with people; and the dignity, patriotism, and humility of a candidate.[52]

Apparently, charismatic qualities have not been much on the minds of the public. The authors found fewer comments on "charisma" than on candidates' competence, integrity, reliability, or personal appearance and demographic characteristics. In addition, perceptions of a candidate's "charisma" were the least important factor in predicting both votes and candidate ratings on the feeling thermometer.[53]

Wattenberg provided an index on the "charisma scale" for candidates in presidential elections from 1952 through 1996.[54] The results appear in Table 4.1. The figures in the far right column represent the net of positive and negative comments for candidates who have served as president.

Dwight Eisenhower, the staid, methodical military manager with the convoluted syntax, had by far the highest scores on the charisma scale. John Kennedy, the handsome, eloquent young proponent of the dynamic New Frontier, on the other hand, achieved only a "1"—while his opponent, Richard Nixon (to whom virtually no one has ever attributed charisma), got a "5" in the same race.

Lyndon Johnson, who complained that his problem was that he lacked charisma[55]and whose appearances before large audiences were notable for their stiffness and awkwardness, came out higher than anyone aside from Eisenhower. Ronald Reagan, The Great Communicator, achieved only a "0" in 1980. Four years later, when the economy was strong, he rose to a "6." Bill Clinton won election in 1992 with a "−2" rating.

An examination of the National Election Studies data shows that public perceptions of "charisma" do not correlate with the conventional wisdom of which presidents possessed charisma. This is not a definitive test of perceptions of charisma, of course. To begin, not everyone will be satisfied with the definition of "charisma" Miller, Wattenberg, and Malanchuk used. We must examine "charismatic" presidents from other perspectives and in more detail.

Consequences of Charisma

Whether one views charisma as something an individual possesses or something others simply perceive that an individual possesses, charisma will be a useful concept to social scientists to the extent that there are *consequences* of it. In an ideal situation, we would investigate charismatic responses to leaders by identifying charismatic leaders and then comparing the response of the public to their leadership with the public's response to similarly positioned noncharismatic leaders. Unfortunately, the research context is far from ideal. To begin, we lack an independent measure of charisma.

Only one study has tried to measure charisma. The author attempted to isolate measurable characteristics of charisma among thirty-four heads of state and then test explanations of the social context of its appearance. The indicators of charisma ranged from pictures of the leader posted in public or in homes and the leader giving long speeches on his sexual prowess and the degree to which females made sacrifices for the leader.[56] This novel attempt at bringing rigor to the study of charisma does not seem to have inspired others to follow and is unlikely to serve our purposes very well.

Although we are unlikely to agree on a measure of charisma, we can compare the public response to leaders to whom we commonly attribute charisma with those to whom we do not. If charisma is a useful resource for leaders, charismatic leaders should evoke different responses from the public than do noncharismatic leaders. The differential responses to charismatic political leaders may include

1. Obtaining unusually high levels of support
2. Obtaining support from unusual sources
3. Obtaining especially intense and committed support that is especially stable and easy to mobilize
4. Successfully leading public opinion, changing the opinions of notable segments of the population on matters of public policy

Such consequences are not necessarily the result of charisma, of course, and there may be additional consequences of charisma. Nevertheless, these are the consequences most commonly attributed to charismatic leaders, and these consequences should reliably occur in response to leaders to whom we attribute charisma.

Charisma and Public Support: John F. Kennedy

We have hypothesized that likely consequences of charisma include obtaining unusually high or stable levels of public support and obtaining support from unusual sources. John F. Kennedy is clearly the post–World War II political leader to whom the term "charismatic" is most frequently applied. Tom Wicker, for example, calls JFK "charismatic."[57] Even Kennedy's critics attribute remarkable personal appeal to him.[58] Thus, Kennedy provides a best-case test for the effect of charisma on popular support. If there is evidence of such an effect, then we should find it here.

Our concern is whether Kennedy's relations with the public indicate any basis for attributing a special rapport with it. There is room for skepticism. For example, in a book of essays published in 1963, Arthur M. Schlesinger, Jr., an admirer of Kennedy's and a principal chronicler of his administration, termed the concept of charisma "mischievous" and irrelevant to the modern world.[59]

THE 1960 ELECTION

Let us begin with the election of 1960. What is most interesting about this election is that Nixon came so close to winning it (perhaps he actually did win). Kennedy, on the other hand, ran well behind the Democratic ticket—despite numerous advantages.

In 1960 only 29 percent of American voters called themselves Republicans, while 45 percent viewed themselves as Democrats,[60] so the Republican should have been a decided underdog without a national hero at the head of the ticket. Moreover, Kennedy ran a very well financed and carefully planned campaign.

In addition, Nixon suffered a seemingly endless list of obstacles (some self-inflicted) to winning the presidency: his dubious choice of Henry Cabot Lodge as his running mate, his knee infection, his pallid appearance in the first presidential debate, his decision not to call Martin Luther King's wife after King was jailed in Georgia—and Kennedy's decision to do so, the story about the loan from Howard Hughes to Nixon's younger brother Donald, the heavy Catholic vote swing to Kennedy, the failure to unleash Eisenhower as a campaigner, the downturn of the economy, his burden of defending the Eisenhower administration, his inability to answer Kennedy's charges on being soft on Cuba in order to protect the plans for the invasion of the island, Eisenhower's "give me a week" remark indicating that Nixon had not made an important contribution to his administration, and his erratic command of himself.

Kennedy was not able to win unexpected states nor was he able even to obtain a majority of the vote cast for president. In addition, there was little in the way of coattails as the Democrats lost twenty seats in the House. This is hardly evidence of a charismatic bond with the electorate.

KENNEDY'S PUBLIC APPROVAL

Once in office, Kennedy enjoyed a much higher level of public support than he experienced during his election (see Table 4.2). Indeed, he achieved the highest average approval rating of any chief executive in the post–World War II era, 71 percent. His lowest yearly average was a remarkably high 64 percent approval. He never fell below 56 percent approval in any individual poll, always maintaining the support of a majority of Americans.

The question for us is whether this level of support provides evidence of charismatic leadership. Was Kennedy able to obtain notably different support than we might expect from a Democratic president? Was he able to mobilize the public behind his initiatives?

One way to evaluate Kennedy's support is to compare it with that of the first

Table 4.2. Average Yearly Approval for Kennedy and Johnson

President	First Year	Second Year	Third Year
Kennedy	76%	72%	64%
Johnson	74	66	51

Source: George C. Edwards III, *Presidential Approval* (Baltimore, MD: Johns Hopkins University Press, 1990).

Table 4.3. Range of Kennedy's and Johnson's Approval Ratings

Kennedy			Johnson		
Year	High	Low	Year	High	Low
1961	79%	72%	1964	79%	69%
1962	79	61	1965	71	62
1963	74	56	1966	61	44

Source: George C. Edwards III, *Presidential Approval* (Baltimore, MD: Johns Hopkins University Press, 1990).

three years of his Democratic successor, Lyndon Johnson, which we do in Table 4.2. Johnson began his tenure with very high approval levels, only slightly lower than Kennedy's, despite the passage of a large number of polarizing policies, including protections for civil rights and the war on poverty. By 1966, however, widespread unrest over the war in Vietnam, civil rights, and other social issues took their toll, and Johnson's approval level fell substantially.

The stability of Kennedy's public approval was less within years than across them. In Table 4.3 we find that, although his public support varied little in his first year in office, the president faced considerable instability in the public's evaluations in 1962 and 1963. There was a general erosion of support among the public over the second and third years of his tenure, much of it due to the loss of approval in the South associated with the issue of the racial integration of educational institutions. However, this decline was punctuated by the Cuban missile crisis in October 1962, which gave him a considerable boost in the polls.

The stability of Johnson's approval, also shown in Table 4.3, was as great as Kennedy's. Kennedy actually had less-stable support during his second year, varying 18 percentage points to only 9 percentage points for Johnson. In their third years, the range of Johnson's approval was 17 percentage points, but Kennedy's was 18 percentage points.

When we disaggregate the public into demographic groups (see Table 4.4), the results are revealing and very similar for both presidents. Differences between the sexes are minimal, while racial differences are significant, especially after the issue of civil rights increased in prominence in 1962 and 1963. Nonwhites were more approving of the presidents, undoubtedly reflecting their commitment to civil rights and the Democratic party identification of most nonwhites.

Table 4.4. Average Approval of Demographic Groups for Kennedy and Johnson

	Kennedy			Johnson		
Group	1961	1962	1963	1964	1965	1966
Party						
Democrats	87%	86%	79%	84%	79%	67%
Republicans	58	49	44	62	49	32
Independents	72	69	61	67	60	44
Gender						
Male	77	72	62	76	67	53
Female	74	72	65	74	66	50
Race						
White	75	71	60	74	64	48
Nonwhite	80	85	86	84	87	76
Region						
East	78	76	71	80	75	61
Midwest	77	73	66	77	69	50
South	72	66	51	69	57	44
West	76	73	65	72	64	49
Religion						
Protestant	72	67	58	73	62	46
Catholic	87	86	81	82	77	63
Education						
Grade school	74	71	63	74	66	53
High school	78	74	66	76	68	52
College	73	67	59	75	64	48
Age						
Under 30	80	81	71	78	70	55
30–49	78	75	67	76	68	53
50+	71	66	57	73	64	49

Source: George C. Edwards III, *Presidential Approval* (Baltimore, MD: Johns Hopkins University Press, 1990).

Support for civil rights also had its costs for both presidents, however. The conservative South, rocked by the tumult over racial integration, gave both presidents lower support than any other region, while the more liberal East continued to accord them both the highest levels of approval.

Religion was a discriminating characteristic in Kennedy's years in office. Not surprisingly for the first Catholic president, Catholics were more supportive than Protestants. In addition, some of the relative lack of Protestant support is probably the result of the lack of support for Kennedy in the largely Protestant South and the fact that Catholics were disproportionately Democrats. Interestingly, the Protestant Johnson continued to receive most of the advantage of his predecessor in obtaining considerably more support from Catholics than from Protestants.

Education was not a particularly important predictor of approval for either president. Younger citizens were slightly more supportive of both presidents than those 30 to 49, and, especially for Kennedy, they were clearly more supportive than those older than 50. Part of the explanation for these differences may also be the fact that older voters were more likely to be Republican, especially in the early 1960s.

Overall, the patterns of the levels, stability, and sources of support for Kennedy and Johnson are quite similar. Kennedy's approval was somewhat higher, especially in the third year, but the patterns are basically the same. Kennedy's support eroded substantially at the time of his death as he became involved in more controversial matters, notably civil rights. Would it have continued to decline if he had lived and pushed through civil rights bills, committed large numbers of troops to fight in Vietnam, and presided over an era of turbulent social protest? We can only speculate, but the data provide little support for the conclusion that his approval would have been immune from a fate similar to his successor's or that he enjoyed a special relationship with the American people.

A CODA ON FDR

Aside from John F. Kennedy, the twentieth-century president to whom people most commonly attribute charisma is Franklin D. Roosevelt. Commentators frequently attribute Roosevelt's early successes in obtaining public support, and thus congressional action, to his charisma, especially as manifested in his radio speeches.

There is much less public opinion survey data on FDR than on more recent presidents, of course. Moreover, FDR served longer than any other president, and his tenure occurred during the unique circumstances of the Great Depression and World War II. All of this makes it difficult to make reasonable comparisons with another president.

Nevertheless, we do know something about Roosevelt's public support. Matthew Baum and Samuel Kernell concluded that "the Roosevelt presidency was unique more in its context than in the president himself." The authors conclude that FDR "was by no means immune to the normal political winds that nip and tug on every president's political support. On a number of occasions, Roosevelt's exceptional political skills failed to insulate him from the negative political consequences of pursuing unpopular policies."[61] There are many examples of such policies, ranging from the attempt to pack the Supreme Court to the president's efforts to move the country from its isolationist tendencies and aid Britain and rebuild its military strength before our entry into World War II.

Charisma and Leading the Public: Reagan and Roosevelt

Perhaps the most important potential consequences of charismatic leadership is moving the public — changing opinions, mobilizing citizens into action, and placing new issues on the public's agenda. Are presidents to whom we attribute charisma, such as Ronald Reagan and Franklin D. Roosevelt, more successful in moving public opinion? Our findings in Chapter 2 provide part of the answer. Even The Great Communicator found it difficult to move his fellow citizens toward his clearly articulated positions on the issues.

REAGAN'S REVOLUTION

It is possible that the effect of charisma is most likely to be manifested in response to the drama of a single speech. The first six months of Ronald Reagan's tenure has become part of the folklore of American politics. The conventional wisdom is that Reagan went on television and by using the bully pulpit mobilized the public to support his tax and spending cuts. The image of Reagan leading the public so successfully is a strong one, and his performance requires that we examine it more closely.

Budgetary Politics, 1981

On February 5, 1981, Reagan made a nationally televised address assessing the nation's economic problems and presenting the broad contours of an economic program. On February 18, he delivered another nationally televised address before a joint session of Congress in which he unveiled his proposals for tax cuts and spending reductions. There is no question that the public was anxious about the state of the economy, which featured high inflation, high interest rates, and rising unemployment. Nevertheless, according to Kernell the public's response "was muted."[62]

On March 30, the president was shot during an assassination attempt. Reagan's approval ratings increased by 7 percentage points after the attempt on his life. Within a week of the president's having been shot, White House deputy chief of staff Michael Deaver convened a meeting of other high-ranking aides to determine how best to take advantage of the new political capital the assassination attempt had created. Ultimately, the plan was for Reagan to make a dramatic nationally televised appearance before Congress, which occurred on April 28. The president showed himself to be recovering from his injuries and vigorously threatened legislators with the wrath of the people if they did not support the Gramm-Latta budget reconciliation resolution, which included the president's proposals.

We lack systematic evidence on the public's response to Reagan's speech. Kernell describes the president's reception in Congress as a "love feast,"[63] and perhaps it was. We do know that there was no upsurge in the president's approval ratings in the Gallup Poll. Indeed, the polls nearest in time before and after the speech produced virtually identical results. Moreover, it is obviously illogical to employ Congress's reception *during* the speech as evidence of public reaction *after* the speech. We also know that in preparation for the president's speech the Republican National Committee stimulated grassroots pressure on Southern Democrats whose districts had voted heavily for Reagan in 1980.[64] The whole point of this effort was to develop support before the speech, and in this the Republicans seem to have been quite successful.

The next stage in the budgetary process was to decide on specific budget cuts. By mid-June, however, the White House concluded that the president could not successfully go public.[65] Nevertheless, the administration won by a narrow margin a crucial procedural vote that allowed the House to consider all the cuts together on a single vote, and then it passed the president's budget.

The most notable recent example of a president mobilizing public opinion to pressure Congress is Reagan's effort to obtain passage of his bill to cut taxes in 1981. On July 27, two days before the crucial vote in the House, the president made a televised plea for support of his tax cut proposals and asked the public to let their representatives in Congress know how they felt. Evidently, this worked, for thousands of telephone calls, letters, and telegrams poured into congressional offices. How much of this represented the efforts of the White House and its corporate allies rather than individual expressions of opinion will probably never be known. Nevertheless, on the morning of the vote Speaker Tip O'Neill declared, "We are experiencing a telephone blitz like this nation has never seen. It's had a devastating effect."[66] With this kind of response, the president easily carried the day.

We must be very careful about inferring the president's success in leading the public from his victory in Congress. The White House was not content to rely solely on a presidential appeal for a show of support. It took additional steps to orchestrate public pressure on Congress. Kernell describes the auxiliary efforts at the mobilization of Reagan's White House in 1981: "Each major television appeal by President Reagan on the eve of a critical budget vote in Congress was preceded by weeks of preparatory work. Polls were taken; speeches incorporating the resulting insights were drafted; the press was briefed, either directly or via leaks. Meanwhile in the field, the ultimate recipients of the president's message, members of Congress, were softened up by presidential travel into their states and districts and by grass-root lobbying campaigns, initiated and orchestrated by the White House but including RNC [the Republican National Committee] and sympathetic business organizations."[67]

Reagan's White House tapped a broad network of constituency groups. Operating through party channels, its Political Affairs Office, and its Office of Public Liaison, the administration generated pressure from the constituents of members of Congress, campaign contributors, political activists, business leaders, state officials, interest groups, and party officials. Television advertisements, letters, and attention from the local news media helped focus attention on swing votes. Although these pressures were directed toward Republicans, Southern Democrats received considerable attention as well, which reinforced their sense of electoral vulnerability. The president also promised not to campaign against Southern Democrats who supported him.[68]

In addition, the administration engaged in old-fashioned bargaining on a wholesale scale. Reagan's budget director David Stockman was quite candid about the concessions that members of Congress demanded in return for their support for the tax cut of 1981, including special breaks for holders of oil leases, real estate tax shelters, and generous loopholes that virtually eliminated the corporate income tax. "The hogs were really feeding," he said. "The greed level, the level of opportunism, just got out of control."[69] Stockman recalled that "the last 10 or 20 percent of the votes needed for a majority of both houses had to be bought, period." Similarly, he termed the trading that went into passing the final budget as "an open vote auction."[70] For example, Reagan agreed to raise sugar price supports to induce representatives from Louisiana to vote for his budget cuts in 1981.[71]

After a careful study, Marc Bodnick concluded that the 1981 tax and budget cuts relied heavily on traditional bargaining and that Reagan's strategy of going public was not as dominant as Kernell indicates. Conservative Democrats supported spending and tax cuts because they agreed with them, not because they were afraid of Reagan's public support. For example, twenty-four of the twenty-nine Democrats who supported the president on specific spending cuts were long-time fiscal conservatives. The other five Democrats had conservative leanings, and each made a deal with the White House. The president's public appeals reinforced deals that were already made. Finally, Bodnick concludes that bargaining had produced a viable tax cut compromise *before* Reagan's public address.[72]

Beyond the Tax Cut

The administration's effort at mobilizing the public on behalf of the tax cut of 1981 is significant not only because of the success of presidential leadership but also because it appears to be a deviant case — even for Ronald Reagan. His next major legislative battle was over the sale of airborne warning and control system (AWACS) planes to Saudi Arabia. The White House decided it could not mobilize the public on this issue, however, and adopted an "inside" strategy working directly with members of Congress to prevent a legislative veto.[73]

Reagan went public one more time regarding the budget in 1981. On September 24, he made a national address arguing for further budget cuts. In a Gallup Poll of October 2–5, 1981, respondents were asked, "In general, are you in favor of budget cuts in addition to those approved earlier this year or are you opposed to more cuts?" Only 42 percent of the public favored such cuts and 46 percent opposed them (12 percent expressed no opinion). The same people were asked, "To reduce the size of the 1982 budget deficiency, President Reagan has proposed cutting $13 billion in addition to the $35 billion in cuts approved earlier in this year. About $11 billion of the new cuts would come from social programs and about $2 billion from defense programs. In general, would you say you approve or disapprove of the President's proposal?" In response to the question posed in this way, 74 percent approved of budget cuts and only 20 percent disapproved (6 percent had no opinion).[74]

Kernell concludes that these results provide evidence of Reagan's remaining a persuasive force with the public.[75] This is unlikely, however. Only 36 percent of Democrats approved of Reagan's job performance, and budget matters were certainly salient at the time and central in evaluations of Reagan's performance as president. It is much more likely that the difference in the responses to the two questions was the result of Gallup raising the issue of budget deficits. In a poll taken just before the president's speech, 67 percent of the public favored a balanced budget amendment to the Constitution, for example.[76] It was the premise of budget cuts being used to reduce the deficit, not the support of Ronald Reagan, that made people willing to support more budget cuts.

In the remainder of his tenure the president went repeatedly to the people regarding a wide range of policies, including the budget, aid to the Contras in Nicaragua, and defense expenditures. He traveled, made television and radio addresses, and held evening press conferences. Despite his high approval levels for much of the time, he was never again able to arouse many in his audience to communicate their support of his policies to Congress. Indeed, it was not

Table 4.5. Reagan's Mistakes in Iran-Contra Affair

Date	Major Mistakes	Minor Mistakes	No Mistakes	No Opinion
3/4/87	46%	47%	4%	3%
3/5–9/87	52	45	3	1
7/21/87	40	48	10	3
8/3–5/87	39	52	6	2
8/12/87	44	49	7	1

Note: ABC News/*Washington Post* Poll question: "Do you think Reagan has made major mistakes in the Iran/Contra affair, made minor mistakes, or do you think he made no mistakes at all?"

long before observers began labeling his budgets as DOA—Dead on Arrival. Most issues hold less appeal to the public than substantial tax cuts.

Although the public relations skills of Reagan's administration were impressive, they could not by themselves create or sustain goodwill. Despite his staff's efforts at promoting a favorable image, he fell below 50 percent approval in the polls after only ten months in office and would not obtain the approval of more than half the public again until November 1983.

Nor was the president more effective in warding off criticism than he was in advancing his initiatives. For example, in 1986 and 1987 Reagan made four nationally televised addresses on the Iran-Contra scandal, the biggest crisis of his presidency. The first two were on November 13 and December 2, 1986. The president's approval fell 16 percentage points in the Gallup Poll from the level he had before the speeches. He lost 6 percentage points after his March 4, 1987, speech. Only following his August 12, 1987, speech did he go up in the polls—4 percentage points. However, after the August 12 speech, 49 percent reported that they were dissatisfied with his explanation and 39 percent thought he lied.[77] Finally, Table 4.5 shows that after his two 1987 speeches regarding the Iran-Contra scandal, the percentage of the public who felt he had made a major mistake *increased*.

Reagan as Facilitator

Rather than serving as an example of the power of a charismatic leader, the early months of Reagan's tenure show the president brilliantly exploiting his opportunities as a facilitator. The president enjoyed favorable conditions for making appeals during his first months in office, including public anxiety over the economy and the perception of a mandate as a result of his surprising margin in the presidential election and the dramatic elevation of Republicans to majority status in the Senate. The same factors drove the Democrats into disarray as they reeled from Reagan's electoral victory and their loss of the Senate. In addition, Reagan advanced a short policy agenda that allowed him to keep a focus on his priorities and made it easier to move rapidly to exploit favorable conditions in the public.

The fundamental conditions of public support in the president's legislatively crucial first year were established outside the White House. When Reagan's views matched the public mood, he effectively used the congruence to his advantage. Yet in the end, there was no charismatic magic. As Kernell concludes, "the supply of popular support rests on opinion dynamics over which the president may exercise little direct control."[78] If charisma is to be a useful concept, it has to last longer than a few months of favorable conditions for public leadership. Reagan was much more effective at exploiting popular support that he was in creating it.

FRANKLIN D. ROOSEVELT

Reagan is hardly alone in failing to move the public. Another great communicator, Franklin D. Roosevelt, had problems of his own—although these have been poorly understood. Historian Doris Kearns Goodwin makes a representative argument when she contends that Roosevelt successfully used his famous fireside chats "to shape, educate and move public opinion at critical moments": "After his first address on the banking crisis . . . large deposits began flowing back into the banking system. When he asked everyone to get a world map and spread it before them as they listened to his description of far-flung battles in the Pacific, map stores sold more maps in several days than they had sold the entire year. When he announced a scrap drive to collect old rubber for reuse, the White House was inundated with old rubber tires, rubber balls, rubber bands and rubber girdles . . ."[79]

None of these examples, however, represents the president asking the people to change their minds. People were not opposed to looking at maps or participating in aiding the war effort. Nor did they offer much resistance to banking. After all, they had their money in the banks in the first place. What they sought was reassurance for their normal inclinations, and Roosevelt provided that reassurance brilliantly. Roosevelt was moving people in the direction they already wanted to go.

Roosevelt recognized the limits of his ability to move the public, even if his many admirers did not, and in the words of historian Richard Hofstadter, "he was content in large measure to follow public opinion."[80] His typical radio address increased his public approval by only about 1 percentage point—and then only during peacetime.[81] He gave only two or three fireside chats a year, and rarely did he focus them on legislation under consideration in Congress. It appears that FDR only used a fireside chat to discuss such matters on four occasions, the clearest example being the broadcast on March 9, 1937, on the ill-fated "Court-packing" bill.[82]

The president responded to changing circumstances like the advent of World War II by seeking popular support from those constituencies most inclined to deliver it rather than by persuading reluctant citizens to support him. For the two years before the U.S. entry into World War II, Roosevelt, fearing a potential backlash if he moved too rapidly, sought to lead public opinion with prudent caution. He knew he was severely constrained by public opinion and that "he was unable to move except in the direction, and largely at the pace, they [the public] wanted to go."[83]

Presidential Personality

There are many dimensions of personality, but for our purposes we are interested in the publicly visible manifestations of personality such as warmth, charm, and humor. The White House goes to extraordinary lengths to orchestrate the president's public appearances, and it does not take a great leap of faith to conclude that these public relations efforts will influence the public's response to the president. Indeed, who would recommend to someone that the way to persuade an audience is to be distant, dour, and dull?

Yet, there is another paradox here. Most presidents elected in the television age, including Harry Truman, Dwight Eisenhower, Lyndon Johnson, Richard Nixon, Jimmy Carter, and George Bush, were not masters of public presentation. Gerald Ford beat Ronald Reagan for the 1976 Republican nomination. Moreover, few would recommend that the president have an affair with a young intern to shore up public support. Yet Bill Clinton did just that and enjoyed high approval ratings for the three years of his presidency that remained after the matter became public.

In addition, there may be little consensus on just what the president's personal characteristics are. Attributions vary according to the ideologies of the commentator. Thus, different people may see the same president as inspirational or passionless, empathetic or insulated, articulate or awkward, a statesman or crass politician. Moreover, different analysts emphasize different ends of the same dimension. They may describe presidents as confident or arrogant, prudent or timid, compassionate or condescending, reserved or callous, responsive or pandering, dignified or regal, warm or corny, decisive or rigid, inspirational or slick.

There is reason to doubt that public relations techniques are at the core of the public's response to presidents. Perhaps the public evaluates presidents on more than their personalities. In this section, we explore the issue of the role of the president's "public personality" in obtaining the public's support.

PERSONALITY OR PERFORMANCE?

The public seems to be able to separate personality from performance in its responses to presidents. Although the public may "like" the president, it still may not approve of his performance as president. In a July 1978 poll, for example, Jimmy Carter's job approval rating was only 39 percent, yet 76 percent of the public felt he was a "likeable person."[84]

Ronald Reagan provides a good test case of the role of personality in presidential approval. Some, especially the president's detractors, ascribed Reagan's standing in the polls primarily to his personal charm and telegenic good looks, his stage presence and professional skills as a television performer (The Great Communicator), the White House's extensive "packaging" of the president's public appearances, or to a Teflon coating that immunized him from accountability for problems of governing and public policy. On the other hand, Richard Wirthlin, the president's primary pollster, argues that Reagan's standing in the polls was not the result of his "nice" personality.[85] Moreover, there is plenty of evidence that Wirthlin is correct.

During the Reagan administration, the Gallup Poll periodically asked respondents whether they approved of the president "as a person" in addition to the standard question of approving of the president's performance "as president." A comparison of the results of asking the same people whether they approved of President Reagan's handling of his job and whether they approved of him as a person can be found in Table 4.6. Throughout his tenure, large majorities in the public, ranging from 67 to 81 percent, "liked" Reagan as a person. On the other hand, the proportion approving his performance in office was consistently lower. The average difference between approval of Reagan as a person and approval of his performance as president was 21 percentage points, representing more than a fifth of the public.

Other data support the conclusion that Reagan's approval levels did not depend on his personality. A study of six ABC News/*Washington Post* national surveys during the period of 1982 through 1984 found that on the average 39 percent of the people liked both Reagan and his policies but an average of 29 percent of the people liked him but disapproved of his policies. People falling into the latter category overwhelmingly planned to vote against the president in the 1984 election.[86] A *Los Angeles Times* national survey in November 1983 also found that 29 percent of the public liked the president personally but disliked most of his policies.[87]

Table 4.6. Comparison of Approval of Reagan as President and as a Person

Date	Job Approval	Approval as Person
1981		
July 17–20	60%	78%
November 13–16	49	73
1982		
February 5–8	47	70
April 30–May 3	44	69
June 11–14	45	67
1983		
August 19–22	43	67
1984		
September 21–24	57	67
1985		
November 11–18	65	81
1986		
September 3–17	63	80
December 4–5	47	75
1987		
January 16–19	48	74
April 10–13	48	75
July 10–13	49	72
1988		
December 27–29	63	79

Source: Gallup Poll.

Equally important evidence that Reagan's approval was not based on his personality is that, contrary to the conventional wisdom, Reagan was not particularly well liked by the American people. In an earlier article, I compared the average favorable or personal approval ratings of recent presidents and found that he was the least well-liked president in the past three decades.[88] Similarly, in a study of the public's attitudes toward winning presidential candidates, Martin Wattenberg found that Reagan was the least popular candidate to win election to the presidency since the election studies began in 1952. In 1980, and especially in 1984, he was "disliked with unprecedented intensity by those who opposed him and supported with an unusual degree of doubt by his backers."[89]

It is plausible that there is some relationship between personal and job approval. This relationship is probably reciprocal. The president's personality may buttress his job approval ratings. It seems equally likely, however, that when Reagan's job performance ratings fell, as in 1982 and 1983, they had a modest negative influence on his personal approval evaluations. In general, however, Americans appear to compartmentalize their attitudes toward the president. They have little difficulty in separating the person from the performance.

To the extent that personality affects the president's success in leading the public at all, it is not likely to be a dynamic influence. The president's personality does not change during his tenure in office, and, as Richard Neustadt argues, the impressions the public holds of the president's personality form early and change slowly.[90] What may be a greater influence on presidential approval and more subject to change is the way the public evaluates some of the job-related traits it attributes to the president. Assessments of characteristics such as the president's integrity, reliability, and leadership ability (as opposed to attributes such as personal warmth and charm) may change as new problems arise or in relation to the president's past performance. Certain characteristics may become more salient in response to changing conditions.

When the Iran-Contra affair became news, President Reagan's decision-making style became a prominent issue, and many people evaluated the same behavior, namely, his focus on the "big picture" and detachment from the details of governing, in a different light. Just as the scandal was breaking in the news, a major business magazine carried a cover story emphasizing the advantages of the president's approach to running the executive branch. Such a story would not appear again. In addition, Reagan's veracity, which had not been an issue during most of his administration, became one, with a majority of Americans concluding that he had lied about his knowledge of the diversion of profits from the arms sales to Iran to the Contras.[91]

Similarly, Jimmy Carter's bent for achieving a command of the details of government would be criticized later as a penchant for the trivial, his deliberateness would be condemned as indecisiveness, and his efforts to rise above politics faulted as naive. The results of two polls, taken about ten months apart, illustrate the potential for change in perceptions of a president's job-related characteristics (see Table 4.7). The figures in the far-right column show that many people changed their minds about Carter's leadership abilities during a relatively short period of time.

The charm of Gerald Ford's unexceptional personal lifestyle soon gave way to questions about his being too common for the presidency. Lyndon Johnson's political cleverness was often viewed as deceitfulness by the end of his tenure. Many presidents find that the same behavior that was once applauded as firmness is later reproached as rigidity.

Table 4.7. Change in Evaluation of Carter's Job-Related Characteristics

Characteristic	Agree		
	Mid-1977[1]	Mid-1978[2]	Change
Decisive, sure of himself	61%	38%	−23%
You know where he stands on issues	42	28	−14
Has strong leadership qualities	62	36	−26
Has well-defined program for moving country ahead	43	29	−14
Uncertain, indecisive, unsure	28	55	+27
Hard to know where he stands	47	66	+19
Lacks strong leadership qualities	27	58	+31
Has no clear-cut program for moving country ahead	44	64	+20

Source: "President Carter's 'Phrase Portrait,'" *The Gallup Opinion Index*, November 1978, p. 9.

[1]September 30–October 3, 1977.
[2]July 21–24, 1978.

Thus, views of the president's job-related characteristics may change over time, and there is evidence that the public's evaluations of them influence their approval of his performance in office. In earlier work, I found that issues of trust and various components of leadership significantly influenced approval of Presidents Nixon, Ford, and Carter.[92]

One of the more interesting phenomena of contemporary politics was President Clinton's high standing in the presidential approval polls in light of a wide range of allegations concerning his personal behavior, both before and after entering the White House. Perhaps even more striking is the president's standing in the polls at the very time that majorities of Americans concluded that he had engaged in behavior of which they disapproved and that he was not peculiarly trustworthy. For example, in a Gallup Poll taken on August 21–23, 1998, only 31 percent of the public felt that Clinton was "honest and trustworthy," 35 percent said he "shows good judgment," and 37 percent responded positively when asked whether the president "shared your values." Yet, 62 percent of the public approved of Clinton's performance as president. A Gallup Poll of October 8–10, 1999, found that only 35 percent of the public approved of Clinton as a person, but 56 percent approved of the job he was doing as president.[93]

The explanation for these seemingly inconsistent opinions is that once again the public compartmentalized its evaluations of the president—but in the opposite direction from its evaluations of presidents such as Carter and Reagan. Job-related characteristics trumped personality. Many approved of the president's performance *as* president, but they did not have high regard for some of his personal characteristics.

The high marks the president received on job-related dimensions helped counter the public's views that he was not a person of integrity. For example, the August 21–23 poll found that 76 percent of the respondents agreed that Clinton "can get things done," 62 percent felt he "cares about the needs of people like you," and 54 percent saw the president as doing a "good job representing America to the world." In addition, polls taken around that time found majorities, sometimes large majorities, approved of the president's handling of a wide range of policies, including foreign affairs, the economy, race relations, and education. As long as people viewed the president as doing a good job as president, Bill Clinton remained high in the polls—no matter how offensive his fellow citizens found his personal behavior.

Conclusion

We began this chapter by raising questions about the common assumption that personal qualities are central to presidential leadership, especially to public leadership. We have attempted to explore in a rigorous manner the issue of whether the messenger matters, and we are now in a position to offer some answers.

We have been unable to find systematic evidence of some special form of leadership that we might characterize as "charismatic." We cannot employ the concept to identify who possesses charisma nor identify any consequences of it. Charisma cannot be used to explain the relative success or failures of presidents to obtain public support. Thus, the concept of charisma does not appear to be either salvageable analytically or helpful empirically. Political consultant and commentator Dick Morris may be correct when he concludes that "charisma is the most elusive of political traits because it doesn't exist in reality, only in our perception once a candidate has made it by hard work and good issues."[94]

One might argue that I have not searched in the right places for evidence of charisma. Perhaps I have not focused on the right leaders, nations, chronological periods, or eras of economic or political development. Perhaps. However, the burden of proof should be on those using the concept of charisma to provide evidence of a distinctive form of leadership and not simply to assume its existence. We ought to have confidence that there is something there before we analyze it, much less attribute significance to it.

Similarly, the public is not as shallow as some commentators seem to think. People are not easy prey for White House public relations techniques and media campaigns; their responses to presidents do *not* seem to be based more on style than on substance. Instead, the evidence is that they can separate the person from the performance—and often do. Although it certainly does not hurt for a president to be likable, this is not necessary for obtaining the public's support and it does not necessarily make the president more persuasive. Indeed, being liked is not necessarily even a guarantee of support.

It does not follow that the individual leader does not matter. Of course leaders matter. They make choices about what policies to pursue, how to frame their presentation to the public, how hard to fight for them, how many other issues to pursue at the same time, and a myriad of other aspects of taking a case to the public. Leaders have important influence over the outcomes of their leadership efforts and may fairly be held responsible for many of their leadership failures.

What we have found is that there is no magic associated with certain leaders. There is much less significance to charisma and personality than the conventional wisdom indicates; personal characteristics are not the key to successfully leading the public. Major changes in public policy require more than just the "right" person in the job and do not necessarily turn on a leader's personal qualities. Public leadership is much more demanding and problematic than the simple solution of placing a charismatic leader at the helm of the ship of state.

Our findings also mean that we need a better understanding of leadership to think sensibly about the role of leadership in a political system. We need to reevaluate how we think about leadership. We have found that the ability of leaders to move the public is limited, and thus the role of the individual leader may be less important than many think. Scholars, then, need to emphasize less personalized and more theoretically meaningful explanations of successful leadership. We should expect less of leaders, focus less exclusively on them, and devote more attention to the context in which they seek to lead.

5

The Politics of Veneration: Do the People Defer?

George Washington is perhaps the most revered political leader in American public life, rivaled only by Abraham Lincoln. Known as "the father of his country," he is the venerated symbol of the founding of the republic. As historian Forrest McDonald puts it, "In Europe as well as in America he was heralded as the Greatest Character of His Age." "It is no exaggeration to say that Americans were willing to venture the experiment with a single, national republican chief executive only because of the unreserved trust in George Washington." Adulation was lavished on him, and McDonald does not exaggerate when he concludes that Washington was "revered as a demigod."[1]

Joseph Ellis adds that "in the America of the 1790s, Washington's image was everywhere, in paintings, prints, lockets; on coins, silverware, plates, and household bric-a-brac. . . . As one popular toast of the day put it, he was 'the man who unites all hearts.' He was the American Zeus, Moses, and Cincinnatus all rolled into one."[2] It is no wonder that in the era before political parties organized the members of the Electoral College to vote for their candidates, Washington twice won election unanimously.

Whether we should characterize Washington as a charismatic figure or simply as a venerated one is not critical for our purposes. What is important is that, without doubt, Washington's persona was at the core of his public support. If personal qualities are at the central to public leadership, Washington was better positioned than any of his successors to dominate American politics.

As we continue our discussion of personal leadership in this chapter, we explore two sets of questions about Washington. First, we focus on how he obtained his peculiar status as a towering figure in the country. Did the public perceive special qualities about Washington? Did his tremendous prestige rest on his charisma or other unique personal factors? Or did Washington obtain public approval as the result of factors largely beyond his control, creating an opportunity that he then exploited to serve his own, quite legitimate ambition for a position of public honor?

We want to examine Washington governing as well as his ascendancy to power. Once in office, did Washington dominate policy making in the new nation? Did the public respond to his leadership in a peculiarly deferential fashion? Did elites, such as members of Congress, shrink from opposing Washington in fear of public reprisals? Or did the environment in which he sought to govern force even the father of his country to play a much more modest leadership role?

The Emergence of Washington as a Hero

Early in his biography of Washington, Barry Schwartz argues that "it is often the case that a revered leader emerges in a time of crisis and collective enthusiasm, when people enter into intense and energizing relationships and ideas take on an irresistible momentum. Inspired into action, people yearn for a leader to carry out their plans. The emergence of the leader serves the needs of the movement generating the crisis; it may be largely independent of the behavior of the person who ascends to the leadership role."[3]

Once the policy of fighting for independence from Britain was determined, the conditions were present for the emergence of such a hero.

His fellow citizens did not recognize Washington as a charismatic figure before they declared their independence from Britain. Until the summer of 1776, Washington was one of many prominent individuals concerned about British abuse of colonists' rights. He first came to widespread public prominence after being named to lead the armed forces of the colonies. Immediately following his appointment as commander in chief, however, he became the best-known and most-admired man in the colonies.

This sudden and dramatic transformation of Washington into a person of heroic proportions was not the result of an appreciation for the quality of Washington's persona or performance. Instead, it was the result of the urgent and strong emotions activated by the decision to resist the British by force and his role in implementing this decision. These passions were the catalyst for transforming Washington's generally ordinary talents and unremarkable characteristics into a heroic image.[4]

Washington was revered before he ever took charge. Enthusiastic crowds delayed him as he traveled to take command of the army in Boston. While encamped there, before a single shot was fired, books were dedicated to him, children were named after him, and ships were named for both him and his wife. Supporters of the Revolution ascribed to him perfections and glossed over or ignored his shortcomings. Appreciation for his virtues and other qualities, such as his noble bearing, was the result rather than the cause of the renown that enveloped him. His military skills were secondary to his symbolic role as defender of the new nation.[5]

A concrete symbol was needed to make the abstract cause of revolution tangible, and Washington fit the bill. According to one of Washington's biographers, "It is a repeating phenomenon of history that a body of men undergoing a major political change find a human being the most persuasive symbol about which to gather."[6] As soon as he took command of the American forces, Washington became the symbol of the revolutionary cause and as such was lavished with praise independent of his performance as commander in chief. Engraved into the collective consciousness of the colonists, he was the most obvious choice to represent the struggle for independence.[7]

Old forms get filled with new content. The monarchy was repudiated as an institution, but it continued to provide the cognitive schema for linking America's masses to a republican state.[8] People could indulge in their habitual adulation of a monarch without reneging on their commitment to republicanism. Partisans of the Revolution made Washington the central symbol of the cause and deliberately substituted him for George III. The veneration of Washington aided in developing a national consciousness and social integration, an urgent concern of the times. Americans transferred their praise and affection from George III to Washington, a native hero, and celebrated him as a way of celebrating themselves.[9]

Washington served as a unifying symbol, a focal point for the new nation. The people celebrated his virtue as an embodiment of the nation's virtue and as a model that would help perpetuate it.[10] The founders believed in the necessity of virtue in the people who ran the government, not just in the structures of government. Thus, Washington's admirers clothed him in religious and classical symbols that satisfied their own political tastes and portrayed his achievements and services as being a manifestation of his virtue.[11]

In exalting Washington, colonists exalted their cause. Americans could demonstrate their support for the war and their attachment to the new nation by extolling Washington as its symbol. By identifying with him, average citizens could articulate their own stake in the war and justify their sacrifice on its behalf. By acclaiming him, Americans could venerate themselves and sanctify the virtues to which they aspired.[12]

At the same time, by investing their impassioned convictions in Washington, the colonists made him into an object of veneration,[13] guaranteeing him a position of political power after the war of independence. Washington's tremendous popularity was an invaluable resource, but at its core, it was not of his own making. Instead, his prestige was a product of the needs of others for a powerful symbol of the new nation.

MANAGING HIS IMAGE

Once Washington had obtained the veneration of the public, how did he maintain it? Ultimately, his public identity was formed and secured insofar as he appropriated for himself and enacted publicly the same moral virtues that others, under the pressure of social circumstances, were induced to attribute to him.[14] He needed to link his image with the political values of his generation if he was to achieve his goal of public recognition.

In other words, Washington depended highly on his environment for obtaining public support. He could not depend on qualities such as charisma to maintain it. Instead, he recognized the demands of his environment and the opportunities it presented for building his public image. Equally important, he possessed the skill to exploit these opportunities to cultivate a favorable public impression.

Washington was an eager, active, and astute politician, who had a great hunger for public honor and concern with the judgment of posterity. He yearned for the approval and praise of the people all his life.[15] To obtain it he methodically fashioned his public self to match the expectations and ideals of his fellow citizens and made himself the embodiment of the revolutionary cause and the new nation.

Washington combined great natural physical endowments, an acute sense of others' responses to him, and a superb understanding of how to shape his performance. He used these traits to create a presence that constituted one of his chief assets: a demeanor that inspired confidence, a bearing that bespoke authority. He was a figure on a stage, a consummate actor whose restrained performance allayed fears of despotism. His mastery of his emotions and tone of detachment, objective and dispassionate, gave citizens confidence in him.[16]

Two related principles dominated the political culture in which Washington's actions were judged: civilian control of the military and decentralized power. Americans at war looked not to their best military man, but to the military man in whom they had the most trust. Washington demonstrated his devotion to civilian control of the military by continually signaling his deference to Congress and his submission to civilian authority, including making it known he would resign any time Congress wished; by not abusing his emergency powers; by quelling the Newburgh mutiny; by protecting civilians through strict control of the army; and, most importantly, by surrendering power at the end of the war. This consistent behavior placed him above suspicion and stilled the fears of those who saw the seeds of tyranny in his prestige.[17]

In addition to presenting himself as a citizen soldier to allay fear of military despotism, Washington demonstrated his commitment to decentralized power in other ways. He avoided obvious self-promotion. Instead, he protested his inadequacy for office and avoided actively soliciting positions. At the same time, he made his availability as commander in chief apparent by wearing his uniform to the Continental Congress. By making offers come to him, he increased his prestige. Another important gesture was accepting no pay for his service in leading the American forces, reinforcing his image of a person sacrificing for his beliefs, with no thought of personal gain.

Ever sensitive to the significance of symbolic gestures, he waited (impatiently) at Mount Vernon for Congress to assemble and tally the electoral votes that everyone knew would select him as the first president. He wanted to avoid appearing eager to obtain power. After an official emissary arrived at Mount Vernon with the news of his election, Washington traveled leisurely to New York to be inaugurated. (He again received a hero's welcome both on his journey to New York and at his inauguration.) After taking office he opened his house regularly to citizens and let it be known that he preferred to be addressed simply as the "President of the United States."[18]

One could take the cynical view that Washington was nothing more than a skilled political chameleon, adopting whatever public posture suited the needs of the time. In a humorous treatment of Washington's refusal to accept payment for his service as commander in chief, Marvin Kitman points out that instead of receiving a salary, he asked that the Continental Congress pick up the tab for his expenses.[19] Thus, instead of the $48,000 he would have received for the eight years of the War of Independence, he turned in an expense account bill of nearly $500,000.

No doubt most of the expenses were perfectly legitimate, but envision a modern-day congressional committee examining the last item on George's expense account: $27,665.30 to pay the expenses of Mrs. Washington's visits to him at his winter headquarters. Evidently, all did not share the rigors of Valley Forge equally. Washington was willing to make every sacrifice for liberty except one — reducing his standard of living. (The good general also bought up deeds to land that Congress was paying the troops in lieu of cash.)

When Washington offered the same deal — no salary, only expenses — to the country after his election as the first president under the Constitution, Congress turned him down and provided a salary of $25,000 per year instead. It was far less expensive.

In private Washington displayed passions and was moody, brooding, pessimistic, correct but not warm, cranky, intolerant, vain, self-righteous, sensitive to criticism, and avoided accepting blame.[20] Nevertheless, he did possess the republican virtues valued by fellow Americans, and his public actions were consistent with these moral values. Washington's skill was not in seeming to be all things to all people, but in his ability to emphasize the virtues he did possess that were also congruent with those Americans were seeking in a leader. Washington possessed and exercised considerable political skill, but there is little evidence that his fellow citizens viewed him as a charismatic figure.

Washington as President: Director or Facilitator?

We have seen that Washington's emergence as a folk hero served the needs of the nascent republic, and he took full advantage of the veneration of the public to obtain the presidency. But once in office, did Washington dominate policy making in the new nation? Did the nature of his leadership allow us to infer that a deferential public gave him unquestioning support as a charismatic or venerated leader, which Washington then translated into elite support for his policies? Or did even the father of his country play a more modest leadership role?

THE PASSIVE PRESIDENT

Washington certainly did not act as though he could dominate the political landscape. Except in matters such as those involving national security policy that fell within the executive's sphere, Washington was outwardly passive toward the legislature.[21] He did not make recommendations to Congress (except in a general way in his annual address), nor did he personally try to influence the passage of legislation. Only once did he wield the veto in a strategic manner to alter or nullify legislation of which he simply disapproved, primarily viewing the veto to be reserved for bills of doubtful constitutionality. Finally, he did not seek to achieve by executive order any matter that the strictest interpretation of the Constitution would find in the legislative domain.[22]

Washington surely did not set the agenda for Congress. When the new government went into operation, it had no funds. It had to act quickly to establish tariffs so it could collect revenue from the spring importing season. Yet it was James Madison as a member of the House of Representatives, not President Washington, who took the lead to fund the government.[23] When it came to passing the Bill of Rights, creating the federal judiciary, determining tariff levels, or even establishing the executive departments and the president's right to remove his own nominees, Washington was a reactor, not a leader of events.[24]

Alexander Hamilton's financial program was the most important domestic policy of the Washington administration. The president's role in it was minimal, however (part of the time during the critical debate over the assumption of the national and state debts, Washington was seriously ill with pneumonia and was not physically able to participate). According to McDonald, "Washington had nothing whatever to do with the preparation of the great Reports: partly out of the observation of the nicety that Hamilton was acting on instructions from Congress, partly because the whole subject was beyond him, the President volunteered neither questions nor suggestions." Thus, Washington's role in creating Hamilton's system, "apart from giving his implied blessing, was nothing at all—except when he very nearly prevented its creation by proposing to veto the charter of the bank."[25]

The most controversial foreign policy issue of Washington's tenure as president, and what has ultimately been considered as one of his chief accomplishments, was Jay's Treaty. Washington was genuinely undecided about the treaty, so he sent it to the Senate without a recommendation. After the Senate had ratified it, he signed the treaty, at least partially in anger at Edmund Randolph's alleged treason.[26]

According to one authority, Washington used his prestige to legitimate the policies and actions of others instead of legitimating his control over government: "He sanctified the new system not by controlling it but by simply identifying himself with it."[27] One noted constitutional historian summarizes Washington's tenure as president as one in which he strove to preside "rather than to lead or to direct."[28]

FRUSTRATIONS WITH CONGRESS

Washington eventually won on the biggest issues of his administration, although, as we will see, often not without a fight. Nevertheless, Congress was not overly responsive to the father of his country. In his annual address in 1791, for example, Washington urged Congress to pass provisions for a uniform militia system; organize the post office and post roads; establish a mint, arsenals and fortifications, and standard weights and measures; and provide for the sale of vacant lands owned by the national government, all of which he had vainly proposed before.[29]

Washington also suffered a number of indignities. The Senate rejected two treaties and five nominations, including that of John Rutledge to be Chief Justice. Following the Whiskey Rebellion, the House would not concur with the Senate in support of Washington's unusual condemnation of the Democratic-Republican societies, which the president believed were responsible for the uprising.[30]

The former commander in chief could never persuade Congress to establish a national militia with uniform training,[31] and it even cut back on his request for an infantry regiment.[32] Nor could the president obtain the establishment of an American university.[33] Even the Federalists could be obstructive, as when supporters of the Bank of the United States held up Washington's request for a slight change in the location of the new capital (closer to Mount Vernon) until he signed the bill.[34]

WHY NOT A DIRECTOR?

There is little question that the way Washington attained the presidency and his performance as chief executive were not consistent with the leadership of a charismatic, director mode of leadership. The question then becomes one of whether or not Washington had discretion in the matter of his leadership. If his deference to Congress was nothing more than his filling what he thought was an appropriate role, then we cannot conclude that Washington's acting as a facilitator rather than a director was the only option open to him.

There is a basis for attributing at least of some of Washington's leadership style to role expectations. He apparently felt his primary task was to serve as a symbol above the political fray and provide the new government with legitimacy in an environment traditionally hostile to central authority.[35] As a symbol of union and restraint, he could encourage attachment to the republic and inspire trust in the new government.

Yet Washington obtained his position because he was already viewed as "above" politics. Conflict and disharmony would not have been the inevitable correlates of a nation responding to the leadership of its revered hero if Washington could have exercised more dominant leadership. The evidence is mixed on Washington's view of the proper role of the presidency in the constitutional system. One biographer argues that he did "not visualize the President as an initiator of policy, a prime mover." Congress was to be the "pivot" of government.[36]

Yet at the same time, Washington had strong views on a wide range of policies, from internal improvements to immigration policy,[37] and he was concerned with obtaining the legislation he desired. He had an assistant keep records of whether Congress had passed his occasional recommendations so he could decide whether he should include the omissions in his next speech to Congress.[38] Even in 1789 Washington was giving his ideas on a national militia plan to Secretary of War Henry Knox so he could incorporate them into a bill for Congress.[39]

James Flexner argues that Washington was a firm adherent to the principle of separation of powers, but the evidence he provides in support of this assertion is meager.[40] Washington had strong views about the Constitution and was not enthusiastic about the separation of powers or federalism. As far as we know, Washington did not speak on the subject of the presidency in the official proceedings of the constitutional convention.[41] He did, however, vote for a strong president with a strong veto.[42] He also rarely and only very briefly mentioned the topic of separation of powers in his writings, never addressing the topic while in office except for a paragraph in his Farewell Address.[43]

He had been exposed to the paralyzing effects of limited government and working with a contentious Congress during the Revolution and desired a government that granted power, not one that limited it. He believed in executive leadership.[44] There is reason to believe that Washington preferred something akin to the British king-in-council form of government, with the Senate as the president's council.[45] In 1814, fifteen years after Washington's death, Jefferson penned his oft-quoted summary evaluation of the first president. Jefferson felt it important to include that Washington wanted a British-style government and was preparing the nation for it.[46]

Washington was scrupulous when the Constitution was clear, but when it was silent or ambiguous, his natural inclination toward unity and cooperation led him to ignore the implicit boundaries between the branches. At the beginning of his term, he was more likely to seek advice from Representative Madison than from Secretary Hamilton or Secretary Jefferson. His use of Chief Justice John Jay as an adviser on a wide range of issues is well-known, as is his use of Jay as his personal diplomatic envoy in the negotiation of what became known as Jay's Treaty. He also sought, unsuccessfully, to use the Supreme Court for advisory opinions.[47]

The king-in-council orientation is also illustrated by Washington's early behavior toward the Senate. His efforts to include the Senate in the negotiation in addition to the ratification of treaties are well-known.[48] Less famous but equally revealing is his reputed response to the rejection of the nomination of Benjamin Fishbourne to be naval officer of the Port of Savannah in 1789. Washington angrily marched to the Senate chamber. Sitting in the vice president's chair, which John Adams vacated for him, the president demanded to be told the reasons for the Senate's action.[49]

In other words, Washington's relatively passive posture toward Congress was unlikely to be the result of a deeply felt view that the doctrine of separation of powers as outlined in the Constitution required that Congress should dominate policy making. Other explanations for his modest leadership of Congress are more compelling.

First, and most important, he was limited by a political culture that was hostile to the exercise of authority. Even though he enjoyed the support of the Federalists, who were probably the most hierarchically inclined major political group the United States has experienced under the Constitution, he ran into substantial opposition. The emerging Democratic-Republicans, led by Madison and Jefferson, were vehemently opposed to executive leadership (at least at that time).

Second, Washington was limited by the independence of Congress. There is no systematic evidence that he could have sustained "control" over Congress, and it is reasonable to expect that an extremely astute politician such as Washington would have recognized the limited potential of his leadership. As Edmund Morgan put it, "Washington's genius lay in his understanding of power."[50] Since he did not like to be refused, a reluctance to face direct opposition to his policies (and a realistic expectation that he would) probably deterred Washington from more active efforts to lead Congress.[51]

When Washington tried to work closely with the Senate early in his tenure, he was disappointed. When he personally asked for advice regarding the negotiation of a treaty with the Creek Indians, he found little deference.[52] In the incident regarding the Senate's rejection of Washington's nomination of Benjamin Fishbourne as the naval officer of Savannah (the precedent for senatorial courtesy), Senator James Gunn of Georgia is reputed to have informed Washington that the Senate was under no obligation to offer any explanation to the president in this case—or in any future case.[53]

We can understand more about the limitations of Washington's ability to rely on public support in his attempts to lead the new nation by exploring how he employed the resources available to him as he tried to influence Congress.

Leading Congress

It goes without saying that the manner of presidential leadership of Congress was different two hundred years ago. The institutionalization of the presidency, the development of technology, and increased expectations of the president, for example, have altered the forms in which presidents attempt to lead Congress. The question here, however, regards the potential and use of leadership resources, not the techniques for employing them. How did Washington use the core leadership resources available to him? Did his leadership indicate public deference to him or did it have much in common with the much less-venerated chief executives of our own day?

PARTY LEADERSHIP

Washington wished to lead by remaining above the political fray and employing his prestige to unify the nation. In this he failed. As we know, the development of American political parties occurred during his presidency.[54] It is especially interesting that the common theme of the growing polarization of parties was opposition to the administration. As John Hoadley put it, "From the economic programs in the First Congress to the anti-Hamilton resolution in the Second to the Whiskey Rebellion in the Third and the Jay Treaty in the Fourth, the most highly partisan issues involved evaluations of actions by the administration."[55]

Washington was unable to prevent the hardening and organization of opposition to his policies, even in the area of national security. Indeed, it was during the dispute over the implementation of Jay's Treaty that the opposition, led by Madison, who in 1789 served as Washington's closest adviser, was first formally organized.[56] Denying the House of Representatives papers regarding the treaty and the House's claim to a role in treaty making was a turning point. The leaders of the opposition, building on the developing polarization of the country, capitalized on Jay's Treaty as a point of disputation over which a two-party system could be nationalized and hardened. The fissure of factionalism had opened so widely that even Washington could no longer straddle it.[57]

Washington abhorred faction and refused to accept the role as party leader.[58] For example, he would not try to influence the outcome of congressional elections. When a candidate for a House seat in Maryland, George Francis Mercer, let it be rumored that the president favored his election, an annoyed Washington wrote him that it would be "highly improper" for the president to try to exercise influence.[59]

What if Washington had been more active as a party leader? Would such a strategy have given him more leverage with Congress? It is impossible to say with certainty, but it is probable that if he had been more aggressive as a party leader, he would have been the catalyst for even earlier development of parties, more organized opposition, and substantially diminished prestige. There is little reason to believe that Washington could have commanded deference as an active party leader.

PUBLIC APPROVAL

Washington's greatest asset was his public prestige, and it served him well. For example, both Washington and Hamilton knew that the president's assent was necessary for the treasury secretary's financial program to be accepted, and that Washington's silence would generally be regarded as approval.[60] Washington's prestige also shielded Hamilton when he came under personal attack, and it gave Congress confidence in allowing Washington to call out the frontier militia.[61]

Jefferson attributed the administration's success in surviving the nationwide protest over Jay's Treaty partly to Washington's prestige. And after the president's victory in obtaining the House's support for implementing the treaty, Jefferson, speaking of Congress, declared, "You will see by their proceedings the truth of what I have always observed to you: that one man outweighs them all in influence over the people, who have supported his judgment against their own and that of their representatives."[62]

Washington worked to obtain public approval. He made public addresses to Congress, a practice abandoned by Jefferson and not revived until the tenure of Woodrow Wilson. In addition, Washington traveled to every state within a few years of taking office, showing the flag of the new government to win support for it—and for himself.[63] As we have seen, he was a master of symbolic politics and continually concerned himself with obtaining the most positive public reaction. For example, on his first goodwill tour, Washington rode in a coach, but mounted his horse when his small traveling party entered a large community: "The relative simplicity of the party was calculated to dispel rumors of monarchism in the new government."[64]

Washington was also concerned about learning of public opinion, so as not to be too far ahead of it.[65] He used his public tours to take the public's pulse on his administration,[66] and he was an "omnivorous" reader of newspapers,[67] which were flourishing in the 1790s.[68] He also employed others to bring him information on what the public was thinking. He once sent Attorney General Edmund Randolph to the South to learn of public sentiment regarding Citizen Genet.[69] Knowing that most of his political and social contacts were with Federalists, he encouraged his personal secretary, Tobias Lear, to keep in contact with the opposition, a suggestion that Lear followed.[70]

Nevertheless, Washington's prestige could carry him only so far. Even the first great issue of controversy, that of debt assumption, was passed only after Hamilton cut a deal with Madison and Jefferson regarding the site of the new capital. His countrymen respected and even revered Washington, but they were not hesitant to oppose him.

Washington's prestige did not immunize him from opposition and criticism. Tension between the monarchial and republican strains in American political culture brought the venerational cult of Washington to an unprecedented level of scrutiny, and the paranoid politics of the time (fed by the fear of a Federalist plot) damaged his reputation.[71]

Starting with Hamilton's economic policies and continuing through the failed military expedition of General Arthur St. Clair, the revolt of western Pennsylvania farmers against a federal excise tax on whiskey (the Whiskey Rebellion), and the controversy surrounding the efforts of the French ambassador, Citizen Genet, to arouse the American public to support France against Britain and oppose Washington's policy of neutrality, the flow of critical commentary transformed from a trickle to a torrent.[72] Philip Freneau's *National Gazette* marked the celebration of the president's sixtieth birthday in 1792 with this report: "The monarchical farce [of Washington's birthday celebration] was as usual kept. . . . The President has been pictured as spotless and infallible, as having no likes or dislikes. The glory and achievement of the late Revolution have been entirely imputed to him, and were he Virtue's self the strains of panegyric could not have been louder." Later that year, Thomas Greenleaf's *New York Journal* charged that "gambling, reveling, horseracing and horse whipping" had been the essentials of Washington's education and that he was "infamously niggardly" in private dealings and a "most horrid swearer and blasphemer" despite his pretended religious piety.[73] Other critics branded him as a despot, embezzler, traitor, and even a murderer.[74]

Reckless and vitriolic partisans now regularly attacked Washington in the newspapers, attempting to arouse the public against his administration. They often succeeded. When Washington issued the Neutrality Proclamation of 1793, mob violence erupted in Philadelphia, New York, and Boston — even in front of Washington's own residence.[75] There was even more widespread criticism and violence in response to Jay's Treaty.[76]

In the last substantive message he ever sent to Jefferson, the president complained of his critics (whom he knew were led by Jefferson), declaring that he was amazed that "every act of my administration would be tortured, and the grossest and most insidious misrepresentations of them be made (by giving one side only of a subject, and that too in such exaggerated and indecent terms as could scarcely be applied to a Nero, a notorious defaulter, or even to a common pickpocket)."[77]

Washington's great prestige did not provide the foundation for him to become a more dominant political figure because of the ambivalent attitudes Americans had (and have) toward political leaders. The very fact that he was so highly esteemed also made Washington the object of enormous suspicion. We must remember that his career is not one in which he would have been accorded positions of leadership under any conditions and was then revered by many because he did not abuse his authority. Instead, his admirers made a virtue of necessity, because the country would not have tolerated an autonomous power as general or president.[78]

Given that his prestige was a valuable, if limited, leadership resource, how did Washington exploit it, and what did he do to increase or maintain his standing in the public? Keeping with the expectations of the time, Washington never addressed the country directly on matters of public policy.[79] Thus, he never personally took his case to the public and made no personal efforts to mobilize public opinion on his behalf. (He is given credit, however, for inventing the executive news leak late in his tenure to explain the recall of James Monroe as minister to France.[80])

Rather than taking his case directly to the people as a charismatic leader, Washington relied on others to engage in persuading his fellow citizens. He benefited from the support of the Federalists, led by Alexander Hamilton, who rallied behind him throughout the country on every major issue. Especially on matters associated with Jay's Treaty, they fought an effective public relations campaign.[81] The Federalist "machine" and the newspapers it published would be the envy of modern presidents.

This last great legislative battle of the Washington administration saw the president's forces pull out all the stops in a coordinated campaign against substantial odds. The Federalists launched a pamphlet campaign and organized a public petition drive in support of the treaty, bankers and insurance companies (who were mostly Federalists) applied pressure to representatives, the Federalist-dominated Senate threatened to hold up other legislation the House desired, and Fisher Ames, the Federalists' most gifted speaker in the House, was designated to lead the debate and made an eloquent and emotional speech on behalf of the treaty. Good fortune also played a role as the popular Pinckney Treaty with Spain was concluded at this time.[82]

McDonald asserts that Washington did not build a system of patronage, preferring to judge potential officials on the basis of their character and commitment to the republic.[83] Yet the outcome of this process was that most of the people appointed to positions in the new government—postmasters, customs officials, and tax collectors—were Federalists. Moreover, most of these officials worked for the Treasury Department, headed by Alexander Hamilton. Many evidently worked for the election of Federalists to office—the first political machine. No wonder Jefferson complained to Washington that he had only a few clerks working for him at the Department of State.[84]

Sometimes Washington was simply clever. On the highly controversial issue of the House's provision of funds to implement Jay's Treaty, Washington delayed sending his request for the money until the opposition had peaked. This infuriated his opponents, who wanted to strike while public furor was greatest, but it may have saved the day for the president. He won in a vote in the Committee of the Whole by one vote.[85]

LEGISLATIVE SKILLS

Washington lacked an institutional mechanism for legislative liaison such as exists in the White House today. Given the small size of Congress and its members' relatively light workloads, there is little reason to think he needed one. Although the president could not be described as a "warm" personality or one who could mix with members of the legislature as a peer, he was not aloof or detached from legislators. Indeed, Washington entertained and dealt with members of Congress on a more regular and personal basis than has any modern president. For example, he gave weekly dinners for government officials, including members of Congress, with invitations issued on a rotational basis.[86]

The evidence is mixed on whether Washington expected his socializing with members of Congress to build bridges between the executive and legislative branches, but he probably had this in mind.[87] There is little evidence that he succeeded, however. His opponents were touched by the president's graciousness, but they remained opponents.[88]

On a broader basis, Washington displayed considerable skill as a legislative leader. Consultation, not confrontation, was his model. He was generally free with sharing information, even embarrassing information, with Congress and tried to cooperate whenever possible.[89] The famous incident of his coming to the Senate to consult on the negotiation of a treaty, although not a successful exercise, is illustrative of his orientation toward Congress.

Bargaining had a prominent role in the Washington administration as well. On the great issue of debt assumption, for example, Hamilton maneuvered, cajoled, and traded his bill through Congress. Not only did he give the South the site of the new capital, but he also increased the nation's indebtedness as he made generous allowances for the calculation of state debts in order to obtain the votes of certain state delegations.[90]

Conclusion

At the beginning of this chapter, I argued that if personal qualities are at the core of public leadership, George Washington was better positioned than any of his successors to dominate American politics. After reviewing his rise to power and his performance in office, we find that Washington obtained public approval as the result of factors largely beyond his control, creating an opportunity that he then exploited to serve his own ambition. More importantly, even with widespread popular approval based on the public's perception of his possessing exceptional personal qualities, a legislature at least initially controlled by allies and without an organized opposition, and an absence of constraining precedents, Washington did not dominate policy making in the new nation. The public did not respond to his leadership in a peculiarly deferential fashion, and elites, such as members of Congress, did not shrink from opposing Washington in fear of public reprisals.

In summing up Washington's administration, historian Forrest McDonald concluded, "George Washington was indispensable, but only for what he was, not for what he did."[91] Even the president who was arguably in the strongest position to serve as a director of national policy did not. And he did not because he could not. When Washington had the opportunity to initiate and set policy on his own, as in the national security area, he did not hesitate to do so.[92] When he was required to obtain the support of Congress, however, he had no choice but to adopt a position of deference and reaction. He could not reshape the contours of the political landscape to pave the way for change.

The challenges Washington confronted in attempting to lead Congress were similar to those faced by presidents two centuries later. He encountered the problem of governing in a political culture that is generally hostile to authority. Even though Washington served during a period in which the hierarchically oriented Federalists were prominent (and the people were accustomed to deferring to a monarch), the emerging egalitarian Democratic-Republicans, with fresh memories of the Revolution, were especially suspicious of anyone holding power.

Washington also had to deal with the separation of powers. Most observers agree that in response to the expansion of the executive branch and perhaps to a loss of institutional comity, Congress over the past generation has prepared itself to participate in all stages of the policy-making process. At the very beginning of the republic, however, Congress also played a central role in the policy-making process, and, reinforced by the different constituencies of the two branches, it zealously guarded that role.

The interplay of political skill and opportunity is central to understanding Washington's emergence as a national leader. He played a modest role in the creation of the emotionally charged political environment of the 1770s. As Garry Wills put it, "Washington did not create the republic, the republic created him."[93] But Washington skillfully exploited the opportunities presented by the Revolution, linking his image with the political values of his generation to obtain public support.

When it came to trying to lead Congress, Washington was much like modern presidents. Despite his distaste for parties and factions, he could not avoid party politics. He was highly dependent on the support of the Federalists, especially during his second term. The Democratic-Republicans were born in opposition to his administration and were often brutal adversaries. Moreover, congressional elections did not present an opportunity for him to rid himself of opponents. These elections were conducted and determined on a local basis, and Washington felt that he could not intervene in them.[94]

As in the case of twentieth-century presidents, Washington's public approval was at the margins of leading Congress. His undoubted prestige was useful in obtaining some congressional support, but it could not change the views of those who firmly held contrary views. Nor could it prevent the emergence of an organized and vocal opposition to his policies.

Feeling more constrained by public opinion than in command of it, Washington made efforts to learn what the public was thinking so he would not stray too far afield. He also made substantial efforts to "go public" and build support for the government and himself. His supporters launched aggressive public relations campaigns on behalf of his policies, but there is little evidence that Washington was able to mobilize the mass public.

Washington adopted a respectful and cooperative orientation toward Congress, especially the Senate, and engaged in regular consultation with its members. Bargaining was also not foreign to his administration. Yet then, as now, personal legislative skills could carry the executive only so far. And neither presidential charm nor executive amenities could make a Hamiltonian out of a Jeffersonian.

In sum, things have not changed much. Two hundred years later, Washington would have pollsters instead of personal envoys reading public opinion; he would approach the public through television instead of the presidential coach; and his administration would bargain over provisions of elaborate social welfare programs instead of the site for the nation's capital. Yet the big picture remains remarkably similar. Systemic factors such as political culture and the structure of the constitutional system determine that Washington, as well as his successors, had to be a facilitator, not a director, of change. He, like they, was not able to create opportunities for change through his personal leadership, no matter how much the public venerated him. *Plus ça change . . .*

PART III

The Message

6

Disseminating the Message: Can the President Focus the Public's Attention?

The second primary component in the communications chain between the president and the public is the president's message. Although some issues force their way onto the president's agenda, presidents have more control over the substance of the messages they communicate to the public — the issues they address, the positions they take on them, and the terms in which they articulate their views — than on any other aspect of the communications process.

The White House's strategic decisions regarding which policies to pursue are beyond the focus of this study; we are concerned with whether presidents are more likely to be successful in moving the public on some issues, national security, for example, than on others. The evidence in Chapters 2 and 3 makes it clear that the topic on which the president communicates does not differentiate success from failure. Presidents fail to move public opinion across a wide spectrum of policy issues.

Similarly, presidents have almost complete freedom in the language they use to express their views on matters of public policy. Commentators often critically evaluate presidents on the quality of their rhetoric, praising "great communicators" such as Ronald Reagan and John F. Kennedy for their prose as well as their style of presentation while criticizing less eloquent presidents such as Lyndon Johnson, Gerald Ford, and George H. W. Bush. The experiences of Kennedy and Reagan, however, offer little support for the view that quality of oratory is a significant advantage in moving public opinion.

There are additional aspects of the president's message that may shed light on the problems the White House experiences in its attempts to lead the public. Before the president can influence *how* the public thinks, he must influence *what* it is thinking about. Influencing the issues that receive serious attention by the public and policy makers has long been viewed as one of the most important sources of political power.[1] In the era of governing by campaigning, presidents often seek to use their messages to focus the attention of the public as a precursor to setting the agenda of policy makers in Washington.

For decades, scholars have maintained that the president has a significant—indeed, the *most* significant—role in setting the policy-making agenda in Washington.[2] In a careful study of the Washington agenda, John Kingdon found that "no other single actor in the political system has quite the capability of the president to set agendas."[3] More recently, Frank Baumgartner and Bryan Jones, in their broad examination of agenda setting, concluded that "no other single actor can focus attention as clearly, or change the motivations of such a great number of other actors, as the president."[4]

Despite the consensus among scholars about the president's influence on the policy agenda, we actually know little about the president's ability to focus public attention on issues of his choosing.[5] Even a brief look at the president's challenges in focusing attention reveals that this is likely to be a daunting task.

The president transmits his messages in an environment clogged with competing communications from a wide variety of sources, through a wide range of media, and on a staggering array of subjects. Even within the domain of politics, Americans are bombarded with political communications every day, many of which originate in the White House. The sheer volume of these communications far exceeds the attentive capacity of any individual.

In addition, the lack of interest in politics of most Americans, as evidenced by the low turnouts even in presidential elections, provides an additional burden on the president's messages. Policy making is a very complex enterprise, and most voters do not have the time, expertise, or inclination to think extensively about most issues (especially those as distant from their everyday experiences as perhaps federal regulations, nuclear weapons, and bureaucratic organization). Even closer to home, after more than two decades of political controversy, nearly half of Americans fail to realize that the nation must import oil.[6] Similarly, the major domestic policy initiative of Ronald Reagan's second term was tax reform, yet as the bill was nearing the end of its legislative path in the Senate, only 40 percent of the public had heard or read even "some" about it.[7] Likewise, Bill Clinton was, understandably, disappointed that even after three years of his administration, nearly half the American people thought that the U.S. annual budget deficit had been going up during his administration, while only one-fifth (correctly) knew it had gone down.[8]

In fact, people generally have only a few issues that are particularly important to them and to which they pay attention.[9] The importance of specific issues to the public varies over time and is closely tied to objective conditions such as unemployment, inflation, international tensions, and racial conflict. In addition, different issues are likely to be salient to different groups in the population at any given time. For example, some groups may be concerned about inflation, others about unemployment, and yet others about a particular aspect of foreign policy or race relations.[10]

In sum, the president faces considerable challenges in using his messages to set the public's agenda. An extraordinary number of communications confront the public, which displays limited interest in those dealing with government and politics. Moreover, the White House can do little to limit the overall volume of messages that citizens encounter or to make the public more attentive to politics.

The president does have a good deal of control over his own messages, however. Setting the public's agenda requires that the president's messages be received by the public and be recognizable amid competing messages. We would expect that a concentration of presidential messages would be more likely to capture the public's attention than would an occasional message or a series of messages dispersed over several years. We would also expect that messages conveyed in an empty communications environment would be more likely to be heard than those transmitted in a congested one.

In this chapter we investigate whether the president's messages are likely to focus public attention on his administration's priorities. Does the president have effective access to the public for his messages? Is he able to cluster messages on a topic so as to increase the probability of making an impression on public opinion through repetition? As a whole, are the president's messages focused on his priorities, or do they span a wide range of subjects, placing the president in competition with himself in his efforts to set the public's agenda?

Although presidents make public statements on a wide range of matters, including hundreds of ceremonial and testimonial proclamations, we concentrate on matters of public policy. It is the effort to bring about changes in public policy, principally through congressional action, that is the primary motivation for going public and attempting to govern through a permanent campaign.

Spreading the Word

As a first step in focusing the public's attention, the president must make the public aware of his position and perhaps that he seeks its support. It is likely that reaching the public will require frequent repetition of the president's views. Given the protracted nature of the legislative process, and the president's need for public support at all stages of it, sustaining a message can be equally important as sending it in the first place. As David Gergen put it, "History teaches that almost nothing a leader says is heard if spoken only once." Administrations attempt to establish a "line of the day" so that many voices echo the same point. Similarly, the skilled communicators in the Reagan White House emphasized a thematic (that is, repetitive) approach to communications.[11]

How well does the White House do in disseminating information about its policy proposals? On one hand, commentary cascades from the White House. One official estimated that the White House produces as many as five million words a year in the president's name in outlets such as speeches, written statements, and proclamations.[12] Tables 6.1 and 6.2 show the president's public remarks for a sample of issues that were important during the Reagan and Clinton presidencies, respectively. (Since the salience of issues varied between the administrations, the issues reported in each table are somewhat different.) The number of presidential statements regarding a prominent policy can exceed two hundred in a year.

To understand the real effect of the president's statements, however, we must disaggregate the figures for total comments. Wide audiences hear only a small proportion of the president's comments. Comments about policy proposals at news conferences and question-and-answer sessions and in most interviews are also usually brief and made in the context of a discussion of many other policies at the same time. Remarks to individual groups and written statements may be focused, but the audience for these communications is modest. In addition, according to Gergen, nearly all of the president's statements "wash over the public. They are dull, gray prose, eminently forgettable."[13]

TELEVISED ADDRESSES

The largest audiences, of course, are for the president's nationally televised addresses, but most of the comments in these addresses are made in the context of remarks about many other policies. There is little opportunity for the president to focus on one issue area. The number and subject of televised addresses by Presidents Reagan and Clinton are shown in Tables 6.3 and 6.4, respectively.

Ronald Reagan made forty-seven nationally televised addresses (Table 6.3). Most of these speeches, however, were either broad communications such as State of the Union messages or narrower reports on military interventions, summit meetings, disasters, and scandals. Only nineteen of these addresses focused on his policy proposals. Consistent with the general strategic view of the Reagan White House, the president focused his policy addresses on a few high-priority policies. Four of these televised addresses sought to obtain support for aid to forces opposing communism in Central America, and four others dealt with other aspects of national security. Nine of the televised addresses centered on the budget and the economy (five of these speeches occurred during the critical months of 1981, when the bulk of the Reagan economic program passed in Congress). The only other addresses on policy proposals, a total of two, were on tax reform and drug control.

Bill Clinton made twenty-eight nationally televised addresses (Table 6.4). Ten of Clinton's national addresses were of a general nature, including his inaugural and State of the Union messages. He also made several addresses regarding military interventions. The president made only six national addresses on legislation before Congress, four of them in 1993. The first two focused on the same issue, his economic stimulus program. The addresses on health care reform and the two budgets also involved issues before Congress. The 1994 address on a Middle Class Bill of Rights occurred after Congress had adjourned and was not focused on legislation before Congress. Instead, it was more of a desperation effort at projecting a tax-cutting image for the White House in the wake of the Republican takeover of Congress. The 1995 address on balancing the budget was also a general plan designed to co-opt the deficit reduction issue from the Republicans. In the remaining five and a half years of his presidency, Clinton never again made a nationally televised address on legislation.

RADIO ADDRESSES

With the advent of television, presidents following Truman generally neglected radio as a medium for communication. The primary explanation for presidents ignoring radio was that the potential audiences for radio addresses are much smaller than for televised addresses. Even though Presidents Nixon and Ford used radio addresses on occasion, not until the Reagan presidency did radio addresses become a nearly regular presidential forum for national communication.

The Reagan White House sought to capitalize on the president's fondness for and experience with radio and began short Saturday broadcasts on a trial basis. When the public and media responded favorably, the administration institutionalized the broadcasts. In all, Reagan made 326 Saturday radio addresses. He typically used them to speak directly to the public in a conversational manner about a particular issue. He divided his attention fairly evenly between domestic and foreign policy, but typically focused on one policy per address. Thus, Reagan delivered a "Radio Address to the Nation on the

Table 6.1. Public Statements of Ronald Reagan on Selected Policy Issues

Year	Total Comments	Televised Addresses	Remarks	Press Conferences	Q&A Sessions	Interviews	Radio Addresses	Written Statements
Abortion								
1981	5	1	3	1	0	0	0	0
1982	11	0	8	1	1	0	0	1
1983	9	0	5	0	2	0	1	1
1984	16	2	5	0	1	4	1	3
1985	10	1	6	0	1	0	0	2
1986	11	1	5	1	0	1	0	3
1987	8	0	4	0	0	0	0	4
1988	18	1	7	0	1	0	1	8
Aid to the Contras								
1981	0	0	0	0	0	0	0	0
1982	0	0	0	0	0	0	0	0
1983	3	0	0	0	1	1	1	0
1984	12	1	0	2	5	4	0	0
1985	25	0	4	2	5	7	3	4
1986	30	1	13	4	7	4	0	1
1987	15	2	1	2	6	2	1	1
1988	17	1	8	2	6	0	0	0
Defense spending								
1981	21	2	8	2	4	1	0	4
1982	48	2	18	5	8	5	5	5
1983	45	3	14	3	14	1	6	4
1984	35	1	17	3	3	7	2	2
1985	43	2	17	3	3	3	10	5
1986	40	2	18	4	2	3	2	9

1987	42	1	20	0	4	0	13	4
1988	46	1	28	3	2	3	4	5
Environmental protection								
1981	7	0	4	0	0	0	0	3
1982	8	2	1	0	0	0	1	4
1983	14	1	4	0	3	0	0	7
1984	15	1	5	1	2	1	1	4
1985	4	0	2	0	0	0	0	2
1986	7	0	2	0	1	0	0	4
1987	16	0	3	0	0	1	2	10
1988	8	0	3	0	0	0	0	5
Grenada								
1981	0	0	0	0	0	0	0	0
1982	2	0	2	0	0	0	0	0
1983	21	3	10	0	2	2	3	1
1984	74	1	60	1	4	3	2	3
1985	6	0	3	0	1	0	1	1
1986	26	1	20	1	1	1	1	1
1987	5	0	4	0	0	0	0	1
1988	19	0	17	0	1	0	1	0
School prayer								
1981	0	0	0	0	0	0	0	0
1982	12	0	9	0	1	0	1	1
1983	7	1	2	0	1	0	2	1
1984	21	1	10	2	1	4	2	1
1985	3	1	2	0	0	0	0	0
1986	3	0	0	0	1	1	0	1
1987	3	0	2	0	1	0	0	0
1988	17	1	15	0	0	0	0	1

Table 6.1. Continued

Year	Total Comments	Televised Addresses	Remarks	Press Conferences	Q&A Sessions	Interviews	Radio Addresses	Written Statements
Strategic Defense Initiative								
1981	0	0	0	0	0	0	0	0
1982	0	0	0	0	0	0	0	0
1983	0	0	0	0	0	0	0	0
1984	0	0	0	0	0	0	0	0
1985	36	2	9	4	3	13	5	0
1986	71	3	38	1	6	5	7	11
1987	58	3	21	2	9	4	4	15
1988	63	1	37	1	2	3	7	12
South Africa								
1981	0	0	0	0	0	0	0	0
1982	0	0	0	0	0	0	0	0
1983	0	0	0	0	0	0	0	0
1984	8	0	4	0	2	0	0	2
1985	18	0	3	2	4	4	0	5
1986	28	0	4	2	4	3	0	15
1987	6	0	3	0	0	0	0	3
1988	8	0	2	1	0	0	0	5
Balanced budget amendment								
1981	1	0	1	0	0	0	0	0
1982	31	2	18	2	5	0	2	2
1983	2	0	2	0	0	0	0	0
1984	46	1	31	1	6	3	2	2

1985	26	0	11	0	2	4	4	5
1986	27	1	14	1	2	1	4	4
1987	41	3	23	0	3	1	7	4
1988	33	1	24	0	2	0	3	3
Spending cuts								
1981	25	3	13	3	2	1	0	3
1982	57	3	39	1	8	2	6	8
1983	34	1	20	2	7	0	3	1
1984	42	2	28	2	6	0	3	1
1985	43	1	20	5	2	5	7	3
1986	28	1	14	2	1	2	6	2
1987	39	0	24	1	3	0	8	3
1988	19	0	12	2	1	0	3	1
Taxes								
1981	54	5	28	5	9	3	0	4
1982	90	3	50	5	13	7	8	4
1983	67	0	37	4	13	2	10	1
1984	73	2	51	2	6	5	5	2
1985	50	4	32	1	4	4	4	1
1986	51	1	36	2	1	0	10	1
1987	31	0	23	1	3	0	3	1
1988	24	0	18	1	2	0	3	0

Source: Public Papers of the Presidents (CD-ROM).

Notes: Remarks are those speeches indicated in the *Public Papers* as "Remarks" to a particular group or about a specific subject. Remarks range from the president's annual prayer breakfast in Washington to campaign rallies throughout the United States. "Toasts" and other spoken words that do not fit in any other category are also considered "remarks."

Q&A includes informal exchanges with reporters as well as question-and-answer sessions with the public or the media.

Written Statements includes written messages to Congress, written statements proclaiming a position, and relevant proclamations.

Table 6.2. Public Statements of Bill Clinton on Selected Policy Issues

Year	Total Comments	Televised Addresses	Remarks	Press Conferences	Q&A Sessions	Interviews	Radio Addresses	Written Statements
Welfare								
1993	126	3	57	4	22	20	19	1
1994	143	2	80	8	25	9	15	4
1995	157	2	91	6	22	6	18	12
1996	239	3	172	4	23	10	17	10
1997	166	1	125	7	17	5	7	4
1998	167	1	140	2	6	6	3	9
1999	184	1	150	3	6	9	6	9
2000	219	1	174	1	5	16	8	14
NAFTA								
1993	128	1	37	16	41	12	10	11
1994	92	1	45	13	9	9	7	8
1995	45	0	24	5	7	5	1	3
1996	21	1	12	1	3	0	0	4
1997	27	0	7	6	6	2	0	6
1998	8	0	2	0	2	1	0	3
1999	14	0	7	2	1	0	0	4
2000	18	0	5	2	2	2	0	7
Environmental protection								
1993	89	1	42	6	17	6	6	11
1994	52	2	22	6	5	1	1	15

1995	164	1	90	9	19	5	12	28
1996	278	3	210	11	13	2	19	20
1997	145	1	98	11	13	1	8	13
1998	182	1	130	5	17	2	7	20
1999	191	1	127	4	13	6	10	30
2000	199	1	139	1	7	12	6	33
Iraq								
1993	29	1	2	6	7	3	0	10
1994	48	1	17	3	3	3	5	16
1995	31	0	11	4	3	3	0	10
1996	39	1	14	2	5	0	3	14
1997	44	0	15	3	14	1	0	11
1998	63	2	20	3	14	5	3	16
1999	21	1	10	0	1	0	0	9
2000	42	1	11	7	2	3	1	17
Economic program								
1993	166	3	57	7	56	25	14	4
1994	60	1	39	3	10	4	1	2
1995	16	0	8	3	3	1	1	0
1996	21	0	13	3	3	1	1	0
1997	14	0	13	1	0	0	0	0
1998	14	0	13	0	1	0	0	0
1999	11	0	10	0	0	0	0	1
2000	22	0	16	0	0	6	0	0

Table 6.2. Continued

Year	Total Comments	Televised Addresses	Remarks	Press Conferences	Q&A Sessions	Interviews	Radio Addresses	Written Statements
Crime								
1993	123	2	55	5	31	18	10	2
1994	242	2	136	7	35	22	30	10
1995	136	1	92	4	15	5	11	8
1996	261	1	214	2	14	3	14	13
1997	175	1	133	2	8	3	9	19
1998	198	1	155	2	8	5	10	17
1999	218	1	163	3	8	6	11	26
2000	248	1	192	2	6	13	7	27
Education								
1993	210	3	110	4	41	17	26	9
1994	200	2	117	8	19	19	24	11
1995	266	2	155	10	40	9	27	23
1996	309	3	242	5	16	4	22	17
1997	261	2	170	10	18	5	21	35
1998	224	1	154	4	24	5	6	30
1999	182	0	122	3	6	6	11	34
2000	202	1	149	2	12	10	11	17
Health care								
1993	267	4	150	13	39	25	26	10
1994	239	2	146	9	21	21	22	18

1995	139	2	94	6	12	7	13	5
1996	225	3	177	4	6	4	16	15
1997	141	2	99	4	13	4	10	9
1998	156	1	124	0	5	3	7	16
1999	183	1	118	6	6	9	10	33
2000	262	1	184	1	9	18	11	38
Minimum wage								
1993	9	0	4	0	4	1	0	0
1994	7	0	3	0	3	1	0	0
1995	54	1	29	5	10	2	5	2
1996	159	1	118	4	15	3	12	6
1997	33	0	26	0	3	1	2	1
1998	53	1	38	1	5	5	0	3
1999	60	1	40	3	4	2	3	7
2000	115	0	76	1	15	2	11	10

Source: Public Papers of the Presidents (CD-ROM).

Notes: Remarks are those speeches indicated in the *Public Papers* as "Remarks" to a particular group or about a specific subject. Remarks range from the president's annual prayer breakfast in Washington to campaign rallies throughout the United States. "Toasts" and other spoken words that do not fit in any other category are also considered "remarks."

Q&A includes informal exchanges with reporters as well as question-and-answer sessions with the public or the media. "Q&A" also includes roundtable discussions and town hall meetings.

Written Statements includes written messages to Congress, written statements proclaiming a position, and relevant proclamations.

Table 6.3. Nationally Televised Addresses of Reagan (1981–1989)

Date	Principal Subject
	General Addresses
January 20, 1981	Inaugural
January 26, 1982	State of the Union
October 13, 1982	State of the economy
January 25, 1983	State of the Union
January 25, 1984	State of the Union
January 21, 1985	Inaugural
February 6, 1985	State of the Union
February 4, 1986	State of the Union
January 27, 1987	State of the Union
January 25, 1988	State of the Union
January 11, 1989	Farewell Address
	Military Interventions
April 14, 1986	Air strike against Libya
September 1, 1982	Middle East
September 20, 1982	U.S. troops to Lebanon
October 27, 1983	Lebanon; Grenada
	Reports on Summits
November 14, 1985	U.S.–Soviet Summit
November 21, 1985	U.S.–Soviet Summit
October 13, 1986	U.S.–Soviet Summit
June 15, 1987	Economic Summit; budget
December 10, 1987	U.S.–Soviet Summit; INF treaty
	Policy Proposals
February 5, 1981	Economy
February 18, 1981	Economy
April 28, 1981	Economy
July 27, 1981	Tax reduction
September 24, 1981	Deficit reduction
April 29, 1982	Budget
August 16, 1982	Budget
October 13, 1982	Economy
November 22, 1982	Arms control; nuclear deterrence
March 23, 1983	Defense spending
April 27, 1983	Central America
January 16, 1984	U.S.–Soviet relations (morning)
May 9, 1984	Central America
April 24, 1985	Budget
May 28, 1985	Tax reform
February 26, 1986	National security

Table 6.3. Continued

	Date	Principal Subject
	March 16, 1986	Nicaragua
	June 14, 1986	Nicaraguan Contras
	September 14, 1986	Campaign against drug abuse
Other		
	December 23, 1981	Christmas; Poland
	September 5, 1983	Soviet attack on Korean civilian airliner
	January 28, 1986	*Challenger* explosion
	July 4, 1986	Statue of Liberty centennial
	November 13, 1986	Iran-Contra
	December 2, 1986	Iran-Contra
	March 4, 1987	Iran-Contra
	August 12, 1987	Iran-Contra

Economic Recovery Program" or a "Radio Address to the Nation on Proposed Natural Gas Deregulation."[14]

George Bush discontinued the use of regular radio communications to the nation, but Bill Clinton made 340 Saturday radio addresses. Clinton's addresses were slightly longer than Reagan's on average and much more likely to focus on domestic policy.[15] They we also somewhat less focused within each address, symbolized by Clinton's titling his speeches as simply, "The President's Radio Address."

Despite the fact that Presidents Reagan and Clinton made a total of nearly seven hundred radio addresses, their efforts were of only marginal value in reaching the public. The addresses were short, averaging about 850 words, and their audiences were typically small. Weekend media paid modest attention to them, with most broadcast and print outlets carrying nothing at all.

STATEMENTS ON PENDING LEGISLATION

Another way to view the extent of the president's efforts to obtain public attention is to explore his statements relative to specific pieces of legislation. Andrew Barrett examined the average number of presidential remarks regarding 253 significant bills on which the president took a position. The results are shown in Table 6.5. Presidents went public an average of 10.5 times during the life of each bill. More than ten specific presidential remarks promoting or denouncing a piece of legislation may seem like a significant number until we consider how long the president had an opportunity to speak out over the life

Table 6.4. Nationally Televised Addresses of Clinton (1993–2001)

Date	Principal Subject
General Addresses	
January 20, 1993	Inaugural
January 25, 1994	State of the Union
January 24, 1995	State of the Union
January 23, 1996	State of the Union
January 20, 1997	Inaugural
February 4, 1997	State of the Union
January 27, 1998	State of the Union
January 19, 1999	State of the Union
January 27, 2000	State of the Union
January 18, 2001	Farewell address
Military Interventions	
June 26, 1993	Air strike against Iraq
October 7, 1993	Somalia
September 15, 1994	Troops to Haiti
September 18, 1994	Troops to Haiti
October 10, 1994	Troops to Iraq
November 27, 1995	Troops to Bosnia
August 20, 1998	Air strike against Afghanistan and the Sudan
December 16, 1998	Air strikes against Iraq
December 19, 1998	Air strikes against Iraq
March 24, 1999	Air strikes in Kosovo
June 10, 1999	End of air strikes in Kosovo
*Other**	
August 17, 1998	Grand Jury testimony
Policy Proposals	
February 15, 1993	Economic program
February 17, 1993	Economic program
August 3, 1993	Budget
September 22, 1993	Health care reform
December 15, 1994	Middle class Bill of Rights (tax cuts)
June 13, 1995	Budget balancing plan

*On December 19, 1998, the president made a short statement on the House vote on impeachment at 4:15 P.M, and on February 12, 1999, he made a short statement on the Senate vote on impeachment at 5:15 P.M. The White House did not view these as national addresses. The president also taped Christmas greetings for rebroadcast in 1996 and 2000.

Table 6.5. Average Presidential Public Statements on Significant Pending Legislation (1977–1992)

	Number of Bills	Average Statements	Statements per Month
Total bills	253	10.5	0.9
Presidential initiatives*	52	20.1	1.9
Congressional initiatives*	173	5.2	0.4
Bills supported by president	176	14.1	1.2
Bills opposed by president	77	2.3	0.3

Source: Adapted from Andrew Barrett, "Gone Public: The Impact of Presidential Rhetoric in Congress," unpublished Ph.D. dissertation, Texas A&M University, 2000.

*Both the president and Congress initiated some bills.

of each bill during a congressional session. When we control for the number of months the president had an opportunity to go public, we find that presidents spoke publicly regarding the bills on average only 0.9 times per month.

There is variance around the mean for all legislation. For example, presidents average 20.1 remarks per bill initiated by their own administration (or 1.9 remarks per month) compared with only 5.2 remarks (or 0.4 remarks per month) for congressional initiatives. Presidents apparently reserve the going public strategy for their own legislative proposals. Similarly, presidents speak out in support of legislation 14.1 times per bill (or 1.2 times per month) more than in opposition (only 2.3 remarks per bill or 0.3 times per month). The president may not need to speak out in opposition to a bill he opposes if that bill appears to be unlikely to pass anyway. In addition, a president may need to go public only once to issue a veto threat to kill successfully a bill since such a threat lifts the bar to passage from a simple majority to a two-thirds vote in both houses of Congress. Finally, since the president always has the veto power at his disposal, he does not need to say anything publicly to kill a legislative proposal he opposes. The bottom line, however, is that even in support of their own most significant legislative initiatives, on which their legacy may be built, presidents speak publicly less than twice a month.

Table 6.6 presents another way to view presidential statements on legislation. We can see that the president speaks out one time or fewer on about one-third of significant bills, and he speaks out five times or fewer on 60 percent of all significant bills. On only 11 percent of these important bills did the president speak publicly more than twenty-five times. On only 26 percent did he speak

Table 6.6. Presidential Public Statements on Significant Pending Legislation (1977–1992)

Times Mentioned	Number of Bills	Percentage of Total
0	58	22.9
1	23	9.1
2–5	71	28.1
6–10	34	13.4
11–25	39	15.4
26–50	15	5.9
51–75	9	3.6
76–100	2	0.8
101+	2	0.8
Total	253	

Source: Adapted from Andrew Barrett, "Gone Public: The Impact of Presidential Rhetoric in Congress," unpublished Ph.D. dissertation, Texas A&M University, 2000.

publicly more than even ten times. The evidence is clear that presidents do not consistently and repeatedly go public regarding most significant legislation.

Focusing Attention

No matter how often the president may speak out on an issue, his messages still occur in a congested communications environment. There are many demands on the public's attention. In addition, the president does not want the public to pay equal attention to all of his messages. Many of these messages are targeted to specific audiences or serve purely symbolic purposes. Although the president will be pleased if these communications bolster his general public support, he does not want them to drown out his efforts to move the public to support his priority policies. If the president's messages are to meet his coalition-building needs, the public must sort through the maze of communications in its environment and concentrate on the president's priority concerns.

To help direct public attention, the president must focus his own messages on his priorities. Setting priorities is also important because the president's political capital is inevitably limited, and it is sensible to focus it on the issues about which he cares most. Moreover, the White House has the capacity to lobby effectively for only a few policies at a time. Focusing, then, can be a critical component of a president's governing strategy.

Focusing is more easily said than done, however. Other powerful influences may affect the public, and there are a number of constraints on the president focusing his own messages on his priorities.

COMPETITION FOR ATTENTION

The presidency is not the only institution that has the potential to focus the public's attention. The president faces many competitors, each of whom has an incentive to obtain the public's support.

Previous Commitments

In the first place, presidents must cope with an elaborate agenda established by their predecessors.[16] The president's choices of priorities usually fall within parameters set by prior commitments of the government that obligate it to spend money, defend allies, maintain services, or protect rights.[17] As Kennedy aide Theodore Sorensen observed, "Presidents rarely, if ever make decisions . . . in the sense of writing their conclusions largely on a clean slate."[18]

The Congress

There is no question that Congress is an important agenda setter, perhaps the central one, in the U.S. political system. Baumgartner and Jones emphasize the importance of Congress in determining and changing the national agenda.[19] Kingdon places Congress second only to the administration as a whole as an agenda setter in Washington.[20] Roy Flemming, B. Dan Wood, and John Bohte find Congress to be the major agenda setter in environmental policy.[21] The public expects Congress to take the initiative,[22] and members of Congress have strong electoral incentives to respond.

Thus, Congress is quite capable of setting its own agenda, and it generally does. Table 6.7 shows the initiators of the major legislative proposals during the period 1953–1996. Congress initiated 66 percent or two-thirds of these proposals. It is not surprising, then, that when President Carter sent his large legislative program to Congress, it had to compete for space on the agenda with congressional initiatives. As a presidential aide put it, "Congress was scheduled up before most of the items arrived."[23]

This aggressive role of Congress is not unusual. Most of the major legislative actions of the 1980s were congressional initiatives.[24] Looking at Ronald Reagan's second term, we find that the major legislative actions of the Ninety-ninth Congress (1985–1986) include the reauthorization of the Clean Water Act, the Safe Drinking Water Act, and the "Superfund" for cleaning up hazardous waste; sanctions against South Africa; reorganization of the Pentagon;

Table 6.7. Initiators of Major Legislative Proposals

Congress	Years	Presidential Initiatives	Congressional Initiatives	Total Bills	Percent Presidential
83rd	1953–54	9	14	23	39.1
84th	1955–56	6	16	22	27.3
85th	1957–58	11	17	28	39.3
86th	1959–60	4	17	21	19.0
87th	1961–62	24	11	35	68.6
88th	1963–64	21	19	40	52.5
89th	1965–66	30	22	52	57.7
90th	1967–68	19	15	34	55.9
91st	1969–70	16	23	39	41.0
92nd	1971–72	17	37	54	31.5
93rd	1973–74	17	39	56	30.4
94th	1975–76	15	40	55	27.2
95th	1977–78	19	21	40	47.5
96th	1979–80	17	18	35	48.6
97th	1981–82	11	25	36	30.6
98th	1983–84	10	25	35	28.6
99th	1985–86	5	27	32	15.6
100th	1987–88	2	35	37	5.4
101st	1989–90	8	31	39	20.5
102nd	1991–92	4	31	35	11.4
103rd	1993–94	15	22	37	40.5
104th	1995–96	0	40	40	0
Total bills		280	545	825	33.9
Average bills/ Congress		12.7	24.7	37.5	

a measure to combat drug abuse; a major revision of immigration law; the Gramm-Rudman-Hollings bill to reduce the deficit; revisions of the law on gun control; the first authorization for water projects in a decade; an extension of daylight saving time; and extended protection against age discrimination. On none of this legislation did the White House take the lead. Instead, it reacted to congressional initiatives. Even the historic Tax Reform Act of 1986 was as much a product of long-term congressional momentum and committee leadership as it was of presidential agenda setting. In 1987, the president found Congress already working on his two primary domestic policy initiatives for his last two years in office, catastrophic health insurance and welfare reform.

Congress was no more deferential to President Clinton. After the Republicans obtained majorities in both the House and Senate in the 1994 midterm elections, the new majority took the lead in proposing major policy initiatives. The aggressive Republican efforts to pass the elements of its Contract with America forced the White House to adopt a defensive posture, and the president offered no major proposals during the entire Congress.

It is not only the opposition party that complicates presidents' efforts to focus their messages. Both George H. W. Bush and Bill Clinton received nearly twice as much criticism as praise in the media *from their own parties* in Congress.[25]

The Media

The public's familiarity with political matters is closely related to the amount and duration of attention these affairs receive in the mass media,[26] especially in foreign affairs. The media also have a strong influence on the issues the public views as important.[27] According to Doris Graber, "Many people readily adopt the media's agenda of importance, often without being aware of it."[28] Moreover, when the media cover events, politicians comment on them and take action, reinforcing the perceived importance of these events and ensuring more public attention to them. In addition, media coverage of issues affects the importance of these issues in the public's assessment of political figures — a topic that we will address in the next chapter.

During the 1979–1980 Iranian hostage crisis, in which several dozen Americans were held hostage, ABC originated a nightly program entitled "America Held Hostage." Walter Cronkite provided a "countdown" of the number of days of the crisis at the end of each evening's news on CBS television; countless feature stories on the hostages and their families were reported in all the media; and the press gave complete coverage to "demonstrations" held in front of the U.S. embassy in Tehran (often artificially created by demonstrators for consumption by Americans). This crisis dominated American politics for more than a year and gave President Carter's approval rating a tremendous, albeit short-termed, boost. In the longer term, however, the coverage destroyed his leadership image. Conversely, when the American ship *Pueblo* was captured by North Korea, there were many more American captives and they were held for almost as long as the hostages in Tehran, but there were also no television cameras and few reporters to cover the situation. Thus, the incident played a much smaller role in American politics.

The president, then, constantly competes with the media in seeking to focus the public's attention. As Martin Linsky concluded in his analysis of a survey of former government officials and interviews with federal policy makers:

"The press has a huge and identifiable impact. . . . Officials believe that the media do a lot to set the policy agenda and to influence how an issue is understood by policymakers, interest groups, and the public."[29]

Recognizing the influence of the media as an agenda setter, the White House invests substantial energy and time in attempting to shape the media's attention.[30] It provides the press with briefings and backgrounders, press releases, and interviews and press conferences with high-level officials, including the president. It also makes efforts to coordinate the news emanating from various parts of the executive branch. Although we have rich descriptions of these efforts,[31] we know very little about their success in influencing the media.

Most examinations of presidential influence on the media's agenda have focused on the State of the Union message. Sheldon Gilberg and his colleagues found that the president was *not* able to influence media stories in the month following the 1978 address. Indeed, they concluded that the media set the president's agenda rather than the reverse.[32] Nearly a decade later, Wayne Wanta and his colleagues reviewed four studies and found mixed results. In two instances the president influenced the media's agenda, but in two instances he did not. Even two studies of the same president, Ronald Reagan, produced different results.[33]

B. Dan Wood and Jeffrey Peake, in a surprising finding, conclude that even in foreign policy, it is the media that influences the president's agenda rather than the other way around.[34] In a broader study focused on the relationships between the president, Congress, and the media, Edwards and Wood found that the president is more likely to react to fluctuations in attention by the media than he is to set the media's agenda. In domestic policy, however, the president has the potential to act in an entrepreneurial fashion to focus the attention of others in the system on major presidential initiatives.[35]

OBSTACLES TO FOCUSING THE MESSAGE

To be effective in leading the public, the president must focus the public's attention on his policies for a sustained period of time. This requires more than a single speech, no matter how eloquent or dramatic it may be. The Reagan White House was successful in maintaining a focus on its top-priority economic policies in 1981. It molded its communication strategy around its legislative priorities and focused the administration's agenda and statements on economic policy to ensure that discussing a wide range of topics did not diffuse the president's message.[36]

Sustaining such a focus is difficult to do, however. Every White House finds that it is impossible to organize the president's schedule for very long around a focus on his major goals, especially when he has been in office for a while. It is even more difficult to coordinate supporters around a message.[37] After 1981, President Reagan had to deal with a wide range of noneconomic policies. Other administrations have encountered similar problems.

Several related forces are at work here. The White House can put off dealing with the full spectrum of national issues for several months at the beginning of a new president's term, but it cannot do so for four years: eventually it must make decisions. By the second year the agenda is full and more policies are in the pipeline, as the administration attempts to satisfy its constituencies and responds to problems it has overlooked.

At the beginning of a two-week period in June 1979, President Carter met with a congressional delegation to try to rally its support for an expected close vote on the implementation of the Panama Canal Treaty. During the course of it, Carter told two congressmen that he would "whip [Senator Kennedy's] ass" if the latter tried to run against him. This statement became a big story on the evening news, overshadowing the Panama Canal issue. Two days later, the president introduced his proposals for national health insurance. Before any campaign could be launched to back his legislation, the president left for Vienna to sign the agreements reached during the Strategic Arms Limitation Talks (SALT). When he returned, he addressed Congress and the nation on the subject of SALT. The president's next appearance on the news took place the following day, when he spoke at a ceremony after the completion of a solar panel for the White House hot-water system. At that time he urged the nation to give its attention to this important alternative to oil. Three days later he left for a world economic conference.[38]

When the Clinton White House tried to put off focusing on welfare so as not to undermine its massive health care reform proposal in 1993–1994, Senator Daniel Patrick Moynihan criticized the president for not being serious about welfare reform. Moynihan, chair of the Senate Finance Committee that had to handle much of health care reform, threatened to hold health care hostage, so the White House had to devote at least some attention to welfare reform.[39]

The degree to which unanticipated issues, including international crises, impose themselves on the president's schedule and divert attention, energy, and resources from *his* agenda[40] will also affect the White House's success in focusing attention on priority issues. As Clinton aide George Stephanopoulos put it: "On the campaign trail, you can just change the subject. But you can't just change the subject as President. You can't wish Bosnia away. You can't wish David Koresh [the leader of the Branch Davidian sect in Waco, Texas] away. You can't just ignore them and change the subject."[41]

President Reagan wanted to focus attention on tax reform in 1985. Yet during a short trip to Alabama he had to react to a Senate vote that day on his request for aid to the rebels in Nicaragua and to the Supreme Court's decision on a school prayer case that had arisen in Alabama. As one presidential aide put it, "You can't go to Alabama and not mention the school prayer decision, and if you go to Alabama and mention the school prayer decision, don't think you are going to get covered on tax reform."[42]

The next year the president was pressing Congress to provide aid to the Contras, but his efforts were again overtaken by other events. According to the White House's communications director, Patrick J. Buchanan, "the Philippines intruded and dominated for two weeks, making it difficult for us to get the contra aid campaign off the ground." In addition, the president had to give a nationally televised speech on behalf of his defense budget, and the explosion of the space shuttle *Challenger* also distracted attention from the president's priorities. As one White House aide put it, "The hardest thing to do is not to get into a reactive mode and have your schedule dictated to you by events, rather than dictating events and having a schedule reflective of your priorities."[43]

When President Clinton tried to press themes he articulated in his 1994 State of the Union message by taking his case to audiences around the country, he was caught up in other issues, such as the trade war with Japan, possible military action in Bosnia, criticism of a former Justice Department official over the crime bill, and cleaning up a last bit of mess from the Tailhook scandal. Later that summer, as the Clinton White House entered the final negotiations over its high-priority bills on crime and health care reform, it had to deal first with the Whitewater hearings and then a huge influx of Cuban refugees.

Ironically, it is the president himself who provides the most important competition for attention to his priorities. There are many demands on the president to act and speak, and when he accedes to these demands, as he must, his words and actions divert attention from his priorities. Focusing attention on priorities is considerably easier for a president with a short legislative agenda, such as Ronald Reagan, than it is for one with a more ambitious agenda. It is also an advantage if the opposition party is in disarray and lacks alternatives to the president's agenda, a situation the Republicans enjoyed in 1981 as the Democrats reeled from Reagan's electoral victory and their loss of the Senate.

Conversely, Bill Clinton took office with a large agenda, which was detailed in his lengthy annual State of the Union addresses.[44] In addition, Democrats had a laundry list of initiatives that had been blocked by George Bush, ranging from family and medical leave to motor voter registration and health care reform. Clinton and his fellow partisans believed in activist government and were predisposed toward doing "good" and against husbanding leadership resources. But no good deed goes unpunished. The more the White House tried to do, the more difficult it was to focus the country's attention on priority issues. "I'm the most impatient person on earth," the president declared. "I've tried to do so many things that sometimes when I do things, no one notices. Most Americans don't know we did family leave or motor voter or national service or changed the environmental policy, because I was always in some other controversy that was getting more ink."[45]

The president may be his own worst enemy in focusing the public's attention. President Clinton had an undisciplined personal style, tremendous energy, a desire to please many sides, a mind stuffed with policy ideas, and a party of interest groups clamoring for policy. Clinton and his advisers understood the virtue of a clear, simple agenda,[46] and the president knew that his defining issues had been overwhelmed as he had engaged in issue proliferation.[47] As he admitted in 1993, "What went wrong was I was not able to keep the public focus on issues that we're working on after I gave the State of the Union address."[48] "It's hard to get more than one message a day across on the evening news to the American people."[49]

He was not able to contain himself, however. He rarely focused on any bill for more than a few days at a time.[50] On November 13, 1993, the last weekend before the NAFTA vote in the House, Clinton made headlines with an emotional appeal in a black church in Memphis on stopping crime. Naturally, this speech, not NAFTA, received the headlines for the Sunday papers and news programs. Shortly after the midterm elections, the president traveled to Indonesia to sign an agreement regarding free trade among Pacific Rim nations. Yet he overshadowed his own success with an off-the-cuff comment on school prayer. Compounding the problem, he made news again the following day as he backed away from his own words.

Similarly, in 1998 Clinton gave a commencement address at MIT on the digital divide. He wanted to focus public attention on the issue of disparities in access to computer technology. Yet the same day as the commencement address he dedicated a nature center at Walden Pond, had pictures taken with several members of the Kennedy family, taped a radio address honoring Robert F. Kennedy, and held a conference call with youth. He also engaged in a discussion of economic strategy as he commented on the latest unemployment figures, and the White House endorsed a new system for allocating "domain names" on the Internet.[51]

The president's personal behavior also played a role in blurring the focus of his public statements. Clinton's chief speechwriter, Michael Waldman, describes how the president kept a very heavy schedule of public appearances and placed a "relentless reliance on the bully pulpit" during the Lewinsky scandal to combat bad publicity. In the process, there were sometimes *two or even three* "messages of the day." In one week, for example, Clinton spoke in public on disaster relief in California, tax reform, drunk driving, food safety legislation, Medicare reform, the economy, and health care, and he announced the naming of the first woman commander of a space shuttle mission.[52]

The Clinton White House understood that the president was speaking on many subjects at once, but it rationalized that he could make up in quantity what he had lost in focus. Indeed, Waldman writes approvingly that Clinton transformed the way the president speaks to the country: "Speeches are no longer thunderbolts hurled from Olympus. Instead, they are a steady purr, one or two or even three a day."[53] Eventually, the president's aides held meetings to try to organize and coordinate the outpouring of presidential messages. They made decisions as to who would speak on a topic, whether remarks would be on the record, what news organizations and media would be kept informed, and, most important, how the message was to be integrated with the desired policy focus.[54] "The bully pulpit is still the president's most powerful tool," Waldman concludes. "But after Clinton, it will be used differently."[55]

The frequency and effect of future presidential public statements is, of course, an open question. A president who follows Clinton's pattern, however, risks undermining rather than reinforcing the effect of his own words.

THE CLINTON HEALTH CARE REFORM PLAN

The defining issue of the Clinton presidency was to have been health care reform, and the White House's handling of this issue illustrates the difficulties the administration had in focusing attention on its priority legislation. To begin, it is difficult to maintain focus on a proposal until a bill is written. The Clinton administration set and then badly overshot its deadline for delivery of a health care reform plan, first arousing and then dissipating public interest. Not meeting its own one-hundred-day deadline created a vacuum that was filled with controversies over issues of lower priority such as gays in the military, the bungled nominations of Zoe Baird and Kimba Wood for attorney general, and public funding for abortion.[56] These issues left an impression of ineptitude and alienated many in the public whose support the president would need for his priority legislation — hardly an auspicious beginning for an administration that had come to office with only 43 percent of the vote.

Clinton later recognized the problem he had created:

> "Republicans made this issue their opening salvo. And they understood — and I didn't understand exactly what I know now — how what we do here plays out in the country. But because it was one of my campaign commitments, I refused to back off. The message out in the country was, 'We elected this guy to turn the economy around, and instead, his top priority is gays in the military.'

> "But that's not true; it was Bob Dole's top priority. His top priority was making this the controversy that would consume the early days of my presidency, and it was a brilliant political move. If it happened to me again, I would say, 'Why is this the Republicans' top priority? I don't want to deal with this now. We can deal with this in six months when the study is done; let's take care of the American people now.' "[57]

Not until September 22, 1993, more than eight months after taking office, did the president make a national address on health care reform, his highest priority legislation. The speech was well received, and polls showed that the public was overwhelmingly supportive of his efforts.[58] Six days later, Hillary Clinton began her testimony on health care reform before five congressional committees, captivating and dominating her audience. But still there was no bill. The pace of rhetoric was out of sync with the pace of lawmaking. The president's September speech had the effect of peaking attention in a legislative battle before the introduction of the bill.

It was not until October 27, 1993, more than nine months after the president appointed his wife to head a panel to prepare health care legislation on January 25, that Clinton submitted his plan — 1,342 pages of it — to Congress. At that point public support was divided evenly, with 45 percent both for and against his bill.[59] Even at this late point, many technical revisions and corrections were required on the massive bill, further blurring the focus on the plan. In addition, the congressional leadership had to sort out committee jurisdiction problems before it could figure out when formally to present the bill. Finally, on November 20, two months after the president's national address, the president health care reform proposal was introduced in both houses of Congress.

In the meantime, there were important distractions from the president's bill. A ninety-minute program from a Sacramento television station ended up focusing on a wide range of issues and concerns, leaving the president little room to lobby for his health care plan. Then on October 3, eighteen American soldiers were killed on a peacekeeping mission in Somalia, and others were wounded or missing. Americans were horrified to see pictures of a dead soldier being dragged through the streets of Mogadishu. So the president returned from his health care trip to California and focused on events abroad. Americans seemed to lose interest in health care at this point. Bill McInturff was doing daily tracking polls from the time of the president's September 22 speech. From that date, "awareness of the plan was going up. Support for the plan was going up." But on October 3, it stopped.[60]

In addition, during this crucial period the president had to devote his full attention and all the White House's resources to obtaining passage of NAFTA, which dominated the news for weeks and which was central to his foreign policy priority of increasing international trade. Moreover, on October 11 the USS *Harlan County,* carrying U.S. troops as part of a United Nations plan to restore democracy in Haiti, was forced to turn around and leave in the face of promilitary gunmen. Thus, Clinton's plan to saturate the country with his message was sabotaged by national and international events.[61]

The president simply did not have time to maintain an intensive public campaign on behalf of his cornerstone policy, and it was beyond the capacity of the White House to coordinate supporters around a message. The president's public outreach on health care was intermittent and declined over time. Moreover, the president's aides could not manage the media to control its content. Thus, by 1994 the White House began to understand that going public was not working and began to focus on directly persuading Washington elites.[62]

Once again, the president realized—and, once again, too late—that he had made a mistake. He came to agree with Senator Moynihan, who had told him that "the system cannot absorb this much change in this short a time." The president reflected that people like Moynihan "thought I was being bullheaded. And I think, in retrospect, they were probably right."[63]

At the same time, the White House was not able to monopolize the dialogue regarding health care reform. Democratic Representative Jim Cooper introduced his own, considerably more modest, health care proposal in the House, and Democratic Senator John Breaux introduced a similar bill in the Senate. In addition, a myriad of voices within the health care industry tried to persuade the public, inundating it with a deluge of direct mail, radio spots, and advertising opposing the president's plan. One set of ads, the "Harry and Louise" ads, received substantial free media coverage as well.

New methods of mass communications and a tidal wave of special interest funding equipped antireform groups of even modest size with the capacity to challenge the president's bully pulpit and redefine the issue of health care. They took full advantage of their opportunities.[64] The media was only too happy to highlight the conflict between the president and his opponents.

A PLETHORA OF MESSAGES

It is difficult, then, for the president to focus his messages on his priorities. The White House faces competition for attention from a preexisting policy agenda, congressional initiatives, media attention to issues, and the campaigns of organized interests. An administration also must overcome the obstacles of coordinating its supporters, dealing with new issues that force their way onto the agenda, and the president's need to speak out on such a wide variety of issues.

We would expect presidents operating in such an environment to lack a focus in their public statements. Looking back at Tables 6.1 and 6.2, we find that presidents make the overwhelming majority of their public statements about public policy in the context of statements about many *other* policies. In addition, even though the data represent only a sample of presidential public statements, they reveal that the president speaks about many different issues regularly and within the same news cycle. Focusing the public's attention is more likely to be an unrealized aspiration of the White House than a well-oiled component of its public relations strategy.

Conclusion

The first step in the president's efforts to lead the public is focusing its attention. People who are not attentive to the issues on which the president wishes to lead are unlikely to be influenced in their views on those issues. If the president's messages are to meet his coalition-building needs, the public must sort through the profusion of communications in its environment, overcome its limited interest in government and politics, and concentrate on the president's priority concerns. It is no exaggeration to conclude that focusing the public's attention is usually a substantial challenge.

The White House can do little to limit the overall volume of messages that citizens encounter or to make the public more attentive to politics. What it can do—in theory—is to repeat its own messages to the public so that they will break through the public's disinterest in politics and the countless distractions from it. In addition, the White House could sustain its flow of messages for the many months of the legislative cycle and concentrate its communications on the president's priorities.

What actually occurs is quite different. Despite an enormous total volume of presidential public remarks, these statements are dispersed over a broad range of policies, and wide audiences hear only a small portion of the president's remarks. The president rarely focuses a televised address on an issue before Congress and actually makes few statements on even significant legislation. In addition, the president faces strong competition for the public's attention from previous commitments of government, congressional initiatives, opposing elites, and the mass media. Even more importantly, the president often provides competition for himself as he addresses other issues, some on his own agenda and others that are forced upon him.

7

Framing the Message: Can the President Structure Choice?

In 1985 Ronald Reagan asked Congress to appropriate funds for twenty-one additional MX missiles. He had been unable to win the money he had sought in 1984 when the debate focused on the utility of the missiles as strategic weapons. He succeeded the next year, however, after the terms of the debate changed to focus on the effect of building the missiles on the arms control negotiations with the Soviet Union that had recently begun in Geneva. Senators and representatives who lacked confidence in the contribution of the MX to national security were still reluctant to go to the public and explain why they were denying American negotiators the bargaining chips they said they required. According to a senior official at the Pentagon: "By the end, we gave up on technical briefings on the missile. . . . It was all based on the unspoken bargaining chip. Without Geneva, we would have died right there."[1]

The program that the president proposed had not changed. The MX was the same missile with essentially the same capabilities in 1985 as in 1984. What had changed were the premises on which discourse on the issue occurred. The burden of proof had shifted from the administration ("MX is a useful weapon") to its opponents ("canceling the MX will not hurt the arms control negotiations"). Structuring of choices is what made the difference, not conversion.

The president is interested not only in what people and policy makers are thinking about but also in *how they are thinking about it.* In other words, presidents not only want the country and Congress to be focused on their priority issues; they also want the debate to be on their terms. In the last chapter I discussed the president's attempts to set the public's agenda by focusing on his priority issues. In this chapter I explore a different aspect of the presidential message. Structuring choice occurs on issues already on the agenda, as in the case of the MX.

What is key here is the president's attempts to influence the public's understanding of what issues are about and the questions it asks about them as it evaluates the president's positions. Structuring the choices about policy issues in ways that favor the president's programs may set the terms of the debate on his proposals and thus the premises on which the public evaluates them. As one leading adviser to Reagan put it, "I've always believed that 80 percent of any legislative or political matter is how you frame the debate."[2]

Framing and Priming

Although we may not think of political discourse in terms of competition over values, much of it is exactly that. Most issues of public policy are complex and involve many dimensions by which individual members of the public may evaluate them. Abortion may be the most controversial issue in American politics. The crux of the decision over which side to support in the debate on abortion is the relative weight one gives to the two well-known values: the life of the unborn and the right of the mother to choose whether to have the child. Those who weigh the rights of the unborn most heavily will oppose abortion, while those weighing the rights of the mother more heavily will support it.

Abortion is an especially contentious issue, one in which opinions are infused with emotions. The same process of weighing competing values occurs over policies less inflamed by passions, however. The minimum wage, for example, is a straightforward policy that simply sets a minimum wage level for workers. Yet the parties contending over this simple policy often seem to be talking past each other. Advocates of increasing the minimum wage focus on *equity:* it is important to pay those making the lowest wages at least enough to support a minimally acceptable lifestyle. Opponents of increasing the minimum wage, on the other hand, focus on *efficiency:* they argue that raising the cost of labor puts businesses that employ low wage earners at a disadvantage in the marketplace and may cause some employers to terminate workers in order to reduce their costs. Each side emphasizes different values in the debate in an attempt to frame the issue to its advantage.

Policy issues are usually complex and subject to alternative interpretations. Both issues within the direct experience of citizens, such as poverty, health care, and racial inequality, as well as issues more remote from everyday life, such as arms control and international trade, are susceptible to widely different understandings.

The sheer complexity of most issues combined with the competing values that are relevant to evaluating them create substantial cognitive burdens for people. How do people, especially the great bulk of people who have limited interest in politics and limited intellectual and information resources, deal with these cognitive challenges?

They cope by acting as cognitive misers and use shortcuts to simplify the decisional process.[3] When people evaluate an issue or a public official, they do not search their memories for all the considerations that might be relevant; they do not incorporate all the dimensions of a policy proposal into the formulation of their preferences. The intellectual burdens would be too great and their interest in politics too limited for such an arduous task. Instead of an exhaustive search, citizens minimize their cognitive burdens by selecting the dimensions they deem to be most important for their evaluations. In this decisional process, people are likely to weigh most heavily the information and values that are most easily accessible. Recent activation is one factor that determines their accessibility.[4]

The cognitive challenges of citizens are both an opportunity and an obstacle for the White House. Because individuals typically have at least two, and often more, relevant values for evaluating issue positions and because they are unlikely to canvass all their values in their evaluations, the president cannot leave to chance the identification of which values are most relevant to the issues he raises. Instead, the president seeks to influence what values citizens employ in their evaluations.

In most instances, the president does not have much effect on the values that people hold. Citizens develop these values over many years, starting in early childhood. By the time people focus on the president, their values are for the most part well established. So the president is not in a position to, say, convince people that they ought to be more generous to the poor or more concerned with the distribution of wealth in the country.

However, people use cues from elites as to the ideological or partisan implications of messages[5] (the source of a message is itself an important cue[6]). By articulating widely held values and pointing out their applicability to a policy issue, event, or his own performance, the president may increase the salience (and thus the accessibility) of those values to the public's evaluations of that issue. In the process, the president is attempting to show the members of the public that his position is consistent with their values. Thus, if the president opposes an expansion of the federal workforce to perform a service, he will probably articulate his opposition in terms of concern for big government, an attitude many in the public already hold.

Through framing, the president attempts to define what a public policy issue is about. A *frame* is a central organizing idea for making sense of an issue or conflict and suggests what the controversy is about and what is at stake.[7] Thus welfare might be framed as an appropriate program necessary to compensate for the difficult circumstances in which the less fortunate find themselves, or as a giveaway to undeserving slackers committed to living on the dole. Similarly, the MX missile discussed above can be framed as a key element in our national security arsenal or as an important bargaining chip for disarmament.

By defining and simplifying a complex issue through framing, the president hopes to activate and make more salient particular considerations that citizens will use for formulating their political preferences. It is not clear whether an issue frame interacts with an individual's memory so as to *prime* certain considerations, making some more accessible than others and therefore more likely to be used in formulating a political preference, or whether framing works by encouraging individuals to deliberately think about the importance of considerations suggested by a frame.[8] In either case, the frame raises the priority and weight that individuals assign to particular attitudes already stored in their memories.[9] The president's goal is to influence which attitudes and information people incorporate into their judgments of his policies and performance.

For example, most people value both being secure against attack and being fiscally responsible. If the president articulates a position in support of a missile defense system in terms of increasing national security against attack and is successful in encouraging people to evaluate this policy on the value of security, the public is more likely to support the president's position. However, if the president's opponents effectively argue that a missile defense system will substantially increase the deficit and thus threaten fiscal responsibility, the public is less likely to support the president.

Similarly, if the president's argument on behalf of Medicaid focuses on compassion for the poor, then those who hold such a value may be more likely to see compassion as relevant to evaluating health care policy and thus be more likely to support the president's position. If, on the other hand, people see other values, such as personal responsibility or frugality, as relevant to federal health care policy, they are more likely to resist the president's appeal for support.

The president may also attempt to prime perceptions of objective circumstances such as the existence of peace and economic prosperity. The White House would prefer to have citizens look on the bright side of their environments so that positive elements will play a more prominent role in their evaluations of the president and his administration.

Framing Issues

Framing and priming have a number of advantages for the president, not the least of which is that they demand less of the public than directly persuading citizens on the merits of a policy proposal. The president does not have to persuade people to change their basic values and preferences. He does not have to convince citizens to develop expertise and acquire and process extensive information about the details of a policy proposal. In addition, framing and priming—because they are relatively simple—are less susceptible to distortion by journalists and opponents than direct persuasion on the merits of a policy proposal.[10]

Instead of trying to persuade the public directly on the merits of a proposal, then, the White House often uses public statements and the press coverage they generate to articulate relatively simple themes. These themes may well have been identified through public opinion research as favoring its positions. The goal is to frame issues and through priming raise the priority and weight that individuals assign to attitudes already stored in their memories, thereby encouraging them to support the president's proposals.

Attempts to frame issues are as old as the republic.[11] Each side of a political contest usually tries to frame the debate to its own advantage. Byron Shafer and William Claggett argue that public opinion is organized around two clusters of issues, both of which are favored by a majority of voters: social welfare, social insurance, and civil rights (associated with Democrats) and cultural values, civil liberties, and foreign relations (associated with Republicans). Each party's best strategy is to frame the choice for voters by focusing attention on the party's most successful cluster of issues.[12] John Petrocik has found that candidates tend to campaign on issues that favor them in order to prime the salience of these issues in voters' decision making.[13] Similarly, an important aspect of campaigning is activating the latent predispositions of partisans by priming party identification as a crucial consideration in their deciding for whom to vote.[14]

Portraying policies in terms of criteria on which there is a consensus and playing down divisive issues are often at the core of efforts to structure choices for both the public and Congress. The Reagan administration framed the 1986 tax reform act as revenue neutral, presenting the choice on the policy as one of serving special interests or helping average taxpayers. Few people would choose the former option. Federal aid to education had been a divisive issue for years before President Johnson proposed the Elementary and Secondary Education Act in 1965. To blunt opposition, he successfully changed the focus of debate from teachers' salaries and classroom shortages to fighting poverty, and from the separation of church and state to aiding children. This change in the premises of congressional decision making eased the path for the bill.[15]

Similarly, Richard Nixon articulated general revenue sharing as a program that made government more efficient and distributed benefits widely. He deemphasized the distributional aspect of the policy, which redistributed federal funds from traditional Democratic constituencies to projects favored by Republicans' middle-class constituents.[16] Dwight Eisenhower employed the uncontroversial symbol of national defense during the Cold War, even when it came to naming legislation, to obtain support for aiding education (the National Defense Education Act) and building highways (the Interstate and Defense Highway Act).

Tragedies occur during every presidency, and the president does not want such events to reflect poorly on his stewardship. Thus, the White House often attempts to frame even disasters in a more positive light. For example, when sixteen Americans were killed during a terrorist bombing of the U.S. embassy in Beirut in 1983, Ronald Reagan needed to interpret the meaning of the event for the public. Among the dead were some Marines, who died while they slept. Nevertheless, the president focused on their courage and sacrifice for their country, reframing the event from one of horror to an instance of heroism. Even more memorably, his speech to the nation following the widely viewed explosion of the space shuttle *Challenger* in 1986 reframed the catastrophe from one of overwhelming shock and grief to a moment of human triumph. Few will forget his evocation of a positive image: "We will never forget them nor the last time we saw them—this morning—as they prepared for their journey and waved goodbye, and slipped the surly bonds of Earth to touch the face of God."[17]

At other times the president must try to frame choices in an atmosphere inflamed by partisanship. Independent Counsel Kenneth Starr issued a report to Congress accusing President Clinton of eleven counts of impeachable offenses, perjury, obstruction of justice, witness tampering, and abuse of power. The president's detractors used the report as a basis for charging that he had broken the law, failed in his primary constitutional duty to take care that the laws be faithfully executed, betrayed the public's trust, and dishonored the nation's highest office. Indeed, they concluded that the gravely aggravated, calculated, and protracted nature of Clinton's lying and obstruction of justice was an assault on the very integrity of the legal process. As a result, they argued, the president should be removed from office through the process of impeachment.

As we know, the White House fought back, framing the issue in an entirely different manner. First, the president apologized to the nation—sort of. Then he engaged in a round of expressions of remorse before a variety of audiences. At the same time, the White House accused Starr of engaging an *intrusive* investigation motivated by a *political vendetta* against the president. The basic White House defense was that the president made a mistake *(personal failing)* in his *private* behavior, apologized for it, and was ready to move on to continue to do the people's business of governing the nation. Impeachment, the president's defenders said, was grossly *disproportionate* to the president's offense. The public found the White House argument compelling and strongly opposed the president's impeachment.

Presidents often use symbols in their efforts to frame issues for the public. Symbols are simple or familiar things that stand for other more complex or unfamiliar things and may be used to describe politicians, events, issues, or some other aspect of the political world. Naturally, symbols are not synonyms for what they describe. The choice of symbols inevitably highlights certain aspects of an issue or event and conceals others, just as in other forms of framing.[18]

Because of the potential power of symbols in shaping public opinion, presidents have encouraged the public to adopt certain symbols as representative of their administrations. Franklin Roosevelt dubbed his administration the "New Deal," and Harry Truman termed his the "Fair Deal." Each symbol was an oversimplification for new and extremely complex policies, but each served to reassure many Americans that these policies were for their good. Similarly, John Kennedy's "New Frontier" and Lyndon Johnson's "Great Society" served as attractive symbols of their administrations.

Many observers feel that a president's failure to lead the public to adopt broad symbols for his administration can cause severe problems in relations with the public. Many commentators criticized Presidents Carter, Bush, and Clinton for lacking unifying themes and cohesion in their programs and for failing to inspire the public with a sense of purpose or idea to follow.[19] Instead of providing the country with a sense of their vision and priorities, they emphasized discrete problem solving.

On the other hand, Ronald Reagan understood instinctually that his popular support was linked to his ability to embody the values of an idealized America. He continually invoked symbols of his vision of America and its past—an optimistic view that did not closely correspond to reality but did sustain public support. He projected a simple, coherent vision for his presidency that served him well in attracting adherents and countering criticism when the inevitable contradictions in policy arose. For example, he maintained his identification with balanced budgets even though he never submitted a budget that was even close to balanced and his administration was responsible for more deficit spending than all previous administrations combined. More broadly, Reagan employed the symbols of an idealized polity to frame his policies as consistent with core American values.[20]

According to Pat Buchanan, who served as the White House director of communications: "For Ronald Reagan the world of legend and myth is a real world. He visits it regularly and he's a happy man there."[21] In his 1965 autobiography, Reagan described his feelings about leaving the military at the end of World War II: "All I wanted to do . . . was to rest up awhile, make love to my wife, and come up refreshed to a better job in an ideal world."[22] The reader would never realize from this that Reagan never left Hollywood while serving in the military during the war! In politics, however, perceptions are as important as reality; consequently, many people responded positively to the president's vision of history and his place therein.

Symbols are also used to describe specific policies. President Johnson declared a "War on Poverty" despite the fact that many saw the "war" as more of a skirmish. Similarly, President Nixon went to considerable efforts to have the public view the January 1973 peace agreement ending the involvement of American troops in Vietnam as "peace with honor," which was clearly a controversial conclusion.

Presidents may manipulate symbols in attempts not only to lead public opinion, but also to deliberately mislead it. Perhaps the most important and effective televised address President Reagan made to the nation in 1981 was his July 27 speech seeking the public's support for his tax cut bill. In it he went to great lengths to present his plan as "bipartisan." It was crucial that he convince the public that this controversial legislation was supported by members of both parties and therefore was, by implication, fair. Despite the fact that House Democrats voted overwhelmingly against the president's proposal two days later, Reagan described it as "bipartisan" eleven times in the span of a few minutes. No one could miss the point.

These illustrations of presidential efforts at framing make setting the terms of debate sound like a silver bullet. All the president has to do is act cleverly to structure the choices of the public and Congress, and he will have his way on policy issues. How, then, is it that presidents usually fail to move the public? There must be more to the story—and there is.

Limits to Framing

At the core of Bill Clinton's successful campaign for the presidency in 1992 was his promise to rejuvenate the economy. Accordingly, his first major proposal as president in 1993 was a plan to stimulate the economy. The Clinton White House wanted the public to view its plan as an effort to get the economy moving again. It would be to the president's advantage for the public to adopt such a perspective because a strong economy is a consensual goal, providing a strong basis of public support that would make it difficult for the Republicans in Congress to oppose the president.

Oppose him they did, however. Republicans felt little fear from a public backlash to their opposition because they had succeeded in defining the president's economic program in terms of wasteful pork barrel expenditures rather than spending essential for the economy. In the end, the president could not obtain the public's support: four months after the bill was introduced, a plurality of the public opposed it, as was shown in Table 2.3. The bill never came to a vote in the Senate.

The White House had to make a strategic decision regarding which to push first, the president's budget or his fiscal stimulus bill. Some Democrats wanted Congress to pass the president's budget with its spending cuts before they were asked to vote for spending increases in the stimulus bill. Although it made sense to provide these Democrats with political cover from the deficit hawks, the move also injected tax increases into the debate over the fiscal stimulus bill. Senate Republicans pointed to tax increases repeatedly in their successful effort to defeat it.[23]

The president's political consultants complained that the Republicans had succeeded in focusing public debate on the president's budget on tax increases rather than economic growth or deficit reduction.[24] Clinton tried to present the issue of taxes as one of fairness, but there is little evidence that this perception was widely shared. When he said his own proposal lacked enough spending cuts and challenged anyone to find more, the discussion focused on whether there were enough cuts rather than economic stimulus or deficit reduction. "The Clinton administration has lost control of its agenda," complained White House pollster Stan Greenberg.[25]

In June 1993, Greenberg wrote to Clinton regarding the administration's contradictory messages. Should it emphasize deficit reduction or economic growth? Should it have a Wall Street message that would not spook business or a populist message that would appeal to middle-class allergies to taxation? Should it pursue a legislative focus according to Congress's agenda or focus on a broader message strategy for influencing Congress through public opinion?

Should Clinton define himself as a social liberal (gay rights, abortion, quotas) or a new kind of Democrat focusing on middle-class values such as rewarding work and responsibility?[26]

We do not know whether Clinton ever replied to the memo, but we do know that the president was well aware of his inability to set the terms of the debate over his proposals. When asked why he was having such a difficult time obtaining the support of the "new" southern Democrats, Clinton responded, "One reason is that in their own districts and states, they've let the Republicans dominate the perception of what we're trying to do . . . the Republicans won the rhetorical debate."[27]

Clinton could not reach the American people—and it frustrated him. Six months after taking office the president reflected on the unexpected dimensions of his job on *Larry King Live:* "The thing that has surprised me most is how difficult it is . . . to really keep communicating what you're about to the American people. . . . That to me has been the most frustrating thing." A few months later he confided to a friend: "I did not realize the importance of communications and the overriding importance of what is on the evening television news. If I am not on, or there with a message, someone else is, with their message."[28]

COMPETING FRAMES

Structuring choice is rarely easy. The challenge that Bill Clinton faced with his economic program is a common one for presidents: the opposition provides one or more competing frames. Just as in agenda setting, there is competition to set the terms of debate over issues. In real life, we know very little about the terms in which the public thinks about issues. Studies that have shown powerful framing effects have typically carefully sequestered citizens and restricted them to hearing only one frame, usually in the context of a controlled experiment.[29] These frames tend to be confined to brief fragments of arguments, pale imitations of frames that often occur in the real world.

The environment in which the president usually operates is fundamentally different from that in an experiment or poll. The president's world is inhabited by committed, well-organized, and well-funded opponents. Intense disagreement among elites generates conflicting messages. John Zaller argues that attitudes on major issues change in response to changes in relation to the intensity of competing streams of political communication. When there is elite consensus, and thus only one set of cues offered to the public, opinion change may be substantial. When elite discourse is divided, however, people respond to the issue according to their predispositions, especially their core partisan and ideological views.[30] Thus, when Paul Sniderman and Sean Theriault offered people competing frames, as in the real world, the people adopted positions consistent with their preexisting values.[31] Donald Haider-Markel and Mark Joslyn also found that predispositions conditioned the effect of framing.[32]

Occasions in which elite commentary is one-sided are rare. Most issues that generate consensual elite discourse arise from external events such as surprise attacks on the United States, such as the terrorist assaults on September 11, 2001, or its allies, such as the invasion of Kuwait in 1990. Consensual issues also tend to be new, with few people having committed themselves to a view about them. In his examination of public opinion regarding the Gulf War, Zaller argues that the president's greatest chance of influencing public opinion is in a crisis (which attracts the public's attention) in which elites articulate a unified message. At other times, most people are too inattentive or too committed to views to be strongly influenced by elite efforts at persuasion.[33]

PUBLIC AWARENESS AND KNOWLEDGE

A fundamental limitation on presidential priming is the public's lack of attention to politics, which restricts its susceptibility to taking cues from political elites. Russell Neuman estimates that in the United States there is a politically sophisticated elite of less than 5 percent of the public. Another 75 percent are marginally attentive and 20 percent are apolitical. Even the marginally attentive lack the background information and rich vocabulary for quick and convenient processing of large amounts of political information. The apolitical 20 percent do not respond to political stimuli in political terms. Even in the middle, he argues, people frequently interpret political stimuli in nonpolitical terms.[34] If attempts to set the terms of debate fall on deaf ears, they are unlikely to be successful.

Levels of interest in and information about politics and public policy vary widely among Americans. From one perspective, those citizens with less interest and knowledge present the most potential for presidential persuasion. Such people cannot resist arguments if they do not possess information about the implications of those arguments for their values, interests, and other predispositions. However, these people are also less likely to be aware of the president's messages, limiting the president's influence. To the extent that they do receive the messages, they will also hear from the opposition how the president's views are inconsistent with their predispositions. In addition, even if their predispositions make them sympathetic to the president's arguments, they may lack the understanding to make the connection between the president's arguments and their own underlying values. Moreover, the more abstract the link between message and value, the fewer people who will make the connection.[35]

In addition, James Kuklinski and his colleagues found that people are frequently *misinformed* (as opposed to uninformed) about policy, and the less they know, the more confidence they have in their beliefs. Thus, they resist correct factual information. Even when presented with factual information, they resist changing their opinions, including those that were the objects of elite framing.[36]

On the other hand, those who pay close attention to politics and policy are likely to have well-developed views and thus be less susceptible to persuasion. Better informed citizens possess the information necessary to identify and thus reject communications inconsistent with their values. They are also more sensitive to the implications of messages. In the typical situation of competing frames offered by elites, reinforcement and polarization of views are more likely than conversion among attentive citizens.[37]

Zaller argues that those in the public most susceptible to presidential influence are those attentive to public affairs (and thus who receive messages) but who lack strong views (and thus who are less likely to resist messages).[38] At best, such people are a small portion of the population. In addition, these people will receive competing messages. There is no basis for inferring that they will be most likely to find the president's messages persuasive. Such a conclusion is especially suspect when we recognize that most attentive people have explicit or latent partisan preferences. The president is leader of one of the parties, and those affiliated with the opposition party must overcome an inherent skepticism about him before they can be converted to support his position.

PERCEPTIONS

For framing to work, people must first perceive accurately the frame offered by the president. We know very little about how people perceive messages from the president or other elites. Nor do we know much about how citizens come to understand public issues or develop their values and other predispositions that the president seeks to prime. (We also do not know whether the potential effect of frames is restricted to priming existing values or whether they may also affect understanding, which may in turn alter opinion.) There is reason to believe, however, that different people perceive the same message differently.[39] With all his personal, ideological, and partisan baggage, no president can assume that all citizens hear the same thing when he speaks.

A related matter of perception is the credibility of the source. Again, the president is likely to be more credible to some people (those predisposed to support him) than others. Many people are unlikely to find him a credible source on most issues, especially those on which opinion is divided and on which he is the leader of one side of the debate. Experimental evidence supports the view that perceived source credibility is a prerequisite for successful framing.[40]

THE NATURE OF ISSUES

The president faces yet other challenges to setting the terms of debate. Although there are occasions on which a president can exploit an external event such as arms control negotiations to structure choices on a single issue, he cannot rely on his environment to be so accommodating. In addition, the White House must advocate the passage of many proposals at roughly the same time, further complicating its efforts to structure choice on any single issue.

INEPTNESS

Attempts to structure decisions may actually hurt the president's cause if they are too heavy-handed and thus create a backlash. In 1986 Ronald Reagan was engaged in his perennial fight to provide aid to the Contras in Nicaragua. The president equated opposition to his aid program with support for the Sandinistas. More graphically, the White House's communications director, Patrick J. Buchanan, wrote an editorial in the *Washington Post* that characterized the issue in stark terms: "With the contra vote, the Democratic Party will reveal whether it stands with Ronald Reagan and the resistance or [Nicaraguan President] Daniel Ortega and the communists." These overt efforts to set the terms of debate were not successful. Instead, they irritated members of Congress and provoked charges that the White House was engaged in red-baiting.[41]

OVERUSE

As in making appeals, the White House can go to the well only so often. In 1986 there was a battle in Congress and in the public over the sale of arms to Saudi Arabia. The president argued, similar to his effort with the MX missile, that a defeat on this highly visible foreign policy issue would undermine his international credibility and destroy his role as a mediator in the Middle East. Despite all his efforts, the president was able to garner only thirty-four votes in the Senate, then controlled by Republicans.[42]

TRANSIENCE OF OPINION CHANGE

In addition, opinion changes that occur may well be likely to be temporary. Even under unusual circumstances when people have participated in intense deliberations with fellow citizens and listened to the testimony of politicians and policy experts, changes of opinion have been found to be largely temporary.[43] Members of the public who are the easiest to sway in the short run are those without crystallized opinions. However, as issues fade into the background or positions on issues are confronted with the realities of daily life or with a better understanding of the implications of support for the president for basic values, opinions that were altered in response to presidential leadership may quickly be forgotten. This slippage is especially likely to occur in foreign policy, the area in which the president's influence on public opinion may be greatest.

THE CLINTON EXPERIENCE

A further look at the Clinton administration illustrates just how difficult it is for the president to frame the debate on policies. From the very start of the administration, the major players in the Clinton White House understood the need for communicating the central values of the administration in a clear and coherent fashion to structure public debate about the Clinton presidency. They also knew that they were not succeeding in doing this. As the months went by, the White House continued to suffer from a lack of coordination between its policy and political messages. Clinton could not seem to create a simple, central message, relating each policy to an overall theme.[44] This failure to set the terms of debate left the administration vulnerable to the vicissitudes of events and to the definitions of its opponents.

Some administrations lend themselves to structuring choice better than others. For example, Ronald Reagan's simple and straightforward conservative philosophy lent itself to structuring the terms of debate on a wide range of issues as for or against big government. It is especially difficult to convey a consistent theme when the president has a large, diverse agenda—as Bill Clinton had. He thought of his legacy primarily in terms of passing legislation, and he wanted to do it on all fronts. Yet every additional policy initiative clouded the public's picture of the administration, allowing side issues such as gays in the military to define it and resulting in caricatures of Clinton and the administration.[45]

Another complicating factor for Clinton was that his views were a complex blend of populism and traditional values. His critics emphasized his liberal stances such as that on health care and "investments." He was branded a social-issues liberal after gays in the military and abortion became the first issues of his administration. Then he was labeled a free-spending liberal after he proposed a $20 billion fiscal stimulus bill as his first economic policy proposal. Yet Clinton also took many conservative, "new Democrat" stances in budget deficit reduction, the crime bill, welfare reform (or its early thrusts), and the like—reflecting traditional values of family, responsibility, work, and reciprocal obligation.

This combination of views made it difficult to establish a central organizing theme for the Clinton administration. It was a challenge for the White House to lead Democrats in the public or Congress with deficit reduction at the core of its policy. As Clinton himself declared sarcastically to aides: "We're Eisenhower Republicans here, and we are fighting with Reagan Republicans. We stand for lower deficits and free trade and the bond market. Isn't that great?"[46] A year later he might have added the crime bill. Thus, it is not surprising that the administration's efforts to frame itself failed to resonate with the public.

It was also challenging to structure choice for the public in a fashion that advantaged the president's more specific policies. On September 22, 1993, the president made a very effective speech outlining his health care proposal, the cornerstone policy of his administration. He articulated six principles as the foundation for his plan: "security, simplicity, savings, choice, quality, and responsibility" and emphasized security. This was an attempt to frame debate over health care and to depict the plan in comforting, affordable terms.

Before the speech, he briefed bipartisan groups of members of Congress for two days, brought 250 talk-show hosts to the White House, and hosted a lunch for select journalists. The day after the speech, the president and the cabinet went on the road to sell the plan to the country, reinforcing a sense that this was the start of an historic process that would culminate in fundamental change. In late September the Gallup Poll found the public split 59 percent–33 percent in favor of Clinton's health care program.[47] It appeared that Clinton had changed the premises of decision from whether to overhaul health care to how to do it.

Opponents did not play dead, however. An aggressive advertising campaign characterized the president's plan as expensive, experimental, providing lower quality and rationed care, and a job killer. Opponents emphasized "big government" to prompt people to put conservative attitudes toward government in the forefront of their minds and use them to evaluate health reform.

Facing such opposition, it was important that Clinton keep the country focused on his terms. But he did not. Instead, the White House failed to follow up effectively on the momentum and national focus of the initial launch of health care, and public support eroded. He gave the critics a chance to organize while the country waited for the details of the plan in October. Calculating that by not offering details in September, he was depriving critics of a target, the president ended up giving them an easy target—the suspicion that he could not figure out how to pay for it.

When the health care reform bill was introduced, the White House decided to keep its sales pitch focused on themes rather than specifics. This seemed like a reasonable approach, because the legislation was so complicated. The public was not willing to make a leap of faith, however; its attention generally focused less on the goals of the president's plan and more on the means he proposed to achieve them. Details such as health alliances had to be defended, even to likely allies. But the White House resisted inquiries about how health alliances would work and talked about its six principles.[48]

The White House was unable to keep the public's attention focused on the inadequacies of the health care system and the broad goals of reform. The dominant public response to the plan was confusion, and the bill's complexity made it difficult to explain. Competing plans in Congress heightened the confusion, as did a myriad of health care industry voices with a deluge of direct mail, radio spots, and advertising, picking out pieces of the plan to oppose. Instead of revolving around a central theme, then, public debate focused on reform's pitfalls.

The White House's most prominent rhetoric focused on obtaining universal coverage for the 15 percent of the public without access to health care (largely those earning $15,000–$30,000 a year). It rarely emphasized the greatest concerns of the middle class (who had some form of health care insurance) — rising insurance costs, fear of a government takeover of health care, rationed health care, and fear of losing coverage.[49]

Because the White House health care reform plan was bureaucratic and complicated, it was easy for opponents to label it a government takeover of the health care system. This threatened the middle class. Gallup polls in August 1994 found that the public saw Clinton's health care reform proposal as a typical Democratic social welfare program, one that helps the poor, hurts the middle class, and creates bigger government. In the end, people were more worried about what would happen if health care reform passed than about losing their health insurance: too much government was a bigger concern than too little health insurance.[50]

So despite unveiling his health care plan with an impressive flourish, the president made little progress in convincing Americans that he had the correct approach. As he lamented in March 1994, "One thing we have not done in an organized and coherent way for the last couple of months is to be very positive in getting out the same message over and over again, and in asking people to compare the alternatives."[51]

The White House recast its six principles to five catchphrases — guaranteed private insurance, choice of doctor, real insurance reform, preservation of Medicare, and guaranteed health benefits at work — but things did not get any better. By August 1994, most Americans wanted to give up and start over again the next year,[52] which is exactly what happened. Even worse, the president's health care bill projected an image of Clinton as a proponent of big government and inflicted substantial damage to his image, especially among Independents.[53]

During the first two years of the Clinton administration, Republicans dominated the symbols of political discourse and set the terms of the debate over policy. In 1994 congressional elections, the Republicans framed the vote choice in national terms, making taxes, social discipline, big government, and the Clinton presidency the dominant issues. They tied congressional Democrats to Clinton, a discredited government, and a deplorable status quo. They set the terms of the debate — and they won.

The Clinton administration was not without success in structuring choice, however. When it appeared that Congress might not vote for NAFTA, the White House repackaged the issue and secured an important legislative victory. It shifted from emphasizing the trade agreement's effect on jobs and began to stress arguments that failure to pass it would undermine U.S. foreign policy. President Clinton told a news conference that if Congress voted down NAFTA, "it would limit my ability to argue that the Asians should open their markets more. . . . More importantly, my ability to argue that the Asians and the Europeans should join with me and push hard to get a world trade agreement through . . . by the end of the year will be more limited."[54] Al Gore went even further: "the consequences of a defeat for NAFTA in the foreign policy arena would be really catastrophic."[55] This strategy increased the stakes of the vote, and thus the risks of losing, but it worked.

The White House also emphasized that support for NAFTA represented a willingness and ability to tackle the future with confidence. As one of Clinton's strategists put it: "We learned something from Ronald Reagan, finally. You need to be right on more than the merits of the case; you need to be right on the presentation. We started to do better when we got off statistics and cast it more broadly . . . as a choice between the future and the past, optimism and pessimism, hope and fear, embracing the modern world and trying to hide from it."[56]

The president won on NAFTA, in large part because of widespread and preexisting Republican support. NAFTA, however, was the exception, not the rule.

The Role of the Media in Structuring Choice

We saw in the previous chapter that the president rarely speaks directly to the public. Most of the time, the president's messages reach the public indirectly through transmission by the mass media. In an ideal world, the president could rely on the media to educate the public about the ambiguities and uncertainties of complex events and issues and provide the background and contextual information that is essential for understanding them.

In addition, the media would inform the public where the president stands, how he has framed an issue, and how that frame relates to the policy under consideration. It does little good, for example, for the president to frame a trade issue as one of increasing economic growth and employment opportunities if the media devote very little attention to the issue and when they do, cover the issue only from the standpoint of the personalities involved on each side of the debate, the strategies they use for achieving their goals, and the implications of their stands for upcoming elections.

It will not take long before the chief executive is disappointed in the media's performance. A common complaint in the White House is that the press is interested in the superficial layer of politics rather than the meat and potatoes of governing. Woodrow Wilson, one of the first presidents to serve in the era of a mass media with a national focus, complained that most reporters were "interested in the personal and trivial rather than in principles of policies."[57] More recently, Jimmy Carter complained to reporters that "I would really like for you all as people who relay Washington events to the world to take a look at the substantive questions I have to face as a president and quit dealing almost exclusively with personalities."[58]

The media are unlikely to adopt uniformly or reliably the White House's framing of issues, however. Instead, the media independently choose which issues to highlight and how to frame them for their viewers and readers. As a result, the media provide powerful competition for the president in his attempts to structure the choices before the public.

QUANTITY OF COVERAGE

Brevity characterizes media coverage of national news in mainline media such as most newspapers and the broadcast networks. Editors do not want to bore or confuse their viewers, listeners, or readers. Stories must be few in number and short in length. The amount of information transmitted under such conditions is inevitably limited, and it is not sufficient for the president to educate the public.

The president experiences the media's mandate for brevity even before reaching the White House. For example, the average length of a presidential candidate's sound bite has continued to slide, falling from 9.8 seconds in 1988 to 7.8 seconds in 2000. The three major networks *together* devoted an average of 12.6 minutes per night to the exceedingly close 2000 presidential election campaign; just half the 24.6 minutes they devoted to the 1992 campaign. Al Gore received a total of less than eighteen minutes of speaking time on the average network for the *entire* campaign. George W. Bush did even worse, receiving less than fourteen minutes on the average network.[59]

Indeed, in the presidential election of 2000 voters had to bypass the network television newscasts and watch the TV talk shows to hear candidates deliver their messages. George W. Bush was on-screen for a total of thirteen minutes during his appearance on the "David Letterman Show" on October 19, which exceeded his entire speaking time on all three network news shows during that month. Similarly, Al Gore received more speaking time on his September 14 Letterman appearance than he did during the entire month of September on the network evening newscasts.[60]

A study of the first sixty days of coverage of the presidencies of Bill Clinton and George W. Bush on ABC, NBC, CBS, PBS, the section fronts and opinion pages of the *Washington Post* and the *New York Times*, and *Newsweek* found 41 percent fewer stories on Bush than on Clinton. *Newsweek* stories on the president had decreased by 59 percent over the eight years, while network coverage was down 43 percent and the *Post* and the *Times* had fallen off by 38 percent.[61] Although the prominence of the president increased after the September 11 terrorist attacks, there is no reason to think the trend toward less coverage of the White House has changed permanently.

SUPERFICIALITY OF COVERAGE

The substance as well as the amount of media coverage hinders the president's efforts to move the public. Rather than focusing on policy issues, the news is becoming more personality-centered, less time-bound, more practical, and more incident-based. About 50 percent of all news stories have no clear connection to policy issues.[62] News organizations demand information that is new and different, personal and intimate, or revealing and unexpected. Most reporting is about events, actions taken or words spoken by public figures, especially if the events are dramatic and colorful, such as ceremonies and parades. According to ABC correspondent Sam Donaldson, "A clip of a convalescent Reagan waving from his window at some circus elephants is going to push an analytical piece about tax cuts off the air every time."[63] In such a news environment, there is little time or space for reflection, analysis, or comprehensive coverage.

The president has to compete with other media priorities while attempting to lead the public. The television networks created distractions during President Clinton's 1997 State of the Union message when they delivered the news of the verdict in the civil suit against O. J. Simpson *during his speech*, and the front page of the *Washington Post* the next day led with the story on Simpson, not the story on the president.

News coverage emphasizes short-run, "instant history." Perspective on the events of the day is secondary. Presidential slips of the tongue or gaffes are often blown out of proportion. For example, in the second debate between Gerald Ford and Jimmy Carter during the 1976 presidential campaign, Ford made a slip and said that Eastern Europe was "free from Soviet domination." Everyone, including the president, knew he had misspoken. Unfortunately for Ford, however, he refused to admit his error for several days while the press had a field day speculating about his basic understanding of world politics. Similarly, when Richard Nixon described the people "blowing up the campuses" as "bums," the press extended the category to all students, something the president had not meant. The uproar following this report can well be imagined.

In its constant search for "news," the press, especially the electronic media, is reluctant to devote repeated attention to an issue even though this might be necessary to explain it adequately to the public. As a deputy press secretary in the Carter administration said: "We have to keep sending out our message if we expect people to understand. The Washington Press corps will explain a policy once and then it will feature the politics of the issue."[64] This is one incentive for the president to meet with the non-Washington press and to address the nation directly on television or radio.

The Body Watch

Most of the White House press activity comes under the heading of the "body watch." In other words, reporters focus on the most visible layer of the president's personal and official activities and provide the public with a step-by-step account. They are interested in what the president is going to do, how his actions will affect others, how he views policies and individuals, how he presents himself, and whose stars are rising and falling, rather than in the substance of policies or the fundamental operations of the executive branch. For example, coverage of the consideration of President Clinton's massive health care proposal in 1993–1994 focused much more on strategy and legislative battles than on the issues of health care.[65]

Editors expect this type of coverage (which they believe will please their readers), and reporters do not want to risk missing a story. As the Washington bureau chief of *Newsweek* said: "The worst thing in the world that could happen to you is for the President of the United States to choke on a piece of meat, and for you not to be there."[66] When President Bush vomited at a state dinner in Japan, television networks devoted great attention to the episode and ran the tape of the president's illness again and again.

Journalists are generally not allowed at Camp David, the presidential retreat. However, about twenty minutes before the president's helicopter lands or departs, a few photographers are allowed to sit in something akin to a duck blind about 150 yards from the helicopter pad and observe the landing and departure. They leave immediately after, without ever speaking to the president. Why do they bother? They are there for the "death watch" — to be on hand in case the president's helicopter crashes.

Human Interest Stories

Human interest stories, especially those about presidents and their families, are always in high demand. Socks, the Clintons' cat, and Buddy, their dog, became overnight celebrities. Such stories are novel and the public can relate to the subjects more easily than to complex matters of public policy such as a presidential tax proposal.

Conflicts between clearly identifiable antagonists (President Clinton versus Speaker of the House Newt Gingrich or independent counsel Kenneth Starr) are highly prized, particularly if there is something tangible at stake such as the passage of a bill or impeachment of the president.

White House reporters are always looking to expose conflicts of interest and other shady behavior of public officials. Scandals involving the president or those close to him receive high-priority coverage in the media, often driving out coverage of news on the president's policies. For example, on April 22, 1994, President Clinton held a press conference on imminent air strikes in Bosnia, which only CNN carried live. On the same day, First Lady Hillary Rodham Clinton held a press conference on the Whitewater investigation, which all the networks carried. When Paula Jones charged President Clinton with sexual harassment (while he was governor of Arkansas), the media devoted extensive coverage to the case, yet even this attention paled compared with the frenzy of coverage devoted to the president's sexual relationship with White House intern Monica Lewinsky. No policy issue received as much attention, especially on television, until the Senate acquitted the president more than a year later.[67] Similarly, the story of George W. Bush's arrest for driving while intoxicated that broke on the last weekend of the 2000 presidential election generated more stories during three days on the three networks than all the foreign policy issues together during the entire campaign.[68]

An emphasis on scandals in an administration, even if the stories are presented in an even-handed manner, rarely helps the White House. (The coverage of the Monica Lewinsky story seems to be an exception, as President Clinton benefited from a backlash against media intrusiveness into his private life. Even here, however, the dominance of the story undermined the president's ability to make substantial progress on his agenda.)

Major news organizations spend a great deal of money covering the presidents, including following them around the globe on official business and vacations. Because of this investment and the public's interest in the president, reporters must come up with something every day. Newsworthy happenings do not necessarily occur every day, however, so reporters either emphasize the trivial or blow events out of proportion. While covering a meeting of Western leaders on the island of Guadeloupe, Sam Donaldson faced the prospect of having nothing to report on a slow news day. Undaunted, he reported on the roasting of the pig that the leaders would be eating that evening, including "an exclusive look at the oven in which the pig would be roasted."[69] Similarly, the White House press often focuses on the exact wording of an announcement in an effort to detect a change in policy, frequently finding significance where none really exists.

Other human interest stories do not involve the White House directly but provide competition in the White House's efforts to obtain scarce space or time in the news. Disasters and incidents of violence (shootings in schools, for example) make for excellent film presentations; they are novel, contain human drama and ample action, and can be portrayed in easily understood terms. The intricacies of Medicare financing are not so intriguing.

MEDIA ACTIVISM

An important limitation on presidential framing is the increasing reluctance of journalists to let the president speak for himself. Instead, reporters feel the necessity of setting the story in a meaningful context. The construction of such a context may entail reporting what was *not* said as well as what was said, what had occurred before, and what political implications may be involved in a statement, policy, or event. More than in the past, reporters today actively and aggressively interpret stories for viewers and readers. They no longer depend on those whom they interview to set the tone of their stories, and they now regularly pass sweeping (and frequently negative) judgments about what politicians are saying and doing.[70]

Our best data about the interpreting role of the press comes from studies of presidential elections. Reporters rather than the candidates have become the center of the story. In 2000, for example, television reporters covering the presidential candidates took three-quarters (74 percent) of spoken airtime while the candidates had a mere 12 percent and other sources had 14 percent. On an average night, reporters spoke for a total of seven minutes of election news airtime on the three network evening newscasts, compared with only one minute for Al Gore and George Bush combined—just under ten seconds per night for each candidate on each network. All other sources combined for an average of one and a half minutes of airtime per night. The three networks were almost identical in their allotment of airtime among candidates, journalists, and other sources.[71]

The White House naturally prefers that the press present the president in a positive context, one that will allow Americans' general respect for the presidency to be transferred to individual presidents. It wishes to have the president framed at a respectful distance by the television camera and portrayed with an aura of dignity and as working in a context of rationality and coherence on activities benefiting the public.

However, even when the president speaks directly to the people, the media present an obstacle to his framing issues in ways that favor his positions. Commentary following presidential speeches and press conferences may influence what viewers remember and may affect their opinions.[72] Although the effect of commentary on presidential addresses and press conferences is unclear, it is probably safe to argue that it is a constraint on the president's ability to lead public opinion. In the words of observers David L. Paletz and Robert M. Entman: "Critical instant analysis undermines presidential authority by transforming him from presenter to protagonist. . . . Credible, familiar, apparently disinterested newsmen and—women—experts too, usually agreeing with each other, comment on the self-interested performance of a politician. Usually the president's rhetoric is deflated, the mood he has striven to create dissipated."[73]

In the past, criticism of presidents was restrained by the reluctance of many editors to publish analyses that diverged sharply from the president's position without direct confirmation from an authoritative source who would be willing to go on the record in opposition to the president. During the famous investigation of the Watergate scandal, the *Washington Post* verified all information attributed to an unnamed source with at least one other independent source. It also did not print information from other media outlets unless its reporters could independently verify that information.[74] Things have changed, however.

When the story broke about charges that President Clinton had sexual relations with Monica Lewinsky, virtually all elements of the mass media went into a feeding frenzy,[75] relying as much on analysis, opinion, and speculation as on confirmed facts. Even the most prominent news outlets carried unsubstantiated reports about charges that had not received independent verification by those carrying the story. If another news outlet carried a charge, it was soon picked up by most of the rest, which did not want to be scooped. For example, unsubstantiated charges that Lewinsky had a dress stained with the president's semen were widely reported, as was the charge that members of the Secret Service had found the president and Lewinsky in a compromising position. Such reporting helped convince the majority of the public that the president had had sexual relations with Lewinsky—despite the absence of direct evidence at the time.

Increasingly, the public receives the news about the president in a negative context, an emphasis that begins during the presidential campaigns. Negative coverage of presidential candidates exceeds positive coverage, and each president since 1976 has received more negative coverage than has his predecessor.[76] In the 1980 election campaign, the press portrayed President Carter as mean and Ronald Reagan as imprecise rather than Carter as precise and Reagan as nice. The emphasis, in other words, was on the candidates' negative qualities. During recent campaigns presidential candidates have received more bad news coverage than good news coverage—a notable change from the past.[77]

To meet their needs for a story containing conflict, reporters routinely turn to opponents of the president when the president makes a statement or takes an action. Thus, it is not surprising that after his election, each president since 1976 has received more negative coverage than his predecessor.[78] President Clinton received mostly negative coverage during his tenure in office, with a ratio of negative to positive comments on network television of about two to one.[79]

The increasing negativism of news coverage of the presidents parallels the increasingly low opinions voters have of them. The media impugn the motives of presidents and presidential candidates and portray them as playing a "game" in which strategy and maneuvers, rather than the substance of public policy, are the crucial elements. This fosters public cynicism and encourages citizens to view presidents and other political leaders in negative terms.[80] The framing of issues in terms of strategy and wheeling-dealing may also undermine efforts to change the status quo by highlighting the risk of deferring to people who engage in such maneuvering.

EVALUATIONS OF THE PRESIDENT

At any one time there are many potential criteria for evaluating the president, ranging from personal characteristics such as integrity to performance on the economy or foreign affairs. The concept of priming is premised on the fact that most of the time the cognitive burdens are too great for people to reach judgments or decisions based on comprehensive, integrated information and the consideration of a large number of criteria. Instead, the public takes short cuts or uses cues. One source of cues is the White House, but another is the mass media.

Media coverage of issues and events may prime the criteria most people select for evaluating the president. In the words of a leading authority on the effect of television news on public opinion: "The themes and issues that are repeated in television news coverage become the priorities of viewers. Issues and events highlighted by television news become especially influential as criteria for evaluating public officials."[81]

The media are more likely to influence perceptions than attitudes. The press can influence the perceptions of what public figures stand for and what their personalities are like, what issues are important, and what is at stake. If the media raise certain issues or personal characteristics to prominence, the significance of attitudes that people already hold may change and thus alter their evaluations of, say, presidential performance, without their attitudes themselves changing. In other words, the media can influence the criteria by which the president is judged.

If the media were simply following the White House's lead in priming criteria for evaluating the president, the media's effect would not pose an obstacle to presidential priming. Instead, it would reinforce the White House's efforts. The media, however, typically follow their own course.

When the media began covering the Iran-Contra affair, Ronald Reagan's public approval took an immediate and severe dip as the public applied new criteria of evaluation.[82] The role of assessments of George Bush's economic performance in overall evaluations of him decreased substantially after the Gulf War began, and it is reasonable to conclude that media priming effects caused a shift of attention to his performance on war-related criteria.[83] Although the president wished the public to continue to weigh heavily his foreign policy stewardship in its evaluations of his performance, the public did not comply. Instead, both the media and the public turned their focus to the economy.[84]

Coverage of the Camp David peace accords boosted the effect of the president's performance in dealing with foreign countries on overall evaluations of the president.[85] Similarly, experiments found that network news affected Jimmy Carter's overall reputation and, to a lesser extent, views of his apparent competence. The standards people used in evaluating the president, what they felt was important in his job performance, seemed to be influenced by the news they watched on television.[86]

When the press gave substantial coverage to President Ford's misstatement about Soviet domination of Eastern Europe, this coverage affected the public. Polls show that most people did not realize the president had made an error until the press told them so. Afterwards, pro-Ford evaluations of the debate declined noticeably as voters' concerns for competence in foreign policy making became salient.[87] A somewhat similar switch occurred after the first debate between Walter Mondale and Ronald Reagan in 1984.[88]

In the days immediately after the first debate between presidential candidates Al Gore and George W. Bush in 2000, by a small margin those who watched the debate were more likely to think that Gore won. However, by a margin of 43 percent to 21 percent, those who did not watch the debate felt Gore had won. One week after the debate, perceptions of the winner among those who did not watch the debate had changed. The advantage for Gore had dropped to 37 percent to 26 percent, halving the original margin of 22 percentage points to only 11.[89] Perceptions among those who watched were stable. It appears that media reports about Gore's lapses and misstatements influenced nonwatchers, who depended on media reports.

Although the public's information on and criteria for evaluating presidential candidates parallel what the media present,[90] the press probably has the greatest effect on public perceptions of individuals and issues between election campaigns, when people are less likely to activate their partisan defenses.

The extraordinary attention that the press devotes to presidents magnifies their flaws and makes them more salient to the public. Even completely unsubstantiated charges against them may make the news because of their prominence. Familiarity may not breed contempt, but it certainly may diminish the aura of grandeur around the chief executive.

The prominent coverage of Gerald Ford's alleged physical clumsiness naturally translated into suggestions of mental ineptitude and became a prominent criterion for evaluating the president. In the president's own words: "Every time I stumbled or bumped my head or fell in the snow, reporters zeroed in on that to the exclusion of almost everything else. The news coverage was harmful, but even more damaging was the fact that Johnny Carson and Chevy Chase used my 'missteps' for their jokes. Their antics—and I'll admit that I laughed at them myself—helped create the public perception of me as a stumbler. And that wasn't funny."[91]

The president's every stumble was magnified as the press emphasized behavior that fit the mold. Ford was repeatedly forced to defend his intelligence, and many of his acts and statements were reported as efforts to "act" presidential.[92] There was a similar theme to the coverage of Vice President Dan Quayle, and as a result, after he misspelled "potato" during the 1992 presidential campaign, it became a widely reported story.

Framing the news in themes both simplifies complex issues and events and provides continuity of people, institutions, and issues. However, as in the case of Gerald Ford, once the press typecasts a president, his image is repeatedly reinforced by news coverage and late-night comedians and is difficult for the president to overcome. Once themes and story lines have been established, the press tends to maintain them in subsequent coverage, and stories that dovetail with the theme are more likely to be in the news. Of necessity, framing the news in this fashion emphasizes some information at the expense of other data, often determining what information is most relevant to news coverage and the context in which it is presented.

George H. W. Bush's privileged background gave rise to a greatly distorting media theme of isolation from the realities of everyday life in the United States. Thus, a story that he expressed amazement at scanners commonly used at supermarket checkout lines was widely reported as further evidence of his isolation — even though the story was incorrect.

Similarly, once the theme of Bill Clinton's weak political and ethical moorings had been established, even the most outrageous tabloid claims of his past misbehavior received media attention, while stories about his policy stances frequently focused on whether or not he was displaying backbone.

In 1992 the press's predominant theme regarding the presidency was that President Bush was in trouble, so it focused on information that would illustrate the theme. Bush received overwhelmingly negative coverage during the year. Indeed, the television networks' portrayal of the economy became more negative even as the economy actually improved. Similar themes were established for President Carter in 1980 and President Ford in 1976.[93]

In addition to framing evaluations of the president in terms of some criteria rather than others, the media also frame individual issues in certain terms. Once again, the media are not agents of the White House. For example, in the debate over Bill Clinton's health care proposal in 1993–1994, the media framed the issue as one of strategy and conflict between the president and his opponents rather than emphasizing the consequences of the issue for the nation. Thus, the media did not mirror the president's attempts to frame the issue.[94] In addition, public support for rebuilding the health care system varied in tandem with changes in media framing.[95]

In general, the media's focus on political conflict and strategy elevates the prominence of political wheeling-dealing in individuals' evaluations of political candidates and policy proposals.[96] Usually, this framing makes it more difficult for the president to garner public support, but there is at least one exception. The media framed the coverage of the Lewinsky scandal in terms of conservative attacks on the president and liberal defenses of him. This frame helped to generate a backlash against Republicans, who the public saw as being motivated by partisan politics.[97] Thus, even though press coverage of the Lewinsky scandal was inherently negative, the cynicism it encouraged inadvertently helped Bill Clinton avoid impeachment.

The Role of the Press in Perspective

Despite the evidence of the effect of media priming criteria for evaluating the president, it is important to keep a perspective. Our examples are of highly visible events, issues, and characteristics. Most potential criteria of evaluation do not reach such prominence. Thus, there are limits to the ability of the media to prime evaluations of the president. It may be that on the few issues that penetrate the consciousness of the broad public, people with only marginal concern for politics may be especially susceptible to the effect of the media because they have few alternative sources of information and less-developed political allegiances. Thus, they have fewer strongly held attitudes to overcome. Similarly, coverage of new issues that are removed from the experiences of people and their political convictions may be more likely to influence public opinion than coverage of continuing issues.

Most people are not very attentive to politics, and many people distrust the media. One study found that priming of the criteria for evaluating the president occurs most for politically knowledgeable citizens (who understand the implications of news stories' messages for their political attitudes) *and* who trust the competence and motives of the media. The number of politically knowledgeable people is small; these citizens are on average exposed to multiple messages (and thus multiple criteria for evaluating the president); and they do not have high levels of trust in the media.[98] Another study found that the content of media coverage of the candidates during the 2000 presidential primaries was not closely mirrored in the polls; the public did not associate strongly either George W. Bush or Al Gore with the principal character themes emphasized in reporting on the candidates since the primary season ended.[99] A great deal of spin is lost on the public. Thus, the media are powerful competitors with the president in framing issues for the public, but they do not necessarily dominate the process.

Conclusion

Presidents make a substantial effort to frame issues in ways that will favor their preferred policy options and to place their own performance in a favorable light. If they succeed in setting the terms of debate on policies and on themselves, they will prime the public to view them as consistent with its core values.

There are substantial obstacles to structuring choices for the American people, however. The White House faces a great deal of competition in its efforts to frame issues. In addition, many people are either unaware of the president's messages or too committed to a different view for the president to persuade them to support his views. Some people will listen but misperceive the president's point. The wide range of issues on which the president attempts to lead, the transience of opinion change, and the potential for overuse and heavy-handedness further complicate the president's efforts.

Perhaps no obstacle to setting the terms of debate is greater than the president's dependence on the mass media to transmit his messages. The media are unlikely to adopt consistently the White House's framing of issues. Instead, they make independent judgments about which issues to highlight and how to frame them for their viewers and readers. Brief, superficial, negative, and interpretive press coverage of the president often leaves the public ill-informed about matters with which the president must deal. In addition, the press often primes criteria for evaluating the president and his policies that do not reflect positively on the White House.

The president, then, cannot depend on structuring the choices about himself or his policies for the public. Persuading the public to think about his policies and his performance in his terms is difficult to do. One can sympathize with Bill Clinton when he declared that "Americans don't want me to help them understand. They just want me to do something about it."[100]

PART IV

The Audience

8

Receiving the Message: Is Anyone Listening?

To this point, we have focused on the first elements of the communications chain, the messenger and the message. At the other end of the chain is the audience for the president's messages. If the president is going to lead the public, it must first *receive* his message. Although commentators on the presidency typically assume that the president can gain the nation's attention whenever he desires to do so, there is little evidence to support such an assumption. Given the problems the president has in disseminating his message, the public's low interest in politics, and the easy access that cable television provides to a large array of alternatives to news programs, we should expect that a large percentage of the public will not be aware of the president's messages.

For the president to influence public opinion, it is not enough for members of the public to receive his message. They must also *understand* it. People must know what opinion the president would like them to adopt, whether it is support for himself or for his policies. We cannot assume that members of the public understand the messages sent by the White House any more than we can assume that they are aware of them. In the first place, an inattentive public is unlikely to be conversant with the president's pleas. Those who are unaware of a message cannot be said to understand it. Even those who pay attention may miss the president's point.

In this chapter I explore the ability of the White House to obtain an audience for its views, focusing especially on the best opportunities available for reaching the public: televised addresses to the nation. I also explore the question of the public's understanding of the president's messages.

The Audience for Televised Addresses

Perhaps the most potentially powerful tool for going public is the nationally televised address. These addresses represent the best opportunity for the president to reach the largest audience of his fellow citizens, because almost every American has access to television and is accustomed to turning to it for news. In addition, when the president addresses the nation, he does so directly (and rapidly), without the mediation of the press. Moreover, in a televised address, the president does not appear as a partisan, but rather as a statesman, usually speaking from the dignified surroundings of the Oval Office or before a joint session of Congress.

To be a useful tool for influencing public opinion, a televised address must first capture the public's attention. To the extent that the president fails to attract an audience, he loses the opportunity to influence public opinion directly. Scholars and other commentators have assumed that the president consistently draws a broad audience for his televised speeches.[1] As a result, studies of the effect of the president's speeches have essentially ignored the actual size of the audience, differences in the audience sizes among speeches, and differences among those who watch presidential addresses and those who do not.

At first glance it seems quite reasonable to assume that because the president is so visible and speaks on such important matters, he will always attract a large audience for his speeches. Wide viewership was certainly common during the early decades of television. Presidential speeches routinely attracted more than 80 percent of those watching television, an audience no one network could command.[2] A study by A. C. Nielsen analyzed ratings of nineteen nationally televised appearances (twelve during prime time) by President Ford. All but three of these appearances *raised* ratings over those of the normal entertainment offerings.[3]

Things have changed, however. When Ronald Reagan urged Congress to adopt his Contra-aid package in March 1986, more than half of the households watching TV viewed something else—the first time in history that a president failed to reach at least 50 percent of U.S. television households. More than sixteen million households that would normally be watching network television defected to cable channels or simply turned off their sets.[4]

On August 3, 1993, President Clinton made a nationally televised address on the budget. Only 35 percent of the public saw even "some" of the speech.[5]

Table 8.1. Audience Share of Televised Presidential Addresses

President	Number of Speeches	Average Audience Share
Nixon	22	75%
Ford	10	81
Carter	12	74
Reagan*	28	62

Source: Adapted from Joe S. Foote, "Ratings Decline of Presidential Television," *Journal of Broadcasting and Electronic Media* 32 (Spring 1988): 227.

*1981–1986

A month later he gave a major address on the defining issue of his administration: health care. Forty-three percent of the public saw little or none of the speech.[6] On November 27, 1995, Bill Clinton made a nationally televised prime-time address to the American public explaining his decision to send U.S. peacekeeping troops to Bosnia. Fifty-five percent of the public did not listen to the president at all, and only 18 percent watched the entire speech.[7] The president's low ratings were not unprecedented. For example, only a minority of those watching television tuned in to see President Bush's triumphal speech to a joint session of Congress after the success of the Gulf War.[8]

How many people do watch the president address the nation? Although we do not have all the data we would like, the data that are available provide a reasonably clear picture. One common measure of viewership in the broadcast industry is the percentage of households *using* television (HUT) who watch a program. This index measures performance in a given time slot. By way of illustration, Table 8.1 shows the results of a study by Joe S. Foote covering the 1969–1986 period during which he used the HUT measure. The data show a declining viewership of presidential televised addresses since Nixon. These differences in percentages represent a large number of people. Whereas Carter averaged sixty-nine million viewers for his prime-time televised addresses, Reagan averaged only fifty-five million.[9] The numbers also seem to indicate, however, that the president obtains the attention of a large percentage of the viewing public.

Such a conclusion would be incorrect, however. The White House is interested in reaching the entire public, not just those who might be watching television. The appropriate measure for audience penetration is the percentage of households *owning* televisions watching the president for an average minute of programming. Nielsen Media Research reports that in 2000, 100.8 million American households owned at least one television. Nielsen reports that in 2000 these households represented 98 percent of all households and comprised 259.9 million people, including 197.7 million adults of least eighteen years of age.[10] The percentage of households owning a television, then, represents virtually everyone in the country.

Examining Nielsen ratings for 128 televised prime-time addresses and news conferences,[11] we find (Table 8.2) that the percentage of households owning televisions that watched the president for an average minute decreased steadily from the Nixon administration through the Clinton years. By the late-1990s, the president was attracting less than a third of homes to watch even his State of the Union message. Even the exceptional curiosity regarding the Monica Lewinsky scandal and the media's extraordinary focus on it right before the 1998 State of the Union message created only a modest spike in viewer interest.

Paradoxically, further developments in the technology that allowed the president to reach mass audiences in the first place have made it easier for these same audiences to avoid listening to the White House. Matthew Baum and Samuel Kernell argue persuasively that the root cause of this drop in viewership is access to alternatives to watching the president provided by cable television.[12] In 2000, 76 percent of all households received cable service, and 85 percent of households owned a VCR[13] (providing yet additional opportunities to avoid watching the president). As cable becomes even more widely available and as the number of channels available to viewers increases, the president is likely to experience more difficulty in attracting an audience for his addresses. New networks such as Fox, WB, and UPN provide yet additional distractions from the president.

The alternatives to network television make it easy for people to tune out the president. Thus, it is not surprising that the decline of watching the president has been more rapid than the erosion of the networks' share of the television audience. In a study of prime-time addresses by Ronald Reagan, Foote found that millions of people (representing on average eleven million households) turned away from the networks but not from viewing television when the president was speaking. Almost all of these people returned to watching the networks after the president finished his speech.[14] As former White House Chief of Staff Leon Panetta points out, presidents who wish to exploit the bully pulpit will have to learn to use the new multichannel system.[15]

Different but equally valuable information on the audience for the president comes from Richard Wirthlin, Ronald Reagan's personal pollster. He polled the public after twenty-two of the president's prime-time nationally televised

Table 8.2. Percentage of Homes Watching Prime-Time Presidential Television Events

Year	Percentage of Homes Watching		
	State of the Union	Address	News Conference
1969	53	36	57
1970	—	54	—
1971	47	43	46
1972	—	46	—
1973	—	47	43
1974	24	51	48
1975	—	61	41
1976	53	48	—
1977	48	48	—
1978	—	45	59
1979	48	53	45
1980	58	54	47
1981	60	46	—
1982	50	37	35
1983	44	—	32
1984	39	—	33
1985	39	36	37
1986	39	41	36
1987	38	—	—
1988	34	—	—
1989	—	32	—
1990	29	33	—
1991	43	36	—
1992	38	—	—
1993	44	29	—
1994	33	30	27
1995	30	28	7[1]
1996	30	—	—
1997	28	—	—
1998	37	—	—

Source: Adapted from data used in Matthew A. Baum and Samuel Kernell, "Has Cable Ended the Golden Age of Presidential Television?" *American Political Science Review* 93 (March 1999): 99–114.

[1]Broadcast by only one television network.

addresses in his first term, inquiring whether people had watched or heard Reagan's speech. To this the respondents could answer that they had either (1) watched or heard all of Reagan's speech, (2) watched or heard part of it, (3) read or heard about the speech afterward, or (4) had not read or heard anything about the speech after the speech was given. Respondents could give only one of these responses, and thus people who said that they watched all of an address could not also be placed in the category that heard or read about the speech later. Table 8.3 presents the results regarding viewership of the president's speeches.

The data in the table indicate that on average, only 21 percent of the public watched all of a Reagan speech, and only another 24 percent heard at least part of them. Sixteen percent of the people who did not watch or hear the addresses heard or read about them after the president delivered them. Fully 39 percent of the public on average did not watch or hear the speeches and never heard or read about them later. In other words, in a typical nationally televised address the president attracted less than half of the public to listen to him directly, and only about one in five citizens sat through his entire speech. (We should also keep in mind that self-reported exposure to the news is prone to considerable exaggeration. Watching the president, for example, is the socially acceptable response to inquiries regarding viewership.[16])Thus, despite the fact that Reagan emphasized making his speeches accessible to his audience (stressing brevity and presentation), he could not reach directly most of the people most of the time.

We do not have systematic poll data for speeches by Presidents Bush and Clinton, but the data that are available tell a similar story to that for President Reagan. Table 8.4 lists twenty presidential speeches by either Presidents Bush or Clinton for which we have poll data regarding viewership. All but two (Clinton's remarks on the House and Senate impeachment votes) were during prime time. The results must be interpreted cautiously because of the nature of the polls (see the table footnotes for details). For example, the results for two of the speeches with the largest audiences (February 17, 1993, and January 27, 1998) are highly biased because the polling organization polled only those who had previously stated that they intended to watch the speech. It is interesting that even then, almost a third of this sample ultimately did not watch. Nielsen reported that fifty-three million people actually viewed the State of the Union message of January 27, 1998—far fewer than 69 percent of the adult public.[17]

Clinton's State of the Union message of January 27, 2000, also received a broad viewership, according to the polls. There is reason for skepticism that the speech attracted a wide audience, however. First, CBS interviewed only

Table 8.3. Public Viewership of Reagan's Televised Addresses

Poll Date	Speech Date	Heard All	Heard Part	Read About Later	Heard/Read Nothing	Speech Topic
2/20–22/81	2/18/81	39%	25%	18%	18%	Budget
9/25–28/81	9/24/81	25	20	19	36	Economy
1/28–31/82	1/26/82	33	22	14	31	State of the Union
4/30–5/3/82	4/29/82	18	21	15	46	Budget
8/25–29/82	8/16/82	20	18	14	48	Taxes
10/14–16/82	10/13/82	10	20	14	56	Economy
11/23–24/82	11/22/82	18	27	11	44	Defense
1/27–29/83	1/25/83	23	27	14	36	State of the Union
4/27–28/83	4/27/83	15	20	6	59	Central America
9/6–9/83	9/5/83	26	22	18	34	Korean airliner
10/26–28/83[1]	10/27/83	27	27	10	36	Grenada
2/2–4/84	1/25/84	20	31	19	30	State of the Union
2/5–10/85	2/6/85	25	23	17	35	State of the Union
4/25–27/85	4/24/85	13	21	11	55	Budget
2/8–9/86	2/4/86	23	21	19	36	State of the Union
3/20–22/86	3/16/86	14	18	27	41	Nicaragua
9/19–21/86	9/14/86	19	28	21	32	Drugs
10/13–17/86	10/13/86	22	29	17	32	Iceland Summit
1/28–29/87	1/27/87	26	23	16	35	State of the Union
8/16–17/87	8/12/87	10	20	23	46	Iran-Contra
12/8–12/87	12/10/87	12	31	18	39	USSR Summit
1/27–30/88	1/25/88	16	24	17	43	State of the Union
Average		21	24	16	39	

Note: Wirthlin Poll, "Did you watch or hear Ronald Reagan's speech? (If 'yes') did you hear or watch all of the speech or just part of it? (If 'no') did you hear or read anything about this speech afterward?"

[1]The poll was conducted to sample opinion on the Grenada invasion. Once Reagan gave his speech, Wirthlin added questions about the speech in the middle of the polling period.

people to whom it had given a Web TV, probably encouraging viewership. In addition, the *New York Times* reported that fewer than half of those watching TV tuned in to hear the president. About nineteen million homes watched the popular ABC game show "Who Wants to Be a Millionaire," which was broadcast right before the presidential address. Presumably those who intended to watch Clinton would remain tuned to ABC, but only ten million did.[18]

Table 8.4. Public Viewership of Bush's and Clinton's Televised Addresses

Poll Date	Speech Date	Poll	Watched	Did Not Watch	Speech Topic
9/7–10/89	9/5/89	Gallup	38%[1]	62%	Drugs
2/1–2/90	1/31/90	Times Mirror	40	60	State of the Union
10/3/90	10/2/90	*Time*/CNN	47	53	Deficit reduction
2/20–23/92	2/20/92	Times Mirror	48	52	State of the Union
2/20–21/93	2/17/93	CBS	70[2]	30	Economic program
8/3/93	8/3/93	CBS	30[3]	70	Budget
9/22/93	9/22/93	ABC/*WP*	54	45	Health care reform
1/28–30/94	1/25/94	CNN/*USA Today*	72[4]	28	State of the Union
9/19/94	9/18/94	CBS/*NY Times*	40[3]	60	Haiti
1/24/95	1/24/95	ABC	58	42	State of the Union
11/27/95	11/27/95	CBS	41[3]	59	Bosnia
1/23/96	1/23/96	ABC	50	50	State of the Union
1/27/98	1/27/98	CBS	69[2]	31	State of the Union
8/17/98	8/17/98	CBS/*NY Times*	64[3]	36	Grand Jury testimony
12/19–20/98	12/19/98	CBS/*NY Times*	45	55	House vote on impeachment
Late 1/99	1/19/99	PEW	59[5]	39	State of the Union
2/12/99	2/12/99	CBS	34[3]	66	Senate vote on impeachment
3/24/99	3/24/99	CBS	38	62	Kosovo
6/10/99	6/10/99	Gallup	38	62	Kosovo
1/27/00	1/27/00	CBS	62[6]	37	State of the Union

Note: Typical questions: "How much of President Clinton's State of the Union speech did you, yourself happen to watch live on Tuesday night—All of it, some of it, only a little, or none at all? Did you watch or listen to President Clinton's speech at the White House after today's Senate vote on impeachment?"

[1]Includes 14 percent of public who watched "only a little" of the speech.
[2]Reinterviews only of people planning to watch the speech.
[3]Reinterviews of people contacted before the speech, asking if can call back after speech.
[4]Includes 18 percent of public who watched "only a little" of the speech.
[5]Includes 35 percent of the public who watched "some" of the speech.
[6]Interviewed a sample previously given a Web TV by CBS.

The CBS News/*New York Times* Poll reinterviewed people that it had contacted before some speeches, perhaps encouraging viewership. Nevertheless, it still found that, except for Clinton's confession of having lied to the public about his relationship with Monica Lewinsky on August 17, 1998, large majorities still did not watch the president's speeches. Moreover, the president's short statement on August 17 was played repeatedly on the news, increasing the chances of people seeing it.

Audiences did not increase when George W. Bush took office. A total of 39.8 million viewers saw at least part of his nationally televised address in February 2001. This audience compares unfavorably with the 67 million viewers for Bill Clinton's first nationally televised address in 1993. Moreover, viewership fell substantially during the president's speech.[19] The terrorist attacks on September 11, 2001, increased interest in the president's messages, however. More than 80 million people watched his address to a joint session of Congress on September 20, 2001, and his 2002 State of the Union message drew nearly 52 million viewers (plus perhaps 1.5 million watching on PBS).[20] A live press conference on October 11, 2001 (his only one that year), drew 64.8 million viewers. However, his address on October 7, 2002, on a possible war with Iraq (discussed below) had an audience of only 16.8 million.[21]

The results in Tables 8.1–8.4 make clear that we should not assume that the president can obtain the public's attention at any given instance or consistently over time. Today, a popular show on one network can command a greater share than the president can by appearing on all of them simultaneously.[22] The president's ability to attract less than half of the public (often substantially less) to watch his televised addresses is yet another obstacle to leading public opinion.

Variation in Audience Size among Addresses

The size of the audience that individual speeches may attract varies widely. Reagan's speech of February 18, 1981, for example, attracted 64 percent of the public to watch at least part of the speech. However, only 30 percent of the public watched his addresses on October 13, 1982[23] and August 12, 1987. Thus, an additional 34 percent of the public watched the February speech and provided the president with the opportunity to influence its opinion. In addition, only 18 percent of the respondents did not hear or read something about the address on February 18, 1981, but this was the case for 59 percent of the respondents regarding his address on April 27, 1983.

It is possible that the audiences for some speeches are larger than for others because people do not know about them beforehand. However, Reed Welch found that the amount of time the media spend previewing a speech, and thus alerting viewers that a speech is coming, is not related to the audience size for an address. It appears that there is widespread notice for almost all presidential addresses.[24]

It is plausible that the topics of presidential speeches may affect the number of people who watch them. People may be more interested in some policy areas than others. For example, it is possible that potential viewers might find domestic policy more relevant than the more remote issues of foreign affairs. Similarly, some topics may be more salient to people than others. A crisis, scandal, or tragedy may attract viewers who would avoid watching a speech about the budget.

Table 8.5 arranges the Reagan televised addresses shown in Table 8.3 by general topic. The figures show that State of the Union messages achieve a somewhat larger audience on average than do other messages. Perhaps their more substantial audiences are the product of a long American tradition and the custom of tuning in to watch them. People are also more likely to be home on a January evening than during less cold nights of the year.

The average viewerships for the foreign and domestic policy addresses in the table are 6 percentage points lower than for State of the Union addresses. Equally important, the audiences for each type of policy address are, on average, identical. There are wide variances among the policy speeches, however, and it is difficult to discern a relationship between salience and viewership of the president's speeches.

The president achieved his highest audience rating (64 percent) with his address on the economy on February 18, 1981. He spoke before a joint session of Congress, unveiling his proposals for tax cuts and spending reductions. As we saw in Chapter 4, the public was anxious about the state of the economy, which was experiencing high inflation, high interest rates, and rising unemployment. Interestingly, both the economy and the president's audiences for his budget and economic speeches continued to decline. Seven months later, on September 24, the president had lost 30 percent of his audience, attracting only 45 percent of the public. By October 13, 1982, he lost another third of his audience, even though the country was in a recession at the time. The only address on domestic policy among our sample that obtained a substantial audience (47 percent) after 1981 was the much-publicized event in which First Lady Nancy Reagan joined the president to advocate "just say no" on September 14, 1986.

In foreign policy, the president obtained relatively large audiences for his addresses regarding the Korean airliner shot down by the Soviet Union, the death of U.S. Marines in Lebanon and the U.S. invasion of Grenada, and the Reykjavik Summit with the USSR in which the president proposed the complete elimination of nuclear weapons. Smaller audiences watched the president's addresses on defense policy in 1982 and the December 1987 US-USSR Summit. Addresses on the fighting in Nicaragua and the Iran-Contra scandal drew even smaller audiences. One might have expected a much larger audience for the latter, given its prominence in the news for the previous nine months.

Table 8.5. Audiences for Reagan's Televised Addresses by Topic

General Topic of Speech	Date of Speech	Watched All or Part of Speech
State of the Union messages		
	January 26, 1982	55%
	January 25, 1983	50
	January 25, 1984	51
	January 6, 1985	48
	January 4, 1986	44
	January 27, 1987	49
	January 25, 1988	40
Average for State of the Union: 48%		
Foreign policy addresses		
Defense policy	November 22, 1982	45
Central America	April 27, 1983	35
Korean airliner	September 5, 1983	48
Lebanon and Grenada	October 27, 1983	54
Nicaragua	March 16, 1986	32
USSR Summit	October 13, 1986	51
Iran-Contra	August 12, 1987	30
USSR Summit	December 12, 1987	43
Average for foreign policy addresses: 42%		
Domestic policy addresses		
Economy	February 18, 1981	64
Economy	September 24, 1981	45
Budget	April 29, 1982	39
Taxes/budget	August 16, 1982	38
Economy	October 13, 1982	30
Budget	April 24, 1985	34
Drugs	September 14, 1986	47
Average for domestic policy addresses: 42%		

The idiosyncrasies of the Bush and Clinton addresses listed in Table 8.4 make it difficult to perform a reliable analysis that parallels the analysis of the Reagan speeches. We can see in Table 8.6, however, that State of the Union messages once again achieve larger audiences on average than other addresses. We also find, as in the case for Reagan, that there do not seem to be patterns to the types of addresses that draw larger audiences.

Table 8.6. Audiences for Bush's and Clinton's Televised Addresses by Topic

General Topic of Speech	Date of Speech	Watched All or Part of Speech
State of the Union messages		
	January 31, 1990	40%
	February 20, 1992	48
	January 25, 1994[4]	72
	January 24, 1995	58
	January 23, 1996	50
	January 27, 1998	69[2]
	January 19, 1999	59[5]
	January 29, 2000	62[6]
Foreign policy addresses		
Haiti	September 18, 1994	40[3]
Bosnia	November 27, 1995	38[3]
Kosovo	March 24, 1999	38
Domestic policy addresses		
Drugs	September 5, 1989	38[1]
Deficit reduction	October 2, 1990	47
Economic program	February 17, 1993	70[2]
Budget	August 3, 1993	30[3]
Health care reform	September 22, 1993	54
Clinton impeachment		
Grand Jury testimony	August 17, 1998	64[3]
House vote on impeachment	December 19, 1998	45
Senate vote on impeachment	January 12, 1999	34[3]

[1]Includes 14 percent of public who watched "only a little" of the speech.
[2]Reinterviews only of people planning to watch the speech.
[3]Reinterviews of people contacted before the speech, asking if can call back after speech.
[4]Includes 18 percent of public who watched "only a little" of the speech.
[5]Includes 35 percent of the public who watched "some" of the speech.
[6]Interviewed a sample previously given a Web TV by CBS.

Who Watches?

The widespread assumption of a large audience for the president's televised addresses has not encouraged researchers to focus on distinguishing between those who watch the addresses and those who do not. Yet we should not assume that those exposed to the president's messages represent a cross section of the public. People vary in their attention to politics and hence in their exposure to political information and argumentation in the media.[25] Thus, we should expect variation in the attention people devote to presidential addresses.

Because many people do not hear the president's messages, it is important to know who does. These are the people that the president is most likely to reach. If the president is primarily preaching to the converted, he is likely to have much less effect than if he reaches a more representative cross section of the public, including many who are predisposed to disagree with him. Reinforcement of existing views is worthwhile, but conversion is more useful because it expands the president's support and reaches into the constituencies of his congressional opponents.

PREACHING TO THE CONVERTED?

We have seen that many people, when given the choice, choose to watch something other than a presidential address. In addition, some people might act to avoid listening to the president's message. Cognitive balance theories hold that people are uncomfortable when exposed to information and ideas that question the validity of their beliefs. To avoid discomfort, people are most attentive to information that is congruent with their existing beliefs and either avoid or screen out (that is, ignore) information that conflicts with the information and attitudes they already have.[26] Doris Graber studied how people process the news, for example, and found that at times people deliberately exclude information with which they anticipate disagreeing.[27]

Cognitive balance theories are consistent with the uses and gratification approach to news choice. Scholars adopting this view argue that individuals pay more attention to news that they find useful and intellectually or emotionally gratifying. More specifically for our purposes, people feel gratified if the media reinforce what they already know and believe.[28]

Roberta Glaros and Bruce Miroff studied reactions to a televised press conference and a televised address of Ronald Reagan. They found that Reagan supporters enjoyed watching him and were "revitalized" by his performances. On the other hand, viewers who did not approve of the president were uncomfortable and even irritated watching him.[29]

If people selectively expose themselves to messages, a message from the president may be a prime target for selectivity. The prominence of the president heightens the salience of a message on a policy and should increase the chances of irritating someone who is sensitive on the matter and who disagrees with the president. Because people do not wish to be irritated and because they have options in watching the president, those who oppose the president may be more likely than others to choose not to watch. Similarly, those who enjoyed the experience of watching a president with whom they agreed may be more likely to make an effort to tune in.

If cognitive consistency theories are correct, people who disagree with the president will avoid exposing themselves to his messages. These are the people whom the president most needs to reach, however. Avoidance behavior would reduce the chances that the president could alter an individual's established beliefs or attitudes and thus expand his support.

However, many scholars now believe that selective exposure to news is not a dominant pattern among the public.[30] A more open stance to the news occurs for several reasons. In the first place, it is difficult to avoid major news stories, such as those involving the president, especially on television. Avoiding dissonant news would require a substantial effort. The typical American lacks the concern for politics necessary to make such a commitment. In addition, many people seem to be curious about discrepant information or pride themselves in being open-minded and receptive to all points of view. People who are especially interested in government and politics may want to know how the opposition is stating its case and the arguments necessary to counter it. Others enjoy hearing news that contradicts their ideas so that they can refute it.

Thus, although people do prefer information that is supportive of their beliefs rather than information that contradicts them, it does not follow that they will not allow themselves to be exposed to nonsupportive information.[31] As Graber summarizes this view, "Apparently exposure to discrepant information is not as universally painful as previously thought." Selective exposure is most likely to occur for those relatively few people who recognize dissonance and find it painful.[32]

Reagan's Core Constituency

Ronald Reagan presents an excellent test of whether people avoid watching the president. Known for his clear conservative policy stances, he increased the polarization of the public along partisan, class, racial, and gender lines. As we can see in Table 8.7, average approval levels for Reagan among important demographic groups were substantially different. The exception is the only slight differences among the average approval levels for Reagan of those in various age groups.

Polarization is evident in the very large differences among the approval levels of groups with different levels of education, perhaps our best indicator of social class. Twenty percentage points separated the approval levels of the most and least educated groups, by far the largest gap to be found among presidents over the past fifty years. A smaller (7 percentage points) but nevertheless significant gap separated the support of union and nonunion house-

Table 8.7. Average Reagan Approval Ratings among Groups

Group	Approval
Male	57%
Female	48
White	57
Nonwhite	22
Grade school	39
High school	51
College	59
Union	46
Nonunion	53
Under 30	54
30–49	54
Over 50	50
Republican	83
Democrat	30
Independent	54

Source: George C. Edwards III, *Presidential Approval* (Baltimore, MD: Johns Hopkins University Press, 1990), p. 156.

holds. These differences undoubtedly reflect the varying responses of different social classes to the president's policies and the predominant party identifications among the groups. The presence of such dissimilarities, but not their size, is consistent with results obtained under previous Republican presidents.

The differences between the subgroups are particularly interesting, and particularly sharp, in the categories of race and gender. The 35-percentage-point difference between whites and nonwhites is unprecedented, larger than even the gaps during the Nixon administration. The president's openly conservative approach to civil rights and social welfare policy issues seems to have exacerbated the tendencies of racial minorities to disapprove of Republicans in the White House.

Finally, there is the "gender gap." For all previous recent presidents, with the exception of a few polls taken under Nixon, the differences in approval levels of men and women had been negligible. For Reagan, however, there was a consistent 9-percentage-point average difference, with men clearly more supportive of the president.

The polarization of the public's evaluation of Ronald Reagan is especially clear in the figures for the approval of party groups. Reagan's average support among Republicans was 83 percent. The figures are dramatically different for Democrats, however, with an average support of only 30 percent. Independents, as we would expect, fall between the partisan groups, with a 54 percent average.

What is most interesting about these figures is the difference between the support of the two parties. Between 1953 and 1980 the absolute difference in approval levels between Democrats and Republicans was 35 percentage points, itself a substantial figure. Independents fell in between, averaging 17 percentage points difference from Democrats and 18 percentage points from Republicans. During Reagan's time in office, however, the gap between Democrats and Republicans widened to 53 percentage points. Independents, still in the middle, on the average approved the president 24 percentage points more than Democrats and 29 points less than Republicans. Partisan identification has always affected how people perceive and react to the president and the events and conditions by which they evaluate him. Under Reagan it became even more salient.

Watching Reagan

Reagan, then, like all other presidents, did not appeal equally to all groups in the public. Instead, he had sources of special strength and weakness in support among particular segments of the public. Was the president's audience notably biased toward his core constituency? We know who approved of Reagan, but how does that compare with who watched his televised addresses? Table 8.8 shows the average viewership of various demographic groups for the twenty-two Reagan televised addresses listed in Table 8.3.[33] Although men were somewhat more likely to watch or hear about the president's speeches than were women, the differences between genders were more modest than they were for approval of the president's job performance.

There are only small differences in direct exposure to the president among those with different levels of education, but there are substantial differences when we factor in hearing or reading about an address after it was delivered. Exposure is directly correlated with levels of education. More educated citizens are more likely to read or watch news pertaining to an address that has already been delivered, because they tend to read newspapers and newsmagazines and keep abreast of the news more than the less educated.

Age also plays a prominent role in the president's efforts to reach the public. Each increment in age corresponds to an increase in people watching his addresses. At the extremes, twice as many people aged sixty-five and older

Table 8.8. Audience Demographics for Twenty-Two Reagan Televised Addresses

Group	Watched All	Watched Part	Heard or Read About Later	Heard or Read Nothing
Gender				
Male	22%	22%	18%	38%
Female	19	24	15	43
Education				
Not high school graduate	20	23	12	45
High school graduate	18	23	15	43
Some college	20	24	19	38
College graduate	23	23	22	32
Postgraduate	27	24	26	24
Age				
18–24	8	24	15	54
25–34	13	24	18	46
35–44	15	23	19	43
45–54	20	26	17	38
55–64	30	23	15	32
65 or older	40	21	12	27
Race				
White	22	23	16	39
Black	12	26	16	47
Other	17	23	15	44
Party identification*				
Republican	24	23	17	34
Independent	19	22	17	42
Democrat	19	24	16	40

Source: Wirthlin Poll.

*Data for party identification available for twenty-one addresses.

watched at least part of the televised addresses on average than those between eighteen and twenty-four years old, and the latter group was twice as likely as the former to have heard or read nothing about a presidential address. This finding is not surprising given that the elderly are the group most likely to watch television.[34]

There is a noticeable difference between blacks and whites in the levels of watching all of a presidential televised address. Variation in education levels among races may account for some of this disparity. A cultural factor may also be involved. Blacks rely less on general mass media for political information than do whites. (Hispanics turn to the mass media even less than do African Americans.)[35] Blacks are also disproportionately young, and younger people in general have lower levels of viewership.

The results for party identification are particularly striking. The differences between Republicans, Independents, and Democrats are modest. The only difference of any note is that Republicans were about 5 percentage points more likely than Independents or Democrats to watch all of a Reagan speech and somewhat less likely not to watch or hear about a speech at all.

Although demographic characteristics often have a strong correlation with political attitudes, the attitudes themselves should be the driving factor in avoidance of presidential addresses. Cognitive balance theories lead us to expect to find that those who were Republican, conservative, and approving of Reagan would be more likely to watch him speak on television.

Reed Welch carefully examined the effect of people's party identification, ideology, and approval or disapproval of Reagan's job performance on their viewing televised addresses. He found that neither ideology nor presidential approval was an important factor in determining who watched and did not watch Reagan's addresses. He also found that although strong Republican identification seemed to encourage watching the Republican president, strong Democratic identification did not discourage watching. These results suggest that people seek out consonant information more than they try to avoid dissonance.[36]

Although Ronald Reagan was a polarizing figure, this did not prevent him from obtaining an audience that included people who were predisposed to disagree with him. There is little evidence that people avoided watching the president to achieve cognitive balance. Although Reagan's audiences were smaller than he preferred, those who did watch provided the president with the opportunity to speak to his opponents and those in the middle as well as to his supporters.

INTEREST AND PARTICIPATION IN POLITICS

People's interest and participation in politics may also affect their attention to televised addresses. The relationship seems to be reciprocal. People who participate display more interest in politics, and political participation enhances a person's awareness of public affairs.[37] Consistent with these expectations, Welch found that people who voted in the 1980 presidential election were more likely to watch Reagan's televised addresses during his first term than were those who did not vote.[38]

These findings are more good news for the White House. If given a choice, the president would prefer to reach those people who vote than those who do not. Aside from the obvious implications for reelection of reaching voters, those who vote are more likely than nonvoters to engage in more time-consuming political activities, such as communicating with members of Congress or speaking to friends about political issues.

There is still much we do not know about who watches the president. For example, we have only glimmers of information on whether those who are personally affected by the problems that the president is addressing are more likely to watch. It is reasonable to speculate, for example, that people who are having trouble supporting themselves and their families will be more likely to watch a televised address in which the president discusses the economy and spells out his economic plan than people who do not perceive themselves as suffering economically.

Understanding the President

For the president to influence public opinion, it is not enough for members of the public to receive his message. They must also *understand* it. People must know what opinion the president would like them to adopt, whether this opinion is support for himself or for his policies. We cannot assume that the public understands the messages sent by the White House any more than we can assume that it is aware of them. In the first place, an inattentive public is unlikely to be conversant with the president's pleas. Those who are unaware of a message cannot be said to understand it.

Even those who pay attention may miss the president's points.[39] Everyday experience shows us that people who have the television on may not be devoting their full attention to it. They may be reading, eating, attending to children, or doing household chores. These and other distractions may hinder people's ability to absorb what the president is saying and to understand the opinions he would like them to hold. Even those who devote their full attention to the president may lack the background to understand what he is talking about.

It is important to distinguish between exposure to the president's message and reception of that message. From the president's perspective, reception of his message requires that his audience comprehends and retains the points he makes. Only people who actually acquire information from the president's speeches can use it in forming and changing their political evaluations, attitudes, opinions, or behaviors. Thus, we need to examine what information people actually acquire from the president's messages.[40]

Some scholars have argued that assessing people's ability to recall information is unnecessary for understanding the effect that messages have on people's opinions.[41] The "on-line" model of attitude formation suggests that people immediately evaluate and integrate new information into a "running tally" to update their attitudes and then discard the information. Thus, for example, campaign information to which people are exposed may affect their overall evaluation of a candidate, even if these people are unable to recall specific points from the information. In such a case, people's recollection of information is not an accurate reflection of the influence that a particular piece of information had on them.[42]

If our interest were limited to the effects of presidential messages on the public's evaluation of the president, we would have less reason to investigate what people remember about the messages themselves. However, we are primarily concerned with the president's ability to influence opinion on public policies. It is difficult to argue that the president can influence public opinion about policies if members of the public cannot remember what he said about these policies and thus are unlikely to have understood what opinions the president wished them to adopt.

It is also important to note that the respondents in the Wirthlin polls did not have to remember Reagan's addresses for long because they were polled shortly after he spoke. Moreover, the topics of the speeches were typically ones Reagan had been addressing for years. In addition, the respondents were asked about their recall of points in a speech immediately after responding to a question of whether they had watched or heard the address or had heard or read about it after it was given. Thus, it is likely that those who replied that they had been exposed to a speech would feel some pressure to actually recall points from that speech.

HOW MUCH DO PEOPLE REMEMBER?

We have long known that the public is not especially attentive to politics. On average, people know little of the details of politics, and their mastery of the facts of public affairs is highly selective and often idiosyncratic. Scholars have found the public unable to recall basic political facts or the characteristics and even names of candidates.[43] Jon Dalager found that only 35 percent of people who claimed to have voted in the 1988 election could correctly identify an issue that was an important campaign theme in the U.S. Senate race in their state. Very few people could correctly identify a second issue.[44]

Table 8.9. Points Remembered from Televised Addresses

Date of Speech	Identified at Least One Point	Identified at Least Two Points	Identified at Least Three Points
September 24, 1981	49%	33%	17%
January 26, 1982	46	37	25
October 13, 1982	28	14	6
January 25, 1983	44	30	17
Average	42	29	16

Source: Wirthlin Poll.
Note: The percentages are cumulative; thus, people who remembered three points are included among those who remembered two points and so on.

Does the president have more success than other elected officials in breaking through this public inattentiveness? To find out, Richard Wirthlin polled the public following four of Ronald Reagan's speeches during the president's first term and asked "what some of the major points of the speech were." Table 8.9 presents the results. On average, 42 percent of the public could identify one point that Reagan talked about in a speech; 29 percent could recall two points; and only 16 percent remembered three points from a speech. Reagan had an especially difficult time getting through to his audience in his speech on October 13, 1982, on the state of the economy. Only 6 percent of the public could name three points from the speech. In addition, we do not know whether the points people remembered were the ones the president raised. We might reasonably assume that most responses were accurate, but it would be overoptimistic to assume that they all were.

A major problem the president faces in communicating his message to the public is the number of people who are exposed to his speeches. The average number of people who did not hear or read anything about the four speeches in the preceding table was 40 percent (see Table 8.3). If we include only those who watched or heard at least part of an address or heard or read about the address after it was delivered, the president's success in communicating his message is more impressive. Table 8.10 shows that 69 percent of the people who were exposed to a speech could name points from a speech. Forty-six percent could identify two points, and 26 percent remembered three.

This is the good news for the president. The bad news is that 31 percent of

Table 8.10. Points Remembered by Those Exposed to Presidential Addresses

Date of Speech	Identified at Least One Point	Identified at Least Two Points	Identified at Least Three Points
September 24, 1981	77%	51%	27%
January 26, 1982	66	54	36
October 13, 1982	64	31	13
January 25, 1983	69	47	27
Average	69	46	26

Source: Wirthlin Poll.
Note: The percentages are cumulative; thus, people who remembered three points are included among those who remembered two points and so on.

the 60 percent of the public who *were* exposed to an address could not identify a single point the president had made. Thus, *a clear majority of the public could not remember anything The Great Communicator had to say, even in the immediate aftermath of a speech.*

WHO UNDERSTANDS?

We have seen earlier in this chapter that not everyone is equally likely to listen to the president. We should also expect that not everyone is equally likely to understand and remember the points the president made. Knowing who understands and remembers the president's points, like knowing who listens to him, is important, because the people who understand the president compose the universe of those whose views he might influence.

Although exposure to the president's message does not guarantee that people will understand what the president had to say, exposure is a necessary requirement for speeches to influence opinion. Welch found that the more people were exposed to a speech, the more likely they were to remember points from the speech. Moreover, people who watched the president's speeches were more able to identify points from the speeches than people who heard or read about the speeches only after he delivered them. Similarly, the more time that the president dedicated to a particular topic in a speech, the more likely it was that people remembered that point and identified it as the major topic of the speech.[45]

Although exposure is necessary for understanding the president's message, even attentive listeners may not understand. As one scholar put it, "The meaning of a message is not 'received,' it is extracted, inferred, worked on, and constructed. The audience member always 'reads into' the message."[46] A number of studies have found that education is strongly related to learning from the news, at least partially because the educated learn new information at a faster rate than the less educated.[47] Other studies find that the background level of political knowledge is the best predictor of recall of events in the news.[48] As Philip Converse put it, "The richness and meaning of new information depends vitally on the amount of past information one brings to the new message. So does the retention of information over time."[49] This phenomenon may underlie the gaps in knowledge identified by educational status.

People with larger stores of knowledge need schemas to organize it. These schemata aid in the acquisition of yet additional information by guiding the interpretation and evaluation of information, thus facilitating the assimilation and retention of information.[50] Less knowledgeable people who lack relevant concepts may be ill-equipped to process new information from the president and may even feel overwhelmed when confronted with it. They are less likely to perceive or remember the points the president made.[51]

We lack information on the schemas of the respondents to Wirthlin's polls, but we can reasonably infer that those with higher levels of education are more likely to posses the necessary cognitive frameworks for understanding Reagan's points. Thus, we expect those with higher levels of education to remember more points from the president's speeches.

The figures in Table 8.11 show the number of points that various demographic groups remembered independent of their exposure to the president's addresses. Here we see that men remember more points than women, the old more than the young, the educated more than the less educated, and whites more than those of other races. However, our earlier findings regarding the demographics of who watches the president's addresses caution against concluding that gender, race, and age explain differences in understanding the president. The differences among demographic groups may be simply a product of differing levels of exposure to the president.

When we control for exposure to the president's televised addresses, most of the differences disappear, as shown in Table 8.12. As expected, the only significant differences among these demographic groups are the greater number of points remembered by those on the higher tiers of the educational scale.

At first glance, it appears that if everyone cannot listen to and understand the president's messages, it is still a considerable advantage to communicate effectively with the more educated and, roughly speaking, the more influential members of society. Moreover, some authors have concluded that it is those people who possess the ability to understand arguments and apply those arguments to their political preferences who will undergo attitude change.[52] From

Table 8.11. Demographics and Points Remembered from Televised Addresses

Group	Identified at Least One Point	Identified at Least Two Points	Identified at Least Three Points
Gender			
Male	45%	32%	22%
Female	39	25	16
Education			
Not high school graduate	34	21	10
High school graduate	36	24	14
Some college	40	26	16
College graduate	49	36	20
Postgraduate	62	47	29
Age			
18–24	29	18	11
25–34	37	24	15
35–44	41	27	15
45–54	46	28	16
55–64	49	35	20
65 or older	52	38	20
Race			
White	48	29	17
Black	35	23	11
Other	39	27	15

Source: Wirthlin Poll.
Note: The percentages are cumulative; thus, people who remembered three points are included among those who remembered two points and so on.

such findings one would infer that those who lack the appropriate background provide the president with little potential for opinion leadership anyway.

The bulk of the evidence on attitude change supports quite a different view, however. The findings of most studies support the view that the most politically aware are *less* likely than others to change their attitudes as the content of public discourse shifts.[53] For example, during the debate over Bill Clinton's health care reform proposals in 1993 and 1994, the preferences of the most highly aware changed less than those of the low- and, especially, medium-awareness groups.[54]

These and similar findings suggest that those people whom the president is most likely to reach and who are most likely to understand his positions are

Table 8.12. Demographics and Points Remembered by Those Exposed to Presidential Addresses

Group	Identified at Least One Point	Identified at Least Two Points	Identified at Least Three Points
Gender			
Male	70%	48%	33%
Female	67	43	28
Education			
Not high school graduate	65	40	20
High school graduate	66	43	25
Some college	70	45	28
College graduate	76	56	32
Postgraduate	82	62	38
Age			
18–24	67	40	24
25–34	71	47	28
35–44	68	44	25
45–54	69	43	24
55–64	72	51	30
65 or older	68	49	26
Race			
White	69	46	27
Black	72	47	23
Other	64	44	24

Source: Wirthlin Poll.
Note: The percentages are cumulative; thus, people who remembered three points are included among those who remembered two points and so on.

the most resistant to attitude change. Although more educated and aware citizens are more likely to receive the communications from the president, they also possess the ability to argue against communications that run counter to their views. Their views are likely to be more firmly grounded than those of less attentive people, and this grounding serves as ballast against rapid conversion to another opinion. In addition, more aware citizens are more likely to receive communications that support their current views as well as those that oppose them, because they receive a larger variety of communications in general.

If many people are unaware of the president's views and if others are resistant to opinion change, who is left? The argument from the literature on opinion change is that those who are moderately aware are likely to experience the greatest attitude change. These citizens are attentive enough to politics to receive political communications. At the same time, their views are less firm and their knowledge is more limited than that of the highly aware. Thus, the moderately aware are less well positioned to resist persuasion efforts, because they lack the ability to argue against messages and they are less likely to encounter communications that support their current views.

Our data do not allow us to pursue this question further among the viewers of Reagan's speeches. At the very least we can conclude, however, that the potential for conversion is modest. Although the president controls how he presents his message to the public, the way that people process the information and the points they remember are beyond his control. Only a small portion of the public is generally open to changing their opinions in response to the president. Achieving an understanding of his message presents yet another challenge for the president in his efforts to move public opinion.

Presidential Access to Television

The White House not only has a problem in obtaining a receptive audience for the president's television appearances. In addition, it must face the obstacle of obtaining television coverage in the first place. Traditionally, presidents could rely on full network coverage of any statement they wished to make directly to the American people or any press conference they wished to be televised. Lyndon Johnson even insisted that the networks keep cameras hot in the White House so he could go on television on short notice. The president can no longer depend on access to network television, however.

The rumblings of network rebellion began in the 1970s and 1980s. On October 15, 1974, President Ford delivered a speech on the economy to the Future Farmers of America. The White House hoped that the television networks would broadcast his speech, but they were not inclined to do so. Finally, the White House made a formal request for airtime, and the networks acceded to the request.

Only ABC carried a speech by Gerald Ford on taxing, spending, and the economy on October 6, 1975. The other networks argued that carrying the president's address would open them to a request for equal time from the Democrats (even though the presidential election would not occur for another year). Although the Democrats did not ask ABC for airtime, Ford never again requested network time.

President Jimmy Carter wanted to address the nation in April 1977 and had to force the issue to receive network airtime.[55] The networks were not as acquiescent the next year when CBS would not preempt a high-budget and highly promoted two-hour special program to broadcast live Carter's national address on the Panama Canal treaty on February 1, 1978. The network did broadcast a taped replay of Carter's message at 11:30 P.M. EST. Later that same year, the networks denied Carter airtime for a speech on the first one and a half years of his presidency that he wished to deliver on July 4.[56]

The only instance during Ronald Reagan's first term in which not all three networks carried a presidential speech upon request occurred on October 13, 1982 (delivered just out of prime time at 7:30 P.M. EST).[57] The networks, with the midterm elections only three weeks away, were troubled with the speech's timing and its potential partisan nature. Only ABC, however, along with a few CBS and NBC affiliates, refused to air the address, with ABC claiming it did not carry the address because the speech was not newsworthy.[58]

The president had a more difficult time obtaining airtime during his second term. Only CNN carried Reagan's June 24, 1986, noontime (EST) speech from the Oval Office on aid to the Contras. The next year the three major networks refused to carry the president's 3:15 P.M. EST address on October 14, 1987, on Robert Bork's nomination to the Supreme Court (CNN carried it). The networks argued that the address was essentially political and the president was saying nothing new. Reagan spoke to the country once again on Contra aid on February 2, 1988. On this occasion his speech was during prime time, and only CNN carried it. This was the only time during his presidency that the networks did not carry a prime-time speech.[59]

Only CNN carried President George Bush's evening press conference on June 4, 1992, one of the few prime-time press conferences the president held. According to press secretary Marlin Fitzwater, there were several instances, such as a planned speech on the economy in late 1991, of the Bush White House canceling speeches or press conferences when it became clear that the networks would not provide coverage.[60]

President Clinton continually ran into difficulty obtaining airtime on the television networks. On June 17, 1993, only NBC among the major networks carried the president's evening press conference, and then only for about thirty minutes before the network resumed its regular programming. ABC carried highlights on *Nightline,* out of prime time. CBS did not carry the president's evening (7:30 P.M. EST) news conference on March 24, 1994. The network chose instead to show an NCAA basketball game. Only CBS among the major networks carried live the president's prime-time news conference on April 18, 1995. As a result, the president reached an audience of only 7 percent of the homes with televisions. (NBC aired parts of the news conference later on *Dateline.*) Given these difficulties, it is not surprising that the president held only four evening press conferences during his eight years in office. The prime-time press conference on August 3, 1994, was the only one for which he obtained live coverage on all the networks.

It took an intense lobbying effort by Vice President Al Gore to convince all the networks to carry the president's June 13, 1995, budget address (the White House press secretary usually makes such calls). As the *Washington Post* put it: "The White House viewed the presidential five-minutes as so vital to the effort to get Clinton back into the budget game that it took the unprecedented step of sending Vice President Gore to negotiate with the networks for live television air time. The major networks had shunned most of Clinton's requests of air time for months, but last night all four of the major networks broadcast the speech from the Oval Office."[61]

Never again during the remaining five and a half years of his presidency would Bill Clinton speak to the American people on a domestic policy issue in a nationally televised address. On five occasions he did speak on military interventions, but when the president requested network airtime to deliver an Oval Office address on United States–China relations in May 2000, he was rebuffed by two of the three networks. Thus he canceled the speech.[62]

As we saw in Table 2.2, most of George W. Bush's prime-time television focused on the terrorist attacks on the United States on September 11, 2001. His only prime-time press conference during his first year in office (held on October 11, 2001) received full network television coverage, as did his short presentations on September 11 and October 7. His major speech to a joint session of Congress on September 20 also received full network coverage. By November 8, however, most networks viewed the president's speech on the U.S. response to terrorism as an event rather than news. Perhaps knowing that it would be refused, the White House did not specifically request airtime. Instead, it informed the networks that the president's speech was available for broadcasting. Thus, CBS, NBC, and Fox chose not to carry the president's speech. Even in the face of terrorist attacks, presidents have no guarantee of airtime.

Nearly a year later, the president faced a similar problem. On October 7, 2002, he made his most comprehensive address regarding the likely need to use force against Saddam Hussein's regime in Iraq. The speech was strictly nonpartisan, the venue for the speech was chosen for the absence of a statewide election in the midterm elections, and the subject focused on what is perhaps the most important decision a nation can take. Nevertheless, ABC, CBS, NBC, and PBS chose not to carry the president's speech. The White House was reluctant to make a special request for airtime out of concern for fanning fears of an imminent invasion, but it would have welcomed coverage.

The networks argued that the president's speech contained little that was new. In the absence of breaking news, the commander in chief was unable to obtain airtime to discuss his thinking about going to war.

Responses to Shrinking Audiences

In response to the increased difficulty of obtaining time on television for presidential speeches and of gaining an audience when television does provide coverage, the White House has tried other means of reaching the public. President Clinton frequently traveled around the country, which brought him substantial local coverage. George W. Bush followed the same pattern, traveling more within the United States early in his term than any of his predecessors.

In addition, the White House has adopted a "rolling" announcement format in which it alerts the press that it will be making an announcement (such as a legislative initiative) in coming days, sparking stories on the upcoming news. Then it makes the announcement, generating yet additional stories. Finally, the president travels around the country repeating the announcement he just made, obtaining both local and network coverage of his media events. George W. Bush's 2001 efforts on behalf of his tax cuts, missile defense, and education policy are recent examples.

The question is whether the increase in local appearances has led to an increase in news coverage for the president and his policies. Early indications are that it has not. A study of the news coverage of the first sixty days of the Clinton and George W. Bush presidencies found that there was a dramatic across-the-board drop-off in coverage on television, in newspapers, and in newsweeklies. As the data in Figure 8.1 reveal, network television coverage was down 43 percent and newspaper coverage was off 38 percent. *Newsweek* magazine had 59 percent fewer stories about Bush in its pages than it carried about Clinton eight years earlier. Although the president was still a dominant figure on op-ed and editorial pages, he was less visible on the front pages, in newscasts, and on financial pages.[63] This lower profile is unlikely to be an asset in advancing the president's agenda.

Other White House attempts to compensate for declining access to national audiences fare no better. Clinton speechwriter Michael Waldman reports that the State of the Union message was the only instance the president could depend on speaking directly to the public. As the president's daily speeches shrank in stature, Clinton "elevated" the State of the Union address into a guide for the next year's initiatives. The increased emphasis on the annual speech, and the corresponding increase in its heft and length,[64] however, undoubtedly discourages viewership, undermining the ability of the president to

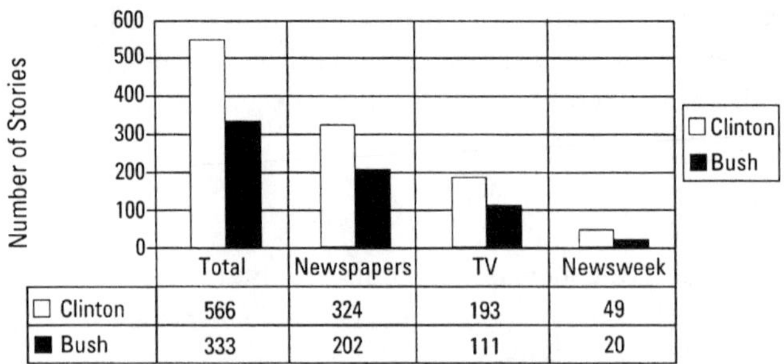

	Total	Newspapers	TV	Newsweek
□ Clinton	566	324	193	49
■ Bush	333	202	111	20

Fig. 8.1. First sixty days' new coverage of Presidents Bill Clinton and George W. Bush. *Source:* Adapted from The Project for Excellence in Journalism, *The First 100 Days: How Bush Versus Clinton Fared in the Press* (2001).

reach the public directly. We saw in the previous chapter that audiences for presidential speeches are *not* increasing to offset the decline in coverage of such speeches on national television.

Conclusion

We began this chapter with the premise that if the president is going to lead the public successfully, it must *receive* his message. The nationally televised address offers the president the best opportunity to reach the largest audience of his fellow citizens in an unmediated fashion and in the context of the dignified surroundings of the Oval Office or a joint session of Congress.

The results of our examination of these addresses reveal yet another obstacle to public leadership. The White House finds it increasingly difficult to obtain an audience for its views. Audiences for the president have been steadily declining, and the options offered by cable television seem to be diverting public attention. No matter what the subject of his speech or press conference, the president can no longer depend on reaching even a bare majority of the public. The fact that those he needs to reach the most, people predisposed to oppose him, are not especially likely to tune him out is small solace for the loss of the bulk of the television audience.

For the president to influence public opinion, members of the public must not only receive his message but understand it as well. Those who are unaware of a message are unlikely to know the president's positions. Even those who pay attention may miss the president's points, and substantial percentages of the public do just that. In addition, individuals' predispositions affect how they process the president's arguments. Thus, only a small portion of the public is generally open to changing its opinions in response to the president.

Compounding the White House's problem, the networks are increasingly likely to refuse airtime to the president. Whereas once the networks automatically broadcast live prime-time presidential policy speeches and press conferences, such events have become relatively rare. Aside from State of the Union messages and statements regarding scandals or military actions, the president is not likely to speak directly to the American people. More than ever, the White House is dependent on the press to deliver its message.

9

Accepting the Message: Can the President Overcome Predispositions?

For the president to lead the public successfully, he must do more than frame issues to his advantage and persuade the public to view issues through those frames. He must do more than disseminate his views widely and ensure that the public receives his messages. The critical final stage in persuading the public is obtaining the public's acceptance of his policy positions and of his own performance.

To gain acceptance, however, the president must overcome the predispositions of the audience. Developed over a lifetime, these views mediate the president's messages. If people perceive the president's stances to be inconsistent with their values and attitudes, they are likely to resist accepting the White House's arguments. Because people do not receive the president's messages with open minds, predispositions present yet another obstacle to the effective use of the bully pulpit.

We saw in Chapter 7 that the White House routinely attempts to frame the president and his positions on issues in ways that are consistent with its audience's predispositions. The president has two goals in these efforts. First, he would like people to perceive that his issue stances are consistent with their values. If people who might otherwise oppose the president's views accept his frames, they will be more likely to change their opinions. As we have seen, however, the prospects for success in these endeavors are not great.

A second goal of appealing to predispositions, through framing or more directly, is to reinforce those who agree with or who are inclined to agree with the White House. Although success in these efforts is less dramatic than changing opinions, reinforcement is also important to the president.

In this chapter I explore the role of predispositions in affecting acceptance of the president's messages. I also explore the possibility that because of their predispositions, some groups are more likely than others to respond positively to the president's arguments—and some may be more likely to respond negatively as well.

Screening the Message

Individuals have orientations that are the result of their backgrounds, experiences, and interests. The orientations of interest to us are people's political values and attitudes, commonly referred to as political predispositions. These predilections are relatively stable and typically not subject to substantial short-term change. Indeed, scholars who have carefully charted over several decades changes in public opinion about policy issues have found that the public displays little change in values and fundamental policy preferences over time.[1]

Predispositions stabilize individual as well as aggregate opinion. Core political predispositions tend to be highly stable through a person's life. Partisan attitudes are highly stable, and changes from one party to the other are uncommon. There is also evidence of increasing attitude crystallization through a person's life, infusing core predispositions with increasing psychological strength over time.[2] Although it is possible that the cumulative effects of small, short-term changes in opinion may ultimately alter predispositions, it is unlikely that the president or other elites affect them significantly or immediately.

The persistence of political predispositions means that presidential messages are not processed by open minds. Predispositions mediate the effect of the presidential messages people encounter directly or in the media. As a result, they may exert a significant influence on the public's acceptance of or resistance to the president's efforts to lead them. As John Zaller succinctly put it, "People tend to resist arguments that are inconsistent with their political predispositions."[3]

Actually, the role of predispositions has permeated our discussion of public leadership. For example, we saw in Chapter 7 that presidential efforts at framing choices for the public are hindered because people respond to issues according to their predispositions, especially their core partisan and ideological views, when offered competing views, as is typically the case on issues on which the president is trying to lead. Chapter 8 showed that the president should find it difficult to change the opinions of those who are most attentive to his messages, because these are the very people who have the most highly developed views and thus are the most resistant to the president's persuasive efforts.

Predispositions make people resistant to opinion change because people selectively process information. A major determinant of this selectivity is the structure of knowledge previously stored in memory. These knowledge structures, generally called "schemata," are based on prior experience and guide the processing and storage of incoming information and the recall and interpretation of information in memory. When the president and other visible political leaders present the public with arguments about the consequences of a policy proposal, only those arguments that are accessible to people and whose assertions agree with citizens' general political beliefs (including the proper scope of government activities and the extent to which the government can solve various social and economic problems) will receive consideration.[4]

In addition, a large body of research has shown that people have a need for cognitive balance, for consistency in their views.[5] We saw in Chapter 8 that people do not seem to expose themselves selectively to presidential messages. Processing information and ideas that question the validity of their beliefs is something else. People are most attentive to information that is congruent with their existing beliefs, reinforcing their relevant predispositions. Conversely, they tend to screen out (that is, ignore) information that conflicts with the information and attitudes they already have, making them resistant to changing their minds.[6]

Of course, in order for predispositions to affect the acceptance of a message, people must recognize the extent of the message's consistency with their predispositions. Possessing a certain amount of contextual information may be necessary to perceiving a relationship between a message and one's predispositions. It would seem to follow that since most people are not very attentive to politics, their predispositions will not be much of a hindrance to presidential persuasion. Not recognizing the implications of messages for their predispositions, they will not resist arguments contrary to them.[7] As we saw in Chapter 8, however, those who are likely to be unaware of the implications of the content of a presidential message for their predispositions are the very people least likely to receive the president's messages in the first place.

There are many types of predispositions, ranging from organizing principles—such as the value of racial equality, economic individualism, or the appropriate role of government in the economy—that lend structure to opinion within a particular issue domain such as civil rights, welfare, or agriculture policy to narrower opinions that are relevant to a single policy such as abortion, the death penalty, and gun control. Ideologies reflect more general orientations that organize a range of values and attitudes on a left-right dimension. To illustrate the effect of predispositions on public opinion regarding the president, I examine perhaps the most important political predisposition: party identification.

Party Identification and Evaluations of the President

Party identification is one of the fundamental orienting mechanisms in American politics. Most Americans develop attachments to one of the major political parties by the time they reach adulthood, and this identification affects how they evaluate the rest of the political landscape.

Party identification influences how individuals view what the president stands for and how well he is performing his job. Affiliates of the president's party tend to attribute their policy positions to him,[8] and they have an incentive to see the chief executive in a favorable light. Conversely, citizens of the opposition party have less need to perceive consistency between their own views and those of the president or to evaluate him favorably. Indeed, their party identification highlights differences with the president.

Members of the president's party are predisposed to approve of his performance and members of the opposition party are predisposed to be less approving. Independents, those without explicit partisan attachments, should fall between the Democrats and Republicans in their levels of approval of the president. Although many of those who identify with the president's party are prone to support his performance because of basic policy agreement with him,[9] there is more at work than simply a congruence of views. Party identification influences as well as reflects political evaluations.

A study of changes in the public's assessment of Dwight Eisenhower, at the time one of the world's most popular men, after he declared himself a Republican in 1952 illustrates the effect of partisan attachments on the evaluation of political leaders. The authors concluded:

> There is no reason to believe that admiration for him had followed any lines of political or social cleavage. Therefore it is noteworthy that our first measurements of public response to Eisenhower drawn after his commitment to the Republican party showed a popular image quite strongly correlated with the individual's own partisan attachment. The stronger the loyalty the voter felt for the Republican party, the more unconditional his respect for Eisenhower. Democrats were much less enthusiastic, and where sense of identification with the Democratic Party was strong enough, evaluated Eisenhower negatively. . . .

> Had Eisenhower chosen instead the Democratic Party, we may assume the relationship would have rotated in the opposing direction: strong Republicans would have decided they disliked Eisenhower.[10]

Public opinion polls clearly reflect the importance of partisan identification as an influence on public evaluations of the president's job performance. Democrats, Republicans, and Independents evaluate the president differently. Table 9.1 shows the average annual level of approval and disapproval of the president for each of these groups from 1953 to 2000.[11]

The average absolute difference between Democrats and Republicans is 41 percentage points, a substantial figure. Independents fall in between, averaging 19 percentage points difference from Democrats and 22 percentage points from Republicans. Members of the president's party are always more likely to approve than disapprove of his performance, usually by very large margins, while in thirty-one of the forty-eight years under study the identifiers with the opposition party are more likely to disapprove than to approve of the president's handling of his job.

Presidents typically receive very high support from their fellow partisans, and this support is usually stable over time. Republican presidents do especially well, averaging 82 percent approval from Republicans in the public. Eisenhower never fell below a yearly average of 82 percent approval from Republicans, while Reagan's lowest yearly average was 77 percent. George Bush fell to 71 percent approval in 1992. In Nixon's first term 79 percent was his lowest average among his party cohorts. Only in the troubled second term did Nixon and then Ford fall to more modest levels of approval, and even then they received on average the support of two out of three Republicans.

Examining the columns of Table 9.1 for disapproval of the president also illuminates the influence of party affiliation on evaluations of the president. Not only do identifiers with the president's party have a strong tendency to approve of his performance in office, but they also are unlikely to disapprove of it. For example, in no year did Eisenhower ever experience even 10 percent of his fellow partisans disapproving of his performance. Ronald Reagan faced only slightly higher disapproval rates among Republicans, while Nixon enjoyed similarly low levels of intraparty opposition until the Watergate story broke. Even then, only about one out of five Republicans failed to approve of Nixon's or Ford's handling of the presidency. Only in 1992 did George Bush suffer more than 8 percent disapproval among Republicans.

Democratic presidents face a more challenging task in obtaining approval from those who identify with their party, averaging 74 percent approval from Democrats in the public. For much of the period covered in Table 9.1, the base of the Democratic party was larger and more diverse than that of the Republican party. Identifiers included most liberals and many moderates and conservatives, making it difficult for a president to please everyone. The Kennedy-Johnson administration did well with Democrats in the public until Vietnam became a major point of contention in 1966. Then approval levels of President Johnson declined considerably among Democratic party identifiers. Jimmy Carter never enjoyed the high levels of party support of his predecessors, and he actually fell to below 50 percent approval among Democrats in 1979. Bill Clinton met with consistently high approval among identifiers with his party, never dropping below 74 percent.

Democratic presidents also encounter greater obstacles in trying to minimize the disapproval of their party identifiers. Democrats in the public are more likely than Republicans to disapprove of one of their own in the White House. Jimmy Carter averaged 30 percent disapproval during his term, and Lyndon Johnson averaged disapproval of almost one in four Democrats during his elected term of 1965–1968. Nevertheless, many more Democrats approve than disapprove of Democratic presidents. Only 13 percent of Democrats on average disapproved of Bill Clinton's performance as president.

We can also see the effect of partisanship on evaluations of the president by examining presidential approval at a cross section of time. In the first week of August 1974, shortly before he resigned, Richard Nixon's overall support stood at 24 percent. Approval among Democrats had diminished to a meager 13 percent, and among Independents he received only a 22 percent approval rating. Yet even at the height of the Watergate crisis, 50 percent of Republicans gave the president their approval.

Five years later, in July 1979, Jimmy Carter, a Democrat, saw his approval level fall to an overall 29 percent. Republican approval stood at only 18 percent. Democrats, on the other hand, were more than twice as likely to support Carter, according him 37 percent approval. Independents were in the middle at 27 percent.

Not only do the absolute levels of presidential approval differ for each group of partisans, they also may shift by different magnitudes or in opposite directions. In other words, Democrats, Republicans, and Independents do not always react the same to the president or to the events and conditions by which they evaluate him. What Democrats see as positive, Republicans may view as quite negative and vice versa. When we correlate presidential approval among Democrats with that among Republicans during Republican presidencies, we obtain an R^2 value of 0.55. During Democratic presidencies, the R^2 value falls to 0.14. In other words, presidential approval among Republicans and Democrats share 55 percent common variance during Republican presidencies and only 14 percent common variance during Democratic presidencies. Although

Table 9.1. Average Yearly Presidential Approval of Partisan Groups (percentages)

Year	President and Party	Democrats		Republicans		Independents	
		Approval	Disapproval	Approval	Disapproval	Approval	Disapproval
1953		56	24	87	4	68	14
1954		50	35	88	6	69	17
1955		56	26	90	4	74	12
1956	Eisenhower—	56	29	93	3	76	12
1957	Republican	47	35	86	7	66	18
1958		37	46	82	9	56	27
1959		48	35	88	6	66	18
1960		44	40	87	7	64	21
1961		87	4	58	22	72	10
1962		86	6	49	35	69	17
1963		79	10	44	40	61	23
1964	Kennedy/Johnson—	84	6	62	21	67	14
1965	Democrat	79	11	49	37	60	24
1966		67	21	32	56	44	40
1967		59	27	26	62	38	46
1968		57	31	26	63	35	53
1969		49	24	82	6	60	17
1970		41	43	82	10	57	28
1971		35	51	79	13	48	38
1972	Nixon/Ford—	40	48	84	10	57	33
1973	Republican	26	63	70	21	42	47

1974		24	63	58	27	35	50
1975		32	51	65	22	44	40
1976		36	50	69	21	50	36
1977		73	12	46	36	60	21
1978	Carter—	57	28	28	59	42	40
1979	Democrat	46	41	24	66	34	52
1980		53	37	25	67	35	54
1981		40	44	85	8	59	26
1982		23	67	79	14	46	42
1983		24	67	78	15	47	41
1984	Reagan—	28	62	89	7	58	30
1985	Republican	36	54	88	7	60	28
1986		40	49	86	9	61	28
1987		25	66	77	15	48	40
1988		30	61	83	12	52	34
1989		50	27	82	6	60	16
1990	George H. W. Bush—	54	33	86	8	64	23
1991	Republican	55	36	88	8	69	22
1992		18	76	71	24	35	54
1993		75	17	24	68	45	41
1994		74	19	21	73	45	45
1995		75	16	22	70	44	42
1996	Clinton—	84	10	23	70	51	36
1997	Democrat	84	10	30	62	54	33
1998		88	9	36	60	64	31
1999		87	11	31	66	60	35
2000		88	10	28	69	61	33

the movement over time of the two groups is related, they are marching to somewhat different drummers.

Some scholars have argued that the strength of party identification as a source of predispositions has diminished in recent decades.[12] The National Election Studies found that 41 percent of the public identified themselves as Independents in 2000, as opposed to 23 percent in 1952. Most scholars, however, have found that parties have resurged in salience since the 1970s and continue to provide a psychological anchoring point for political attitudes.[13] The effect of the increasing percentage of self-identified Independents, they argue, is more apparent than real. Most Independents actually lean toward one of the parties and act similar to partisans.[14] In 1996, for example, only 9 percent in National Election Studies neither affiliated with nor leaned toward either political party. In 2000, the figure was 12 percent, with 28 percent claiming to be Independents but leaning toward one of the parties.

The introduction of many new people into the electorate in the 1960s and 1970s when the post–World War II baby boom generation reached adulthood and the unique political traumas of those years may have caused a temporary decrease in the effect of party on presidential approval. Yet partisanship has proved to be resilient,[15] and party identification remains an important intermediary between the president and the public. It significantly affects how the public perceives and reacts to the chief executive and the events and conditions by which they assess him.

Despite the influence of party identification, it is clear that it functions as only a partially effective perceptual screen. Perceptions that are inconsistent with party identification escape its mediating effects and influence individuals. The data in Table 9.1 indicate, for example, that many members of the opposition party support the president. On average, a Republican president receives a 39 percent approval rating from Democrats, while a Democratic president receives a 34 percent approval rating from Republicans. Predispositions such as party identification are not controlling but they are difficult obstacles for presidents to overcome in their quest to lead public opinion.

Adjusting toward Equilibrium

We have seen the effect of predispositions on a particular attitude, presidential approval. We can also see the effect of predispositions by taking a broad view of public opinion about public policy. In their sweeping "macro" view of public opinion, Robert Erikson, Michael MacKuen, and James Stimson show that opinion always moves contrary to the president's position for the entire span of their analysis, 1952–1996. They argue that a moderate public always gets too much liberalism from Democrats and too much conservatism from Republicans. Because public officials have policy beliefs as well as an interest in reelection, they are not likely to calibrate their policy stances exactly to match those of the public. Therefore, opinion movement is typically contrary to the ideological persuasion of presidents. Liberal presidents produce movement in the conservative direction and conservatives generate public support for more liberal policies.[16]

The public continuously adjusts its views of current policy in the direction of a long-run equilibrium path as it compares its preferences for ideal policy with its views of current policy to produce a policy mood.[17] Thus, the conservative policy period of the 1950s produced a liberal mood that resulted in the liberal policy changes of the mid-1960s. These policies, in turn, helped elect conservative Richard Nixon. In the late 1970s, Jimmy Carter's liberal policies paved the way for Ronald Reagan's conservative tenure, which in turn laid the foundation for Bill Clinton's more liberal stances.

These findings are consistent with those of Christopher Wlezien, who argued that public opinion is a like a thermostat—becoming conservative when public policy is too liberal for its tastes and demanding more liberal policies when government is too conservative. In other words, the public is always moving toward restoring the equilibrium between public preferences and government policy.[18]

Loss Aversion

Research in psychology has found that people have a broad predisposition to avoid loss[19] and place more emphasis on avoiding potential losses than on obtaining potential gains. In their decision making they place more weight on information that has negative, as opposed to positive, implications for their interests. Similarly, when individuals form impressions of situations or other people, they weigh negative information more heavily than positive. Impressions formed on the basis of negative information, moreover, tend to be more lasting and more resistant to change.[20]

Risk and loss aversion and distrust of government make people wary of policy initiatives, especially when they are complex and their consequences are uncertain. Since uncertainty accompanies virtually every proposal for a major shift in public policy, it is not surprising that people are naturally inclined against change.[21] Further encouraging this predisposition is the media's focus on political conflict and strategy, which elevates the prominence of political wheeling-dealing in individuals' evaluations of political leaders and policy proposals.[22] The resulting increase in public cynicism highlights the risk of altering the status quo.

The predisposition for loss aversion is an obstacle for presidential leadership of the public. Most presidents want to leave some substantial change at the core of their legacies. Yet those proposing new directions in policy encounter a more formidable task than advocates of the status quo.[23] Those opposing change have a more modest task of emphasizing the negative to increase the public's uncertainty and anxiety to avoid risk.

Michael Cobb and James Kuklinski found in an experimental study of opinion change on NAFTA and health care that arguments *against* both worked especially well.[24] They found people to be both risk and loss averse, and arguments against change, which accentuate the unpleasant consequences of a proposed policy, easily resonated with the average person. In addition, they suggest that fear and anger, which negative arguments presumably evoke, are among the strongest emotions and serve as readily available shortcuts for decision making when people evaluate an impending policy initiative.[25]

Disaggregating Opinion

We have found that the public's views of public policy rarely move in the direction the president is attempting to lead. In their extensive treatment of trends in public opinion, Page and Shapiro and Erikson, MacKuen, and Stimson found that there is a uniformity of preference change, with movement in public opinion coming from all strata.[26] Nevertheless, it is possible that the aggregate national data in our study mask movement that occurs among subgroups of the population. Perhaps the president's leadership does change a small but important segment of public opinion — those predisposed to support him. Or perhaps predispositions polarize responses to the president, with the opinions of some moving markedly toward the president while the opinions of others are moving in the opposite direction.

To examine these possibilities, I have selected four issues that I discussed in Chapters 2 and 3. The data available on these issues allow us to disaggregate opinion and search for opinion change below the surface of the national totals.

GOVERNMENT SERVICES AND SPENDING

Perhaps nothing is more representative of the differences between the political parties than their basic level of support for government services and spending. Tables 9.2 and 9.3 examine public support for government services and spending during the Reagan and Clinton presidencies. They disaggregate the data presented earlier in Tables 3.11 and 2.5, respectively. The figures represent the average response for each group on the seven-point scale reflected in the question.

Reagan

Table 9.2 provides data from the Reagan administration, a period when the president advocated fewer services and less spending. I also include data from 1980, right before Reagan took office, as a baseline. Because the sample size for each demographic group is smaller than that for the entire population—and thus the sampling error is greater—we expect more volatility among years than when we use the fully aggregated data set. The change from 1980 is listed in the second column from the right. Because Reagan opposed increased spending on domestic programs, a minus sign indicates movement in the president's direction.

There is no obvious measure of a real change in opinion. However, a change of 0.5 might be a sensible indicator of real movement on a seven-point scale. As the second column from the right shows, there is only one example of opinion changing in the president's direction by 0.5 in the 1980–1988 period. The exception is blacks (the next largest change was among those aged fifty-six and older, who moved 0.46 of a point toward the president's position). It is difficult to argue that blacks were especially responsive to Reagan. The explanation for their opinion change seems to be their extraordinarily high support for government services in 1980, which provide more potential for moving in the president's direction, even as they remained the group most supportive of government services in 1988. It is also the case that blacks compose the smallest group in the table, increasing the likelihood of measurement error—and thus opinion volatility.

Differences in opinion change among categories of each grouping are small, with the possible exception of Democrats, who moved toward the president while Republicans, and especially Independents, moved in the opposite direction. What is especially interesting is that opinion among those most predisposed toward the president, Republicans, conservatives, and those with high incomes, moved against the direction of the president's attempts at public leadership. During Reagan's tenure, these groups became marginally *more* supportive of government services.

The year of 1980 was unusual in recent American history because the country experienced unusually high inflation, interest rates, and unemployment. If support for government services and spending was unusually high, it would distort opinion change. We would anticipate a moderating (and thus lessening) of support for government services and spending during prosperity. This

Table 9.2. Public Support for Government Services, 1980–1988

Group	1980	1982	1984	1986	1988	Change, 1980–1988	Change, 1982–1988
Gender							
Male	4.25	3.55	3.83	4.30	3.96	−0.29	+0.41
Female	4.46	3.98	4.19	4.67	4.30	−0.16	+0.32
Race							
White	4.20	3.67	3.90	4.29	4.10	−0.10	+0.43
Black	5.72	5.06	5.09	5.53	4.97	−0.75	−0.03
Education							
High school or less	4.52	3.92	4.15	4.71	4.36	−0.16	+0.44
Some college	4.16	3.79	4.01	4.42	4.04	−0.12	+0.25
College graduate	4.14	3.42	3.64	4.14	3.78	−0.36	+0.36
Age							
18–35	4.52	3.92	4.13	4.66	4.40	−0.12	+0.48
36–55	4.13	3.69	3.68	4.45	4.03	−0.10	+0.34
56+	4.41	3.66	4.02	4.32	3.95	−0.46	+0.29
Income							
$0–10,000	4.86	4.24	4.51	4.75	4.82	−0.04	+0.58
$10–25,000	4.37	3.84	4.02	4.55	4.24	−0.13	+0.40
$25–50,000	4.08	3.58	3.83	4.33	4.04	−0.04	+0.46
$50,000+	3.62	3.04	3.45	4.19	3.79	+0.17	+0.75
Party							
Republican	3.46	3.06	3.39	3.77	3.49	+0.03	+0.43
Independent	4.07	3.71	4.03	4.32	4.37	+0.30	+0.66
Democrat	5.09	4.26	4.52	4.96	4.69	−0.40	+0.43
Ideology							
Conservative	3.76	3.28	3.69	3.98	3.86	+0.10	+0.58
Moderate	4.52	3.90	4.02	4.60	4.24	−0.28	+0.34
Liberal	5.05	4.43	4.32	4.92	4.73	−0.32	+0.30

Notes: Yearly figures represent mean scores on a seven-point scale. National Election Studies question: "Some people think that government should provide fewer services, even in areas such as health and education, in order to reduce spending. Other people feel that it is important for the government to provide many more services even if it means an increase in spending. Where would you place yourself on this scale?" (1 = Fewer services; 7 = More services) opinion change would be independent of the president's leadership, further undermining the effect on public opinion attributable to the president.

The year 1982 was also unusual, as the United States experienced its last serious recession. One might expect that demands for government services and spending would be high. However, examining the column for 1982 shows that the opposite was true. Support decreased substantially compared with 1980. We might attribute this change to the president's leadership of a conservative revolution in public policy. The fact that the president was below 50 percent in the polls for the entire year of 1982 should make us skeptical of this explanation. We also need to investigate opinion change in the remaining six years of Reagan's presidency.

Despite the president's famous consistency in his conservative stands and message, public support for government services and spending was substantially volatile. The last column in Table 9.2 shows changes in opinion among demographic groups during the 1982–1988 period. In *every* category, opinion changed against the president over the last six years of his tenure. Many of these changes are substantial, headed by the 0.75 change for those in the highest income group, the 0.66 change for Independents, and the 0.58 changes for those in the lowest income group and conservatives. It does not seem logical to attribute the change in opinion from 1980 to 1982 to Reagan's leadership and then ignore the widespread turn in opinion against the president over the following six years.

It is more reasonable to attribute the changes in opinion to broad swings in the public mood beyond the influence of the president. We saw in Chapter 2 that Reagan arrived at the White House on the crest of a preexisting wave of conservatism. Conservative opinion on government services and spending seems to have peaked in 1982. Afterwards, the country reverted to its more typical (and moderate) opinion.

Clinton

Table 9.3 provides the levels of public support for government services and spending among demographic groups during the Clinton presidency. Bill Clinton spent much of his presidency fighting for more spending and expanded public services against congressional Republicans who opposed his policy preferences. Thus, a positive sign in the last column indicates opinion movement in the president's direction.

The only period during Clinton's presidency when either house of Congress had a Democratic majority was 1993–1994. It was during these years, his first two in office, that the president offered his most important legislative initiatives and made the greatest efforts to lead the public to support them. We

Table 9.3. Public Support for Government Services, 1992–2000

Group	1992	1994	1996	1998	2000	Change, 1992–2000
Gender						
Male	4.14	3.43	3.68	4.09	4.16	+0.02
Female	4.69	3.98	4.09	4.49	4.71	+0.02
Race						
White	4.25	3.59	3.76	4.21	4.31	+0.06
Black	5.23	4.72	5.00	5.07	5.34	+0.11
Education						
High school or less	4.60	3.95	4.11	4.41	4.72	+0.12
Some college	4.32	3.62	3.88	4.36	4.42	+0.10
College graduate	4.19	3.44	3.62	4.02	4.03	−0.16
Age						
18–35	4.75	3.86	4.04	4.60	4.70	−0.05
36–55	4.10	3.68	3.82	4.17	4.38	+0.28
56+	4.36	3.61	3.87	4.16	4.30	−0.06
Income						
$0–10,000	5.05	4.29	4.74	4.57	5.23	+0.18
$10–25,000	4.58	3.93	4.22	4.43	4.88	+0.30
$25–50,000	4.34	3.59	3.76	4.29	4.42	+0.08
$50,000+	4.00	3.41	3.51	4.12	4.25	+0.25
Party						
Republican	3.88	3.06	3.11	3.73	3.61	−0.27
Independent	4.40	3.87	3.83	4.33	4.45	+0.05
Democrat	4.74	4.21	4.54	4.66	5.08	+0.34
Ideology						
Conservative	4.03	3.25	3.51	3.93	4.18	+0.15
Moderate	4.40	3.88	4.20	4.18	4.51	+0.11
Liberal	4.73	4.28	4.46	4.72	4.84	+0.11

Notes: Yearly figures represent mean scores on a seven-point scale. National Election Studies question: "Some people think that government should provide fewer services, even in areas such as health and education, in order to reduce spending. Other people feel that it is important for the government to provide many more services even if it means an increase in spending. Where would you place yourself on this scale?" (1 = Fewer services; 7 = More services) can see in Table 9.3 that between 1992 and 1994, the public's support for government services and spending *decreased* (contrary to the president's efforts) among people in every demographic category in the table. Moreover, these changes were substantial, exceeding 0.5 for every group except those aged thirty-six to fifty-five (0.42) and liberals (0.45). After 1994 and throughout the remainder of Clinton's tenure, however, public support for government services and spending increased steadily.

This pattern is the opposite of the one for Ronald Reagan. For Reagan, public opinion moved in his direction for two years and then against him for the remaining six years of his presidency. We clearly cannot attribute the changes in opinion between 1992 and 1994 to Clinton's leadership, because public opinion moved against him. The public response may have been in reaction to the administration's liberal policies such as the president's health care proposal or to Newt Gingrich's efforts to move the country to the right. For our purposes, the main point is that the public did not respond to the White House's call for support.

Can we attribute the increase in public support for government services and spending after 1994 to a more effective use of the bully pulpit? It is difficult to do so in the face of Clinton's failure to lead the public during 1993–1994. In addition, opinion in 1994 was an aberration (the figures for gender, party, and ideological groups are very similar to the figures for that other aberrational year, 1982). To understand opinion change during the Clinton presidency, we must compare opinion in 1992 with that in 2000.

Most of the opinion changes between 1992 and 2000 are small, and none reach even 0.4. Most interesting are the differences in the responses of Republicans and Democrats, indicating some opposite responses during the highly polarized Clinton years. Republicans moved a modest 0.27 away from the president's views, while Democrats, more predisposed to support the president, moved 0.34 in the other direction. The views of Independents were unchanged. There was little net change in national opinion because people on average were as likely to move away from as toward the president's views. People in the different ideological groupings moved in similar fashion.

In the end, these changes in opinion are modest and cannot bear the burden of much analysis. Table 9.4 shows the change in opinion on support for government services and spending over the twenty years after 1980. It excludes the education, age, and income groups, as the meaning of a level of education or income changes substantially over a generation and entirely different people occupy the first two age cohorts over such a period. The results of comparing 1980 with 2000 are striking. After all the tumult and polarization of the 1980s and 1990s, public opinion regarding government services and spending

Table 9.4. Public Support for Government Services, 1980–2000

Group	1980	2000	Change, 1980–2000
Gender			
Male	4.25	4.16	−0.09
Female	4.46	4.71	+0.25
Race			
White	4.20	4.31	+0.11
Black	5.72	5.34	−0.38
Party			
Republican	3.46	3.61	+0.15
Independent	4.07	4.45	+0.38
Democrat	5.09	5.08	−0.01
Ideology			
Conservative	3.76	4.18	+0.42
Moderate	4.52	4.51	−0.01
Liberal	5.05	4.84	−0.21

Notes: Yearly figures represent mean scores on a seven-point scale. National Election Studies question: "Some people think that government should provide fewer services, even in areas such as health and education, in order to reduce spending. Other people feel that it is important for the government to provide many more services even if it means an increase in spending. Where would you place yourself on this scale?" (1 = Fewer services; 7 = More services)

changed very little. Indeed, support for public services and spending among Democrats and Republicans in 2000 was virtually identical to what it was in 1980. Liberals and, especially, conservatives moved toward the mean, while moderates stood just where they did twenty years before. It seems, then, that we should interpret the changes in opinion over the 1992–2000 period as a reflection of a return to core predispositions.

REAGAN AND DEFENSE SPENDING

No government activity was as important to Ronald Reagan as national defense, and he tirelessly advocated increases in defense spending. Table 9.5 shows public support for defense spending among demographic groups. A positive sign in the last column indicates opinion movement in the president's direction.

All the signs in the last column of the table are negative, however, and all the changes in opinion over Reagan's presidency exceed 1.0 on the seven-point scale. In other words, opinion moved substantially, and in a direction contrary

Table 9.5 Public Support for Defense Spending, 1980–1988

Group	1980	1982	1984	1986	1988	Change, 1980–1988
Gender						
Male	5.37	4.08	4.14	3.98	4.06	−1.31
Female	5.07	3.72	3.89	3.60	3.83	−1.24
Race						
White	5.26	3.91	4.05	3.83	3.98	−1.28
Black	4.74	3.65	3.65	3.39	3.49	−1.25
Education						
High school or less	5.29	4.11	4.07	3.85	4.02	−1.27
Some college	5.24	3.73	4.08	3.86	3.96	−1.28
College graduate	4.89	3.57	3.73	3.50	3.66	−1.23
Age						
18–35	5.13	3.66	3.97	3.77	3.81	−1.32
36–55	5.27	4.04	4.13	3.84	4.01	−1.26
56+	5.26	4.06	3.96	3.70	4.00	−1.26
Income						
$0–10,000	5.03	3.87	3.72	3.71	3.88	−1.15
$10–25,000	5.30	3.90	4.08	3.71	4.01	−1.29
$25–50,000	5.23	3.92	4.02	3.83	3.89	−1.34
$50,000+	5.19	3.92	4.23	4.00	3.95	−1.24
Party						
Republican	5.57	4.34	4.51	3.05	4.46	−1.11
Independent	5.15	3.77	3.92	3.79	3.71	−1.46
Democrat	5.00	3.68	3.67	4.26	3.61	−1.39
Ideology						
Conservative	5.56	4.28	4.29	4.22	4.20	−1.36
Moderate	5.15	3.85	3.97	3.79	3.95	−1.20
Liberal	4.61	3.10	3.58	3.13	3.41	−1.20

Notes: Yearly figures represent mean scores on a seven-point scale. National Election Studies question: "Some people believe that we should be spending much less money on defense. Others feel that spending should be greatly increased. Where would you place yourself on this scale?" (1 = Decrease; 7 = Increase)

to the president's wishes. Equally important, the differences among different categories of each grouping are modest. No group seemed especially responsive to the president and thus resisted the national trend against defense spending substantially more than another.

Although conservatives and liberals changed nearly identically, one could argue that conservatives had more room to decrease their support because they began with higher levels. Such an argument is akin to that which points out that there is less potential for those who already approve of the president to rally to his side than for those who disapprove of his performance.[27] In the case of movement on a seven-point scale (as opposed to an either/or choice of approve or disapprove), however, there is plenty of room for movement in either direction. It is difficult to make the case that Reagan's fellow conservatives were more likely to respond to him than were liberals.

In Chapter 3, we found that 1980 represented an unusual high point for support for defense spending in the wake of the Soviet Union's invasion of Afghanistan and the holding of American hostages in Iran. Measuring change from such an unusual point may present an unreasonably high hurdle for presidential leadership. When we examine opinion change between 1982, when opinion had returned to normal, and the end of Reagan's tenure in 1988, we find remarkable stability. Only those with some college education and liberals move as much as 0.2 during the six years. In sum, support for defense spending decreased substantially after Reagan became president and stayed there the remainder of his tenure.

CLINTON AND HEALTH CARE

Because of its prominence, I have frequently discussed Bill Clinton's 1993 health care initiative. The White House made a full-court press over ten months for its centerpiece legislation, and we can compare those who supported it at the beginning and the end of the effort to see whether some people were especially responsive to the president's appeals. Table 9.6 presents the results of Gallup polls taken immediately after the president made his nationally televised address on his proposal on September 22, 1993, and the middle of July 1994, when it became clear that neither house of Congress would bring it to a vote and the bill was dead. (Gallup did not ask for ideological preferences in these polls).

Examining the column on the far right of the table reveals that *every* group except blacks, the most loyal of Clinton's followers, decreased their support of his health care proposal by more than 10 percentage points over the ten months. Comparing the 1994 opinion among categories of each demographic grouping, we find that it closely reflects what we would expect to be the predispositions for those of different income levels, party preferences, races, and ages. Those with low incomes, Democrats, blacks, and the young (who would be the greatest beneficiaries of the proposed changes in health care) were the most supportive. We might have expected women to stick with Clin-

Table 9.6. Public Support for Clinton's Health Care Reform

	September 24–26, 1993			July 15–17, 1994			Change,
Group	Favor	Oppose	Unsure	Favor	Oppose	Unsure	1993–1994
Gender							
Male	57%	36%	7%	41%	56%	3%	−16
Female	61	29	10	39	55	6	−26
Race							
White	58	34	8	35	61	4	−23
Black	70	21	9	76	21	3	+6
Education							
High school or less	59	33	8	42	52	6	−17
Some college	62	29	9	34	60	6	−28
College graduate	57	37	6	39	58	3	−16
Age							
18–35	56	35	9	45	52	3	−11
36–55	59	33	8	38	57	5	−21
56+	64	29	7	35	58	7	−29
Income							
$0–10,000	66	20	14	49	44	7	−17
$10–30,000	61	31	8	46	49	5	−15
$30–50,000	58	35	7	36	61	3	−22
$50,000+	50	43	7	32	65	3	−18
Party							
Republican	35	56	9	13	84	3	−22
Independent	55	34	11	39	56	5	−16
Democrat	83	13	4	69	26	5	−14

Source: Gallup Poll.

ton more than men, given their generally higher levels of support for him, but they did not. Education levels did not systematically differentiate support for the president's proposal.

The president was unable to increase or maintain the support of any group shown in the table, with the exception of blacks. However, some groups were less likely than others to decrease their support. In general, the groups most likely to support the health care initiative in the first place were also the groups less likely to drop their support substantially. For example, the president lost 61 percent of the modest support he had originally among Republicans, but he only lost 17 percent of the much greater original support among Democrats. Similar but less dramatic differences occurred for those with different ages and income levels.

We cannot determine from the available data whether the greater stability of support among original supporters of Clinton's health care proposal was the consequence of (1) their living in more uniformly supportive environments of friends, neighbors, and coworkers, (2) a stronger commitment originally, (3) a general inclination to follow the president's lead because of their broad political predispositions, or (4) a combination of these factors. The results do show that predispositions among those inclined to support him can be an advantage to the president at the same time that predispositions among opponents present an important obstacle to his leadership.

Conclusion

The final link in the chain of communications from the president to the public is a weak one. The president must overcome the predispositions of his audience if he is to change their minds about his policies or his performance. This is very difficult to do. Most people ignore or reject arguments contrary to their predispositions. Nor can the president depend on those predisposed toward him to be especially responsive or to resist national trends opposed to the president's positions.

Presidents, then, find it very difficult to move the public. Usually they fail. If this is the case, why do they keep trying?

PART V

Conclusion

10

Going Public in Perspective: What Should the President Do?

Presidents go public for many reasons. In this book I have focused on presidents' efforts to encourage positive evaluations of themselves, promote their legislative initiatives, rally the public behind their military interventions, and defend themselves against charges of malfeasance or misconduct. Although sometimes they are able to maintain public support for themselves and their policies, presidents typically do not succeed in their efforts to change public opinion. Even "great communicators" usually fail to obtain the public's support for their high-priority initiatives.

Moreover, the bully pulpit has proved ineffective not only for achieving majority support but also for increasing support from a smaller base. Similarly, presidents usually fail to move to the general public and are frustrated in their attempts to move those who should be most attuned to their messages. Maintenance of existing support is also usually not enough, as opinion is generally not where the president wishes it to be. Even when support for the president is at a high level, it may not be enough. For example, Bill Clinton was quite successful in maintaining substantial public opposition to Congress impeaching him. He was not able to forestall impeachment, however, because he could not obtain support from Republicans in the public, who formed the core electoral constituencies of members of the majority party in each house of Congress.

Americans do not defer to the chief executive, and they are not swayed by supposedly charismatic personalities. In addition, the president faces a number of obstacles to focusing the public's attention, framing issues to his advantage, obtaining an audience for his messages, and overcoming the public's predispositions.

Meeting with repeated failure, why do presidents persist in basing their strategy for governing on going public? Is there an alternative to the permanent campaign?

Why Do Presidents Persist?

In Chapter 1, we saw that the nature of the American political system provides presidents with strong incentives to increase their persuasive resources by seeking public support. In the next eight chapters we have seen that they usually fail to achieve this goal. Why do people at the pinnacle of power persist in expending scarce time and energy on what appears to be a futile mission?

THE ROUTINES OF POLITICS

There is a strong inertial component to presidential behavior. Presidents *become* president by going public. To reach the White House, they make dozens of commercials, commission hundreds of polls, deliver thousands of speeches, and shake tens of thousands of hands. This process now extends for at least two years as candidates endure the rigors of the lengthy process to achieve their party's nomination.

The primary and general election campaigns for president are only the tip of the iceberg. Every president elected in the past two generations has experienced extensive campaigning for other offices before seeking the presidency. It is difficult to imagine a candidate reaching the White House in any other way. John F. Kennedy, Lyndon Johnson, Richard Nixon, and Gerald Ford began running for office at an early age and never stopped. Jimmy Carter served in a variety of local offices, including the school board, the state legislature, and then as governor.

Ronald Reagan developed his political persona giving speeches for General Electric and came to the public eye as a political figure in 1964 after making a nationally televised speech on behalf of Barry Goldwater's candidacy. The success of this speech among conservatives propelled him to the governorship of California. Bill Clinton ran for office continuously in Arkansas, a state with short terms and a tradition of retail politics. George H. W. Bush ran for the U.S. Senate twice and served two terms in the House in between. Then he chaired the Republican National Committee and served eight years as vice president—going public constantly along the way. Even the relative neophyte George W. Bush ran for Congress and then twice for governor of the second largest state.

For each of these men, the result of all this public activity was winning the presidency, the biggest prize in politics. This success reinforces the routine of going public. The fact that campaigns influence the vote choices of only a small percentage of the public[1] and that elections, unlike legislative battles, always yield a winner does not diminish the proclivity of new presidents to keep doing what got them to the White House in the first place.

James David Barber identified three political roles that all presidents must perform: rhetoric, personal relations, and homework. The habitual way of performing these roles is what he terms presidential *style*.[2] The relative emphases in a president's style reflect not only the president's strengths but also his perceptions about the requirements of effective leadership.

Not all presidents have a natural inclination for rhetoric, and not all presidents have personalities well suited to going public. Candidates who emphasize rhetoric, however, such as Kennedy, Reagan, and Clinton, are more likely to receive a nomination than those who do not, increasing the probabilities of those inclined toward the rhetorical style becoming president.

Those presidents whose political styles are not characterized by rhetoric typically attain the presidency by less direct routes. Lyndon Johnson and Gerald Ford were both accidental presidents. Richard Nixon and George H. W. Bush were vice presidents who succeeded to the presidency, having established their credentials primarily with government service rather than on the campaign trail.

Equally important, even presidents who have not emphasized rhetoric in their political styles have felt it necessary to devote substantial attention to going public. One of President Johnson's closest aides, Jack Valenti, came to the White House from the advertising business and went into the motion picture industry when he left. It is not an exaggeration to maintain that Richard Nixon, the most reclusive of presidents, was obsessed with public relations. His chief of staff, H. R. Haldeman; his press secretary and later close adviser, Ron Ziegler; and several other aides came to the White House from advertising firms. Jimmy Carter, another president who emphasized homework, put Gerald Rafshoon, the advertising director for his 1976 campaign, on the White House staff.

Once a president occupies the Oval Office, another routine bolsters the permanent campaign. Since the Nixon administration, the White House has institutionalized a public relations infrastructure to aid the president in going public. Although the personnel change between and during administrations, the expectation of the normal way of doing business is well established across presidencies.

PREACHING TO THE CONVERTED

Not all of the White House's public relations efforts are designed to alter opinions. Instead, the audience for much of the permanent campaign is those who already agree with the president. Preaching to the converted, by definition, does not change opinions and is not what most political commentators have in mind when they advocate that the White House employ the bully pulpit. Yet perhaps the most important function of a coalition builder, in an election or in dealing with a legislature, is consolidating one's core supporters. This may require reassuring them as to one's fundamental principles, strengthening their resolve to persist in a political battle, or encouraging them to become more active on behalf of a candidacy or policy proposal.

Maintaining preexisting support or activating those predisposed to back him can be crucial to a president's success. Important policies usually face substantial opposition. Often, opponents are virulent in their criticism. No president will unilaterally disarm and remain quiet in the face of such antagonism. They feel they must engage in a permanent campaign just to maintain the status quo. As we saw in Chapter 7 and reiterated in Chapter 9, priming may be successful in framing choices when people are offered only one side of an argument. When offered competing views, they are likely to respond according to their predispositions. Thus, the White House must act to reinforce the predispositions of its supporters.

Presidents also go public to demonstrate preexisting public support when that support lies in the constituencies of members of Congress who are potential swing votes. George W. Bush's travels early in his tenure seemed motivated more by demonstrating his support in states where he ran well in the election than in convincing more skeptical voters of the soundness of his proposals. He did not travel to California until May 29, 2001, and visited New York even later. Instead, the White House gave priority to states that Bush had won and that were represented by Democratic senators, including Georgia, Louisiana, Arkansas, Missouri, North and South Dakota, Montana, and North Carolina.

Preaching to the converted may have an additional advantage. Sometimes new policies arise on which there is little or no existing opinion. President Reagan's proposal for a defensive missile shield is an example. If the president is able to activate latent policy views by linking his initiative to existing views, such as support for a strong national defense, he may be able to obtain rapidly a sizable core of supporters for his program.

More broadly, public opinion about matters of politics and policy is often amorphous. It lacks articulation and structure. It requires leadership to tap into it effectively, give it direction, and use it to bring about policy change. The president must sense the nature of the opportunity at hand, clearly associate himself and his policies with favorable public opinion in the minds of political elites, and approach Congress when conditions are most favorable for passing legislation. As Richard Hofstadter said of Franklin D. Roosevelt, he was not able to move the public, but "he was able to give it that necessary additional impetus of leadership which can translate desires into policies."[3]

Presidents, even those skilled in the rhetorical arts, are unlikely to be directors of change, reshaping the political landscape to pave the way for change. Instead, they are facilitators, whose greatest skill is recognizing and exploiting opportunities for change in their environment. Being a facilitator rather than a director of change has advantages, however. Following rather than molding public opinion makes presidents and their staffs attuned to how issues resonate with the public and thus the potential for exploiting public support to bring about change.

INFLUENCING ELITES

It is also possible that the effect of public leadership may be in realms other than that of the general public.[4] The real influence of public leadership may be on elite debate, journalistic coverage, or congressional deliberation. These relationships require a separate study, but they could play a decisive role in policy making.

The White House invests substantial energy and time in attempting to shape the media's attention.[5] It provides the press with briefings and backgrounders, press releases, and interviews and press conferences with high-level officials, including the president. It also makes efforts to coordinate the news emanating from various parts of the executive branch. Although we have rich descriptions of these efforts,[6] we know very little about their success in influencing the media.

What we do know should introduce a note of caution into our discussion. We saw in Chapter 6 that the president has many powerful competitors in agenda setting. In a study covering 1984–1994, B. Dan Wood and I found that the president was generally *not* able to set the agendas of the media and Congress with his public statements, even in foreign policy. Instead, most (but not all) of the time, the president was more likely to react to fluctuations in attention to issues in the media than he was to set the media's agenda.[7]

When it comes to setting Congress's agenda, the president is more successful. We have found that the president's proposals for potentially significant legislation virtually always make it on to the congressional agenda.[8] We do not know the extent to which the president's public statements facilitate this process. By speaking out in favor of an initiative, the president may draw enough attention to the issue that members of Congress feel the need to do something about it. The president is especially likely to go public on his most important legislative proposals. To provide an *incentive* for Congress to act, the president must influence what the public thinks is important. We are just beginning to make progress in understanding presidential influence on public opinion, but Jeffrey Cohen found that presidents' State of the Union messages do seem to influence the public's policy agenda (views of the most important problem), although not for a sustained period of time. Cohen also found, however, that more substantive policy rhetoric did not influence the public's agenda.[9] Furthermore, Kim Hill found that although the president could affect the public's agenda in the short term, real-world phenomena were far more important.[10]

It is also possible that presidential public statements serve as cues for members of Congress[11] and the bureaucracy.[12] Busy policy makers may respond to cues from the chief executive regarding his priorities, his threshold of acceptable legislation, and his willingness to fight to get his way. Studies of this area are in their infancy but hold promise for enriching our understanding of policy making.

What Should Presidents Do?

The failure of presidents to change the public's mind does not mean that presidents should not go public. As we have seen, there are reasons to continue to speak out. It does mean, however, that presidents should not base their strategies for governing on the premise of substantially increasing the size of their public support. Such strategies are prone to failure. As historian E. H. Carr put it, "the men who are popularly said to 'make history' are dealing with highly intractable material, . . . which includes the wills of their fellowmen, [which] can be moulded only in accordance with certain existing trends, and . . . the statesman who fails to understand, and refuses to comply with, those trends dooms himself to sterility."[13]

DO NO HARM

Presidents not only fail to create new political capital by going public, but their efforts at persuading the public may also *decrease* their chances of success in bringing about changes in public policy. When political leaders take their cases directly to the public, they have to accommodate the limited attention spans of the public and the availability of space on television. As a result, the president and his opponents often reduce choices to stark black-and-white terms. When leaders frame issues in such terms, they typically frustrate rather than facilitate building coalitions. Such positions are difficult to compromise, which hardens negotiating positions as both sides posture as much to mobilize an intense minority of supporters as to persuade the other side. *The permanent campaign is antithetical to governing.*

The enormous amount of money required to run a permanent campaign also discourages building broad coalitions. In Bill Clinton's first year in office, the Democratic National Committee spent more than $3 million promoting the fiscal year 1994 budget and another $4 million advertising on behalf of the president's health care proposal.[14] By June 1996, before the national convention, the committee had spent an estimated $34 million on issue advocacy advertising for Clinton.[15] To raise such sums, presidents need to tailor their messages to attract those most predisposed to support them, those with "special interests," instead of focusing on building support within broad coalitions.

In addition, it is often the case that frightening people about the evils of the opposition is the most effective means of raising money. Such scare tactics encourage harsh attacks on opponents while discouraging the comity necessary for building coalitions. Interest groups, which provide substantial funds for the permanent campaign, enforce ideological rigidity by closely monitoring policy makers and rapidly attacking deviations from the group's line.[16] As fund-raising structures are institutionalized and produce ever-increasing amounts of money for the permanent campaign, we should not be surprised that policy making is more ideologically charged and personally hostile and resembles sustained political warfare more than democratic consideration of policy alternatives.

Indeed, as Hugh Heclo argues, campaigning to govern is antideliberative. Campaigning focuses on persuasion, competition, conflict, and short-term victory. Campaigns are waged in either/or terms. Conversely, governing involves deliberation, cooperation, negotiation, and compromise over an extended period. Campaigns prosecute a cause among adversaries rather than deliberate courses of action among collaborators. Campaign communications are designed to win rather than to educate or learn. Thus, the incentives for leaders are to stay on message rather than to engage with opponents and to frame issues rather than inform their audience about anything in detail. Similarly, campaigning requires projecting self-assurance rather than admitting ignorance or uncertainty about complex issues and counterattacking and switching the subject rather than struggling with tough questions. It is better to have a campaign issue for the next election than deal with an issue by governing. Thus, Heclo concludes, the more campaigning infiltrates into governing, the more we should expect the values of a campaign perspective to dominate over values of deliberation.[17]

Similarly, David Brady and Morris Fiorina argue that governing by campaigning too often revolves around destroying enemies rather than producing legislative products broadly acceptable to the electorate. The tendencies are for civility to lose out to conflict, compromise to deadlock, deliberation to sound bites, and legislative product to campaign issues.[18] Norman Ornstein and Thomas Mann add that in the permanent campaign, political leaders do not look for ways to insulate controversial or difficult policy decisions from their vulnerability to demagoguery and oversimplification.[19]

Given the nature of White House efforts at public persuasion, it is not the case that even a failed effort at going public will be useful for educating the public and thus pave the way for eventual passage of proposals. Major initiatives have few second chances in contemporary America. In addition, as we have seen, there is little evidence that public relations campaigns, as they are currently executed, actually do much educating. The public is more likely to respond to what they experience in their everyday lives than to the urgings of the chief executive in the permanent campaign.

These narrowing and antideliberative propensities of the permanent campaign are exacerbated by the increasing ideological distinctiveness of the two major parties, which encourage presidents and members of Congress to view those on the other side of the aisle as enemies to defeat rather than opponents with whom to compromise. Moreover, the media is oriented toward viewing politics as a game and more likely to cover communications that are critical and conflictual, providing additional incentives to publicity hungry officials.

Traditionally, presidents attempted to build coalitions in Congress through bargaining. The core strategy was to provide benefits for both sides, allowing many to share in a coalition's success and to declare victory. Going public is fundamentally different. The core strategy is to *defeat the opposition,* creating winners and losers in a zero-sum game. In going public, the president tries to intimidate opponents by increasing the political costs of opposition rather than attracting them with benefits. If going public is not a successful strategy and actually makes coalition building more difficult, polarization, gridlock, and public cynicism, which characterize American politics today, are the likely results.

A DIFFERENT APPROACH

Related to decreasing the chances of success is the failure to exploit opportunities. Adopting going public as a core governing strategy, as we saw in Chapter 1, may encourage presidents to underestimate their opponents and eschew necessary compromises in the mistaken belief that they can move the public. In the process, the White House may suffer significant opportunity costs as it overlooks less dramatic, but more realistic, chances for success. This is unfortunate, because the ability to identify and exploit opportunities is the key to presidential legislative success.

Exploiting Opportunities

The most productive periods of presidential-congressional relations have occurred when the president had a large partisan majority and moved rapidly to exploit the political capital that the previous election had handed him. When Congress first met in special session in March 1933 after Franklin D. Roosevelt's inauguration, it rapidly passed the new president's bills to control the resumption of banking, repeal Prohibition, and effect government economies. This is all FDR originally planned for Congress to do; he expected to reassemble the legislature when permanent and more constructive legislation was ready.[20] Yet the president found a situation ripe for change. James MacGregor Burns described it as follows:

> A dozen days after the inauguration a move of adulation for Roosevelt was sweeping the country. Over ten thousand telegrams swamped the White House in a single week. Newspaper editorials were paeans of praise. . . . A flush of hope swept the nation. Gold was flowing back to financial institutions; banks were reopening without crowds of depositors clamoring for their money; employment and production seemed to be turning upward.
>
> "I will do anything you ask," a congressman from Iowa wrote the President. "You are my leader."[21]

Roosevelt decided to exploit this favorable environment and strike repeatedly with hastily drawn legislation. This period of intense activity came to be known as the Hundred Days.

Lyndon Johnson also knew that his personal leadership could not sustain congressional support for his policies. He had to exploit the opportunities provided by the assassination of President Kennedy and the election of 1964. That election produced a rarity in American politics: a liberal majority. He told his aide Jack Valenti early in his presidency, "I keep hitting hard because I know this honeymoon won't last. Every day I lose a little more political capital. That's why we have to keep at it, never letting up. One day soon . . . the critics and the snipers will move in and we will be at stalemate. We have to get all we can now, before the roof comes down."[22] Thus in February 1965, after his landslide victory, Johnson assembled the congressional liaison officials from the various departments and told them that his victory at the polls "might be more of a loophole than a mandate," and that because his popularity could decrease rapidly, they would have to use it to their advantage while it lasted.[23]

Johnson followed his own advice. At the end of an extraordinarily productive session of Congress in 1965, he tried to push through Congress a bill providing for home rule in the District of Columbia, a feat that several presidents had attempted unsuccessfully. When an aide asked him why he was working seven days a week on the bill when the same liberal majority would be returning in January, he replied that he knew the odds were greatly against his success and that it was the only chance he would have. Despite the returning liberal majority, "they'll all be thinking about their reelections. I'll have made mistakes, my polls will be down, and they'll be trying to put some distance between themselves and me. They won't want to go into the fall with their opponents calling 'em Lyndon Johnson's rubber stamp."[24]

The administration of Ronald Reagan realized from the beginning that it had an opportunity to effect major changes in public policy, but that it had to concentrate its focus on its highest priority (tax cuts and defense spending) and move quickly before the environment became less favorable. The president and his staff moved rapidly in 1981 to exploit the perceptions of a mandate and the dramatic elevation of Republicans to majority status in the Senate. Similarly, within a week of the president's having been shot, Michael Deaver convened a meeting of other high-ranking aides at the White House to determine how best to take advantage of the new political capital the assassination attempt had created.

Sometimes Congress may be closely divided but the president can rely on unified party support to achieve passage of important legislation, such as George W. Bush's tax cut in 2001. Bush was not intimidated by the narrowness of his election or the nature of its resolution. Although his tone was one of reconciliation, he ignored those who urged him to strike a bipartisan posture and hold off on his major initiatives. The White House correctly understood that the one policy that both unified and energized Republicans was tax cuts. Although most congressional Democrats would oppose the cuts, a majority of the public, including Independents and even some Democrats, would support or at least tolerate them. Equally important, tax cuts, unlike most other major policies, could be considered under rules that prohibited a filibuster. Thus, a united, although slender, majority could prevail—and it did.

Thus even presidents who appeared to dominate Congress were actually facilitators rather than directors of change. They knew that they were unlikely to change opinion and that opinion alone could not sustain their leadership of Congress. They understood their strategic positions, and when their goals, majority party coalitions, and public opinion were congruent, they consciously took advantage of opportunities in their environments. Working at the margins, they successfully guided legislation through Congress.

"Staying Private"

In the absence of favorable party configurations in Congress, and lacking the ability to use public opinion to pressure legislators, presidents might consider an alternative route that focuses more on attracting support in Congress by providing benefits than on increasing the costs of opposition. At the core of this strategy is quiet negotiations—the opposite of going public, what we may term "staying private." The Balanced Budget Act of 1997 provides an illustration.

Throughout President Clinton's first term, budget battles were at the center of conflict between Clinton and congressional Republicans. The president's fiscal 1994 budget, his first, passed Congress without a single Republican vote.

The new Republican congressional majority that came to power in 1995 was determined to make a balanced budget and tax cuts their vehicle for radically reshaping the federal government. But they underestimated Clinton's will and his ability to stymie them. By the time the Republicans conceded defeat in budget talks that dragged into 1996, they had triggered two federal shutdowns that closed much of the government and brought them a drubbing in the public opinion polls. They also made it easier for the president to present himself to the public as a moderate protecting the country from irresponsible reversals in well-established policies.

The residue of those battles—and of the ensuing fall 1996 elections, during which Democrats tarred Republicans as Medicare killers—was a deep bitterness that seemed likely to poison the relationship between the White House and Congress indefinitely. Yet within a few months both sides reached an historic agreement on achieving a balanced budget within five years.

Several environmental factors contributed to this success. In the first place, a balanced budget was achievable only because of the plummeting federal deficit. The primary cause for the deficit's dramatic drop was the surging economy. Also essential to the agreement was the groundwork laid by the budgets of 1990 and 1993. Both budgets structured decision making on taxing and spending in a way that substantially constrained deficit spending.

This foundation had been costly for presidents, however. In 1990, President George Bush bit the bullet and reversed his election pledge not to raise taxes. He agreed to a budget deal with the congressional Democrats that succeeded in reducing the deficit and limiting spending. In 1992, he lost his bid for reelection. In 1993, President Clinton followed Bush's precedent and reversed his promise to lower taxes with a program of higher taxes and spending constraints. In the 1994 elections, Republicans castigated Clinton and the Democrats for increasing taxes in support of a bloated federal government. In the end, they won majorities in both houses of Congress for the first time since the election of 1952.

Yet despite the unsettling history of recent budget battles, efforts to obtain a budget agreement succeeded. First, everyone was exhausted from brutalizing each other over the past four years. The fighting was an obstacle not only to dealing with the budget but also to accomplishing anything else.

In addition, both sides needed an agreement. The president needed a legislative achievement for his legacy, and the Democrats needed credibility on the issue of fiscal responsibility if they were to retake Congress and retain the White House in 2000. The Republicans needed to show that they could govern as a majority party and make moderate rather than radical changes in policy.

In this environment, both sides departed from the warfare over the budget that had preoccupied Congress for most of the previous generation. Low-keyed, good-faith negotiations began shortly after the president submitted his fiscal year 1998 budget, and senior White House officials held a series of private meetings with members of Congress. Unlike the political posturing in late 1995 and early 1996, *neither side focused on moving the negotiations into the public arena*. In the end, this made it easier for them to reach an agreement on the budget.

Equally important, both sides were willing to compromise, and they each gained from it. The negotiations culminated in an agreement to balance the budget by 2002, and Congress adopted a broadly supported, bipartisan budget resolution to guide its tax and spending decisions. This in turn paved the way for two reconciliation bills, including the Balanced Budget Act of 1997, and thirteen fiscal 1998 appropriations bills.

For Republicans, the budget agreement capped a balanced-budget and tax-cutting drive that had consumed them since they took over Congress in 1995. They got tax and spending cuts, a balanced budget in five years, and a plan to keep Medicare solvent for another decade. Thus, although they did not win a radical overhaul of entitlement programs, they did make substantial progress toward their core goals.

For Clinton, the budget agreement represented perhaps his greatest legislative triumph. He left the bargaining table with much of what he wanted, including an increased scope for the child tax credit, a new children's health initiative, restoration of welfare benefits for disabled legal immigrants, increased spending for food stamps, and a host of other incremental increases in social spending.

These compromises did not satisfy everyone, of course. Clinton had to walk a fine line between compromising with Republicans and maintaining the support of Democratic liberals who did not like budgetary constraints and did not want to hand the Republicans a positive accomplishment. They were also upset that they were not included in the negotiating process. Similarly, Republican leaders had to deal with die-hard conservatives, who did not want to compromise at all with the president.

The dramatic shift from the rancorous partisan warfare that had dominated the consideration of the budget during the 104th Congress to the bipartisan compromise of the 105th Congress paid substantial dividends. Building on a strong economy and two earlier rounds of deficit reduction, President Clinton and the Republican majority in Congress struck an historic agreement to balance the budget in five years, while cutting taxes and increasing spending for some administration priorities such as children's health care.

To succeed, all leaders must accurately identify the possibilities in their environments for accomplishing their goals. In 1997, President Clinton recognized both that it was in the interests of both Democrats and Republicans to reach an agreement on the budget and that such an agreement was possible. He also concluded that the political risks of antagonizing liberals on his left and being outmaneuvered by his heretofore-implacable opponents on the right were less than the prospects of a notable agreement.

Leaders must also adopt a strategy for governing appropriate to the environment in which they are operating. As we have noted, when political leaders take their cases directly to the public, they often frustrate rather than facilitate building coalitions. Such positions are difficult to compromise, and there is less emphasis on providing benefits for both sides, allowing many to share in a coalition's success and to declare victory.

The decision of President Clinton and the Republican congressional leaders to quietly negotiate and compromise, letting everyone claim victory, made the budget agreement possible. In addition, the success of these executive-legislative negotiations paved the way for additional talks of a similar nature on Social Security and Medicare that may have ultimately proved fruitful if it were not for the confounding influence of the impeachment inquiry in 1998.

There are many other examples of the White House and Congress strategically engaging in quiet negotiations to produce important legislation. The Clean Air Act Amendments of 1990 and the No Child Left Behind Act of 2001 are important examples. So is the budget agreement of 1990. Despite the exaggerations of the bill's negative effect on George H. W. Bush's reelection, there is no doubt that the act made the most important legislative contribution to the disappearance of the federal deficit in the late-1990s, dramatically affecting net revenues and structuring the consideration of future budgets.

"Staying private" will not change the incentives to defeat opponents. Nor will it narrow the ideological differences between the parties or produce unified government. Moreover, there are times when a president can rely on unified party support to achieve passage of important legislation, such as the examples cited earlier in this chapter. However, staying private is likely to contribute to reducing gridlock, incivility, and, thus, public cynicism and deserves a more prominent role in the president's strategic arsenal.

Notes

Chapter 1. The Permanent Campaign

1. See Samuel Kernell, *Going Public,* 3d ed. (Washington, DC: Congressional Quarterly Press, 1997).

2. Bob Woodward, *The Choice* (New York: Simon & Schuster, 1996), p. 344. These funds were spent through the Democratic National Committee.

3. Michael Waldman, *POTUS Speaks* (New York: Simon & Schuster, 2000), p. 16. See also Marc Lacey, "Guarding the President's Words and, Maybe, His Legacy," *New York Times,* January 24, 2000, p. A12.

4. Kernell, *Going Public,* p. 121.

5. Woodward, *The Choice,* pp. 54, 126; Elizabeth Drew, *Showdown: The Struggle Between the Gingrich Congress and the Clinton White House* (New York: Simon & Schuster, 1996), pp. 19, 34–35.

6. Lou Cannon, *Reagan* (New York: Putnam, 1982), p. 319.

7. See, for example, Jeffrey K. Tulis, *The Rhetorical Presidency* (Princeton, NJ: Princeton University Press, 1987).

8. See, for example, Kernell, *Going Public.*

9. Sidney Blumenthal, *The Permanent Campaign: Inside the World of Elite Political Operatives* (Boston: Beacon Press, 1980), pp. 38–42.

10. Sidney Blumenthal, "Marketing the President," *New York Times Magazine,* September 13, 1981, p. 114.

11. Drew, *Showdown,* p. 19.

12. Quoted in Woodward, *The Choice,* p. 22.

13. Quoted in Bob Woodward, *Shadow* (New York: Simon & Schuster, 1999), p. 513.

14. Quoted in Joan Hoff, *Nixon Reconsidered* (New York: Basic Books, 1994), p. 17.

15. Dick Morris, *The New Prince* (Los Angeles: Renaissance Books, 1999), pp. 75, 72.

16. Sidney Blumenthal, *The Permanent Campaign*. Rev. ed. (New York: Simon & Schuster, 1982), pp. 23, 24.

17. Blumenthal, *The Permanent Campaign,* p. 24. See also pp. 297–298.

18. See, for example, Theodore J. Lowi, *The Personal President* (Ithaca, NY: Cornell University Press, 1985).

19. David Gergen, *Eyewitness to Power: The Essence of Leadership* (New York: Simon & Schuster, 2000), p. 210.

20. Gergen, *Eyewitness to Power,* p. 348.

21. Blumenthal, *The Permanent Campaign,* p. 284.

22. Lawrence R. Jacobs and Robert Y. Shapiro, *Politicians Don't Pander* (Chicago: University of Chicago Press, 2000), pp. 45, 106, 136.

23. See, for example, Tulis, *The Rhetorical Presidency;* David Zarefsky, *Lincoln, Douglas, and Slavery: In the Crucible of Public Debate* (Chicago: University of Chicago Press, 1990); Craig Allen Smith and Kathy B. Smith, *The White House Speaks: Presidential Leadership as Persuasion* (Westport, CT: Praeger, 1994); Martin J. Medhurst, *Dwight D. Eisenhower: Strategic Communicator* (Westport, CT: Greenwood Press, 1993); Roderick P. Hart, *The Sound of Leadership: Presidential Communication in the Modern Age* (Chicago: University of Chicago Press, 1987); Karlyn Kohrs Campbell and Kathleen Hall Jamieson, *Deeds Done in Words: Presidential Rhetoric and the Genres of Governance* (Chicago: University of Chicago Press, 1990); Mary E. Stuckey, *Playing the Game: The Presidential Rhetoric of Ronald Reagan* (New York: Praeger, 1990); and Theodore Otto Windt, Jr., *Presidents and Protesters: Political Rhetoric in the 1960s* (Tuscaloosa: University of Alabama Press, 1990).

24. George C. Edwards III, "Presidential Rhetoric: What Difference Does It Make"? in *The Future of the Rhetorical Presidency,* ed. Martin J. Medhurst (College Station: Texas A&M University Press, 1996).

25. Quoted in Victor Gold, "George Bush Speaks Out," *The Washingtonian,* February 1994, p. 41.

26. Ronald Reagan, *An American Life* (New York: Simon & Schuster, 1990), p. 471.

27. Jacobs and Shapiro, *Politicians Don't Pander,* pp. 76, 81–83, 105, 115–116, 136, 149, 152.

28. Jacobs and Shapiro, *Politicians Don't Pander,* p. 115.

29. Jacobs and Shapiro, *Politicians Don't Pander,* pp. 115, 149.

30. Drew, *Showdown,* p. 66.

31. Quoted in Blumenthal, *The Permanent Campaign,* pp. 292–293.

32. George C. Edwards III, *At the Margins: Presidential Leadership of Congress* (New Haven, CT: Yale University Press, 1989), chapter 11.

33. See Sarah A. Binder, "The Dynamics of Legislative Gridlock, 1947–96," *American Political Science Review* 93 (September 1999): 519–533.

34. David W. Rohde, *Parties and Reform in the Postreform House* (Chicago: University of Chicago Press, 1991); John H. Aldrich and David W. Rohde, "The Consequences of Party Organization in the House: The Role of the Majority and Minority Parties in

Conditional Party Government," in *Polarized Politics: Congress and the President in a Partisan Era,* ed. Jon R. Bond and Richard Fleisher (Washington, DC: Congressional Quarterly Press, 2000).

35. Richard Fleisher and Jon R. Bond, "Partisanship and the President's Quest for Votes on the Floor of Congress," in *Polarized Politics: Congress and the President in a Partisan Era,* ed. Jon R. Bond and Richard Fleisher (Washington, DC: Congressional Quarterly Press, 2000).

36. Edwards, *At the Margins*; Jon R. Bond and Richard Fleisher, *The President in the Legislative Arena* (Chicago: University of Chicago Press, 1990).

37. Edwards, *At the Margins,* chapter 9; Bond and Fleisher, *President in the Legislative Arena,* chapter 8.

38. George C. Edwards III and Andrew Barrett, "Presidential Agenda Setting in Congress," in *Polarized Politics: Congress and the President in a Partisan Era,* ed. Jon R. Bond and Richard Fleisher (Washington, DC: Congressional Quarterly Press, 2000).

39. George C. Edwards III, Andrew Barrett, and Jeffrey Peake, "The Legislative Impact of Divided Government," *American Journal of Political Science* 41 (April 1997): 545–563; Sarah A. Binder, "The Dynamics of Legislative Gridlock, 1947–96," *American Political Science Review* 93 (September 1999): 519–533.

40. George C. Edwards III, *The Public Presidency* (New York: St. Martin's, 1983), pp. 83–93; Gregory N. Flemming, "Presidential Coattails in Open-Seat Elections," *Legislative Studies Quarterly* 20 (May 1995): 197–212.

41. Alan I. Abramowitz and Jeffrey A. Segal, *Senate Elections* (Ann Arbor: University of Michigan Press, 1992), pp. 121, 233, 238; Lonna Rae Atkeson and Randall W. Partin, "Economic and Referendum Voting: A Comparison of Gubernatorial and Senatorial Elections," *American Political Science Review* 89 (March 1995): 99–107; James E. Campbell and Joe A. Sumners, "Presidential Coattails in Senate Elections," *American Political Science Review* 84 (June 1990): 513–524.

42. See Jeffrey E. Cohen, Michael A. Krassa, and John A. Hamman, "The Impact of Presidential Campaigning on Midterm U.S. Senate Elections," *American Political Science Review* 85 (March 1991): 165–180.

43. Leon D. Epstein, *Political Parties in Western Democracies* (New York: Praeger, 1967).

44. Edwards, *At the Margins;* Bond and Fleisher, *President in the Legislative Arena.*

45. Kenneth E. Collier, *Between the Branches* (Pittsburgh, PA: University of Pittsburgh Press, 1997); Abraham Holtzman, *Legislative Liaison* (Chicago: Rand-McNally, 1970); Charles O. Jones, *The Trusteeship Presidency* (Baton Rouge: Louisiana State University Press, 1988); Stephen J. Wayne, *The Legislative Presidency* (New York: Harper & Row, 1978).

46. Edwards, *At the Margins;* Bond and Fleisher, *President in the Legislative Arena.*

47. Quoted in Michael Oreskes, "Approval of Bush, Bolstered by Panama, Soars in Poll," *New York Times,* January 19, 1990, p. A20.

48. Quoted in David E. Rosenbaum, "Clinton's Plan for Economy May Hinge on His Popularity," *New York Times,* April 29, 1993, p. A1.

49. Quoted in R. W. Apple, Jr., "Vote Against Crime Bill Is Lesson on Clout," *New York Times,* August 17, 1994, pp. A1, B6.

50. Alan P. Balutis, "The Presidency and the Press: The Expanding Presidential Image," *Presidential Studies Quarterly* 7 (Fall 1977): 244–251; Elmer E. Cornwell, Jr., "Presidential News: The Expanding Public Image," *Journalism Quarterly* 36 (Summer 1959): 275–283; Herbert J. Gans, *Deciding What's News* (New York: Vintage, 1979), p. 9; Michael B. Grossman and Martha J. Kumar, *Portraying the President* (Baltimore, MD: Johns Hopkins University Press, 1981), pp. 258–259, 265; Richard Davis, "News Coverage of American Political Institutions," paper presented of the annual meeting of the American Political Science Association, Washington, DC, August, 1986; Norman Ornstein and Michael Robinson, "The Case of Our Disappearing Congress," *TV Guide,* January 11, 1986, pp. 4–6, 8–10.

51. See George C. Edwards III, *Presidential Approval* (Baltimore, MD: Johns Hopkins University Press, 1990).

52. Collier, *Between the Branches,* p. 1.

53. Fred I. Greenstein, *The Hidden-Hand Presidency* (New York: Basic Books, 1982), p. 99.

54. Bryce Harlow, Oral History, Lyndon B. Johnson Library, Austin, TX, p. 53.

55. See, for example, Richard Rovere, *Affairs of State: The Eisenhower Years* (New York: Farrar, Strauss, 1956), pp. 261–262; Harry McPherson, *A Political Education* (Boston: Little, Brown, 1972), pp. 105–106.

56. Neil MacNeil, *Dirksen: Portrait of a Public Man* (New York: World, 1970), pp. 138, 142.

57. Lyndon B. Johnson, *The Vantage Point: Perspectives of the Presidency, 1963–1969* (New York: Popular Library, 1971), p. 443.

58. McPherson, *A Political Education,* pp. 246–247.

59. Richard M. Nixon, *In the Arena: A Memoir of Victory, Defeat and Renewal* (New York: Simon & Schuster, 1990), p. 282.

60. H. R. Haldeman, *The Haldeman Diaries: Inside the Nixon White House.* New York: G. P. Putnam's Sons, 1994), p. 532.

61. Richard M. Nixon, *RN: The Memoirs of Richard M. Nixon* (New York: Grosset and Dunlap, 1978), p. 753.

62. Quoted in William Safire, *Before the Fall: An Inside View of the Pre-Watergate White House* (New York: Doubleday, 1975), p. 284.

63. Quoted in Stephen E. Ambrose, *Nixon: The Triumph of a Politician, 1962–1972* (New York: Simon & Schuster, 1989), p. 287.

64. Kenneth Collier, "The President, the Public and Congress," paper delivered at the annual meeting of the Midwest Political Science Association, Chicago, April 6–8,1995, p. 6.

65. William E. Timmons, *Memorandum for the President,* December 31, 1973. Folder: "Executive-Legislative Relations—93rd Congress, 1st Session," William E. Timmons Files, Box 3, Gerald R. Ford Library, Ann Arbor, MI, p. 3.

66. Quoted in Peter Goldman, with Eleanor Clift and Thomas M. DeFrank, "Carter Up Close," *Newsweek,* May 2, 1977, p. 35. Also see the statement of Hamilton Jordan in the same article.

67. Quoted in Barry M. Hager, "Carter Seeks More Effective Use of Departmental Lobbyists' Skills," *Congressional Quarterly Weekly Report,* March 4, 1978, pp. 585.

68. Quoted in Tom Mathews, with Henry W. Hubbard, Rich Thomas, Eleanor Clift, and David Martin, "Slings and Arrows," *Newsweek,* July 31, 1978, p. 20.

69. Quoted in Sidney Blumenthal, "Marketing the President," *New York Times Magazine,* September 13,1981, p. 110.

70. Quoted in James A. Barnes, "White House Notebook: They Can Sell, but Can They Close?" *National Journal,* March 20, 1993, p. 712.

71. Quoted in Alison Mitchell, "Clinton Seems to Keep Running Though the Race Is Run and Won," *New York Times,* February 12, 1997, p. A12.

72. Jacobs and Shapiro, *Politicians Don't Pander,* pp. 104–105.

73. Dick Morris, *Behind the Oval Office* (New York: Random House, 1997), pp. 33, 324; Mitchell, "Clinton Seems to Keep Running Though the Race Is Run and Won."

74. Morris, *The New Prince,* p. 71.

75. News release, CBS News/*New York Times* Poll, October 30, 1986, tables 21, 27.

76. Glenn R. Parker, "Cycles in Congressional District Attention," *Journal of Politics* 42 (May 1980): 547.

77. William Schneider, "It's Payback Time for GOP and Press," *National Journal,* March 19, p. 696.

78. Walter D. Burnham, "Insulation and Responsiveness in Congressional Elections," *Political Science Quarterly* 90 (Fall 1975): 418; "1974 Support in Congress: Ford Low, Nixon Up," *Congressional Quarterly Weekly Report,* January 18, 1975, pp. 148.

79. John R. Alford and John R. Hibbing, "The Conditions Required for Economic Issue Voting: Actions Speak More Loudly than Partisan Affiliation," paper presented at the annual meeting of the Midwest Political Science Association, Chicago, April 1984.

80. Gary C. Jacobson, "The 1994 Midterm: Why the Models Missed It," *Extension of Remarks,* APSA Legislative Studies Section, 1994; David W. Brady, John F. Cogan, and Douglas Rivers, *How Republicans Captured the House: An Assessment of the 1994 Midterm Elections* (Stanford, CA: Hoover Institution, 1995).

81. Alan I. Abramowitz and Jeffrey A. Segal, *Senate Elections* (Ann Arbor: University of Michigan Press, 1992), pp. 121, 233, 238; Atkeson and Partin, "Economic and Referendum Voting."

82. Quoted in Paul C. Light, *The President's Agenda: Domestic Policy Choice from Kennedy to Carter (with Notes on Reagan)* (Baltimore, MD: Johns Hopkins University Press, 1983), p. xiii.

83. Kernell, *Going Public,* pp. 144–154.

84. Richard Neustadt, *Presidential Power and the Modern Presidents* (New York: Free Press, 1990), p. 264.

85. Quoted in Dom Bonafede, "The Strained Relationship," *National Journal,* May 19, 1979, p. 830.

86. Nigel Bowles, *The White House and Capitol Hill* (New York: Oxford University Press, 1987), pp. 99, 102, 104.

87. See Darrell M. West, "Activists and Economic Policymaking in Congress," *American Journal of Political Science* 32 (August 1988): 662–680; Gerald C. Wright, Jr., "Policy Voting in the U.S. Senate: Who Is Represented?" *Legislative Studies Quarterly* 14 (November 1989): 465–486; John W. Kingdon, *Congressmen's Voting Decisions* (New York: Harper & Row, 1973), p. 34; Warren E. Miller and Donald E. Stokes,

"Constituency Influences on Congress," *American Political Science Review* 57 (March 1963): 45–56; Lewis A. Dexter, "The Representative and His District," in *New Perspectives on the House of Representatives,* 2d ed., ed. Robert L. Peabody and Nelson W. Polsby (Chicago: Rand-McNally, 1969), p. 330; Duncan MacRae, *Dimensions of Congressional Voting* (Berkeley: University of California Press, 1958), p. 264; Aage R. Clausen, *How Congressmen Decide: A Policy Focus* (New York: St. Martin's, 1973), pp. 126–127, 182, 188; Morris P. Fiorina, *Representatives, Roll Calls, and Constituencies* (Lexington, MA: Lexington Books, 1974); Richard F. Fenno, Jr., *Home Style* (Boston: Little, Brown, 1978); John S. Stolarek, Robert M. Rood, and Marcia Whicker Taylor, "Measuring Constituency Opinion in the U.S. House: Mail Versus Random Surveys," *Legislative Studies Quarterly* 6 (November 1981): 589–595; Keith T. Poole and Howard Rosenthal, "The Polarization of American Politics," *Journal of Politics* 46 (November 1984): 1061–1074; Amihai Glazer and Marc Robbins, "Congressional Responsiveness to Constituency Change," *American Journal of Political Science* 29 (May 1985): 259–273; Gregory Markus, "Electoral Coalitions and Senate Roll-Call Behavior: An Ecological Analysis," *American Journal of Political Science* 18 (August 1974): 595–608; Bruce I. Oppenheimer, "Senators' Constituencies: Suggestions for Redefinition," paper presented at the annual meeting of the American Political Science Association, Chicago, September 1971; Christopher H. Achen, "Measuring Representation," *American Journal of Political Science* 22 (August 1978): 475–510; Charles S. Bullock III and David W. Brady, "Party, Constituency, and U.S. Senate Voting Behavior," paper presented at the annual meeting of the Southern Political Science Association, New Orleans, November 1977.

88. Martin P. Wattenberg, "The Democrats' Decline in the House During the Clinton Presidency: An Analysis of Partisan Swings," *Presidential Studies Quarterly* 29 (September 1999): 685–689.

89. See, for example, Edwards, *At the Margins,* chapter 6; Bond and Fleisher, *President in the Legislative Arena,* chapter 7.

90. Neustadt, *Presidential Power,* p. 78; Edwards, *At the Margins,* pp. 109–114.

91. Neustadt, *Presidential Power,* p. 74.

92. Neustadt, *Presidential Power,* pp. 75, 77.

Chapter 2. Presidential Persuasion, Part I

1. Theodore C. Sorensen, *Kennedy* (London: Hodder and Stoughton, 1965), p. 392.

2. George C. Edwards III, *At the Margins: Presidential Leadership of Congress* (New Haven, CT: Yale University Press, 1989).

3. Lee Sigelman, "Gauging the Public Response to Presidential Leadership," *Presidential Studies Quarterly* 10 (Summer 1980): 427–433. See also Pamela Johnston Conover and Lee Sigelman, "Presidential Influence and Public Opinion: The Case of the Iranian Hostage Crisis," *Social Science Quarterly* 63 (June 1982): 249–264.

4. Dan Thomas and Lee Sigelman, "Presidential Identification and Policy Leadership: Experimental Evidence on the Reagan Case," in *The Presidency and Public Policy Making,* ed. George C. Edwards III, Steven Y. Shull, and Norman C. Thomas (Pittsburgh: University of Pittsburgh Press, 1985), pp. 37–49. See also, a poll of Utah residents found that although two-thirds of them opposed deploying MX missiles in Utah and Nevada,

an equal number said they would either "definitely" or "probably" support President Reagan if he decided to go ahead and base the missiles in those states.

5. Lee Sigelman and Carol K. Sigelman, "Presidential Leadership of Public Opinion: From 'Benevolent Leader' to Kiss of Death?" *Experimental Study of Politics* 7 (No. 3, 1981): 1–22.

6. Jeffrey J. Mondak, "Source Cues and Public Approval: The Cognitive Dynamics of Public Support for the Reagan Administration," *American Journal of Political Science* 37 (February 1993): 186–212.

7. Roberta Glaros and Bruce Miroff, "Watching Ronald Reagan: Viewers' Reaction to the President on Television," *Congress and the Presidency* 10 (Spring 1983): 25–46.

8. George C. Edwards III, *The Public Presidency* (New York: St. Martin's, 1983); Theodore J. Lowi, *The Personal President* (Ithaca, NY: Cornell University Press, 1985).

9. Samuel Kernell, *Going Public,* 3d ed. (Washington, DC: Congressional Quarterly Press, 1997); Jeffrey K. Tulis, *The Rhetorical Presidency* (Princeton, NJ: Princeton University Press, 1987); Richard J. Ellis, *Presidential Lightning Rods: The Politics of Blame Avoidance* (Lawrence: University Press of Kansas, 1994); Edwards, *The Public Presidency*; Lawrence R. Jacobs and Robert Y. Shapiro, "Issues, Candidate Image, and Priming: The Use of Private Polls in Kennedy's 1960 Presidential Campaign," *American Political Science Review* 88 (September 1994): 527–540; Thomas Cronin, "The Presidency Public Relations Script," in *The Presidency Reappraised,* ed. Thomas E. Cronin and Rexford G. Tugwell (Praeger, 1974); William Lammers, "Presidential Attention-Focusing Activities," in *The President and the Public,* ed. Doris Graber (Institute for the Study of Human Issues, 1982); Bruce Miroff, "The Presidency and the Public: Leadership as Spectacle," in *The Presidency and the Political System,* 4th ed., ed. Michael Nelson (Washington, DC: Congressional Quarterly, 1995); Matthew A. Baum and Samuel Kernell, "Has Cable Ended the Golden Age of Presidential Television?" *American Political Science Review* 93 (March 1999): 99–114; John A. Hamman and Jeffrey E. Cohen, "Reelection and Congressional Support: Presidential Motives in Distributive Politics," *American Politics Quarterly* 25 (January 1997): 56–74; M. Stephen Weatherford, "The Interplay of Ideology and Advice in Economic Policy-Making: The Case of the Political Business Cycle," *Journal of Politics* 49 (November 1987): 925–952.

10. Michael B. Grossman and Martha J. Kumar, *Portraying the President* (Baltimore, MD: Johns Hopkins University Press, 1981); and John Anthony Maltese, *Spin Control: The White House Office of Communications and the Management of Presidential News* (Chapel Hill: University of North Carolina Press, 1992).

11. George C. Edwards III, *Presidential Approval* (Baltimore, MD: Johns Hopkins University Press, 1990); Richard A. Brody, *Assessing the President: The Media, Elite Opinion, and Public Support* (Stanford, CA: Stanford University Press, 1991); Samuel Kernell, "Explaining Presidential Popularity," *American Political Science Review* 72 (June 1978): 506–522; Donald R. Kinder, "Presidents, Prosperity, and Public Opinion," *Public Opinion Quarterly* 45 (Spring 1981): 1–21; George C. Edwards III, William Mitchell, and Reed Welch, "Explaining Presidential Approval: The Significance of Issue Salience," *American Journal of Political Science* (February 1995): 108–134; Richard Lau and David O. Sears, "Cognitive Links Between Economic Grievances and Political Responses," *Political Behavior* 3 (No. 4, 1981): 279–302; Jon A. Krosnick and Donald R.

Kinder, "Altering the Foundations of Support for the President through Priming," *American Political Science Review* 84 (June 1990): 497–512; Jon A. Krosnick and Laura A. Brannon, "The Impact of the Gulf War on the Ingredients of Presidential Evaluations: Multidimensional Effects of Political Involvement," *American Political Science Review* 87 (December 1993): 963–975; John E. Mueller, *War, Presidents, and Public Opinion* (New York: Wiley, 1970).

12. Lyn Ragsdale, "The Politics of Presidential Speechmaking, 1949–1980," *American Political Science Review* 78 (December 1984): 971–984. See also Lyn Ragsdale, "Presidential Speechmaking and the Public Audience: Individual Presidents and Group Attitudes," *Journal of Politics* 49 (August 1987): 704–736.

13. Paul Brace and Barbara Hinckley, *Follow the Leader* (New York: Basic Books, 1992), pp. 56.

14. Benjamin I. Page and Robert Y. Shapiro, "Presidential Leadership through Public Opinion," in *The Presidency and Public Policy Making,* ed. Edwards, Shull, and Thomas,, pp. 22–36; Benjamin I. Page, Robert Y. Shapiro, and Glenn R. Dempsey, "What Moves Public Opinion?" *American Political Science Review* 81 (March 1987): 23–44; Roy L. Behr and Shanto Iyengar, "Television News, Real-World Cues, and Changes in the Public Agenda," *Public Opinion Quarterly* 49 (Spring 1985): 38–57. Cohen (see below), however, found little effect of approval on public leadership.

15. See Samuel Kernell, "The Presidency and the People: The Modern Paradox," in *The Presidency and the Political System,* ed. Michael Nelson (Washington, DC: Congressional Quarterly Press, 1984), pp. 250–253; Lee Sigelman, "The Commander in Chief and the Public: Mass Response to Johnson's March 31, 1968 Bombing Halt Speech," *Journal of Political and Military Sociology* 8 (Spring 1980): 1–14.

16. Dennis M. Simon and Charles W. Ostrom, Jr., "The Impact of Televised Speeches and Foreign Travel on Presidential Approval," *Public Opinion Quarterly* 53 (Spring 1989): 58–82.

17. Jeffrey E. Cohen, *Presidential Responsiveness and Public Policy-Making* (Ann Arbor: University of Michigan Press, 1997).

18. Kim Quaile Hill, "The Policy Agendas of the President and the Mass Public: A Research Validation and Extension," *American Journal of Political Science* 42 (October 1998): 1328–1334.

19. Kernell, *Going Public.*

20. Eugene J. Rossi, "Mass and Attentive Opinion on Nuclear Weapons Tests and Fallout, 1954–1963," *Public Opinion Quarterly* 29 (Summer 1965): 280–297; Robert S. Erikson, Norman R. Luttbeg, and Kent L. Tedin, *American Public Opinion: Its Origins, Content, and Impact,* 2d ed. (New York: Wiley, 1980), p. 144; Mueller, *War, Presidents, and Public Opinion,* pp. 69–74; CBS News/*New York Times* Poll, October 28, 1983, p. 2; Benjamin I. Page and Robert Y. Shapiro, *The Rational Public* (Chicago: University of Chicago Press, 1992), p. 182; and Barry Sussman, "Reagan's Talk Gains Support for Policies," *Washington Post,* October 30, 1983, sec. A, pp. 1, 18. However, compare Page and Shapiro, *The Rational Public,* pp. 242, 250.

21. As reported in Bob Woodward, *The Agenda: Inside the Clinton White House* (New York: Simon & Schuster, 1994), pp. 248, 141.

22. Charles O. Jones, *Clinton and Congress, 1993–1996* (Norman: University of Oklahoma Press, 1999), pp. 90–91.

23. Matthew A. Baum and Samuel Kernell, "Economic Class and Popular Support for Franklin Roosevelt in War and Peace," *Public Opinion Quarterly* 65 (Summer 2001): 218, 223.

24. Quoted in Jack Nelson and Robert J. Donovan, "The Education of a President," *Los Angeles Times Magazine,* August 1, 1993, p. 14. See also "The President at Midterm," *USA Weekend,* November 4–6, 1994, p. 4.

25. "Democrats Look to Salvage Part of Stimulus Plan," *Congressional Quarterly Weekly Report,* April 24, 1993, pp. 1002–1003.

26. Michael Waldman, *POTUS Speaks* (New York: Simon & Schuster, 2000), p. 41.

27. "Health Care Reform: The Lost Chance," *Newsweek,* September 19, 1994, p. 32.

28. Woodward, *The Agenda*, p. 285.

29. "Switchboards Swamped with Calls over Tax Plan," *New York Times,* August 5, 1993, p. A18.

30. Greg M. Shaw and Robert Y. Shapiro, "The Polls—Trends: Poverty and Public Assistance," *Public Opinion Quarterly* 66 (Spring 2002): 105–128.

31. Caution is appropriate in interpreting the figures for the September 15 poll because only four hundred people were reinterviewed after the president's September 15 speech.

32. Gallup Poll, November 9, 1993.

33. See, for example, Waldman, *POTUS Speaks,* pp. 65–66.

34. See, for example, Waldman, *POTUS Speaks,* pp. 178, 220–221.

35. White House transcript of interview of President Clinton by WWWE Radio, Cleveland, October 24, 1994.

Chapter 3. Presidential Persuasion, Part II

1. "Reagan Bids Nation Farewell: 'We've Made a Difference,'" *Congressional Quarterly Weekly Report,* January 14, 1989, p. 95.

2. Haynes Johnson, *Sleepwalking Through History* (New York: Norton), p. 167.

3. Martin Anderson, *Revolution: The Reagan Legacy* (Stanford, CA: Hoover Institution Press, 1990), p. 7.

4. Anderson, *Revolution,* pp. xviii–xix.

5. Johnson, *Sleepwalking Through History,* p. 49. Johnson (p. 79) also argued that Reagan's election as governor of California in 1966, during the period of discord over the war in Vietnam, civil rights, and campus unrest, occurred because "through Reagan the public had a vehicle to express resentment at both national disorder and political leadership."

6. William A. Niskanen, *Reaganomics* (New York: Oxford University Press, 1988), p. 22.

7. James A. Stimson, *Public Opinion in America: Moods, Cycles, and Swings* (Boulder, CO: Westview, 1991), pp. 64, 126–127.

8. Benjamin I. Page and Robert Y. Shapiro, *The Rational Public* (Chicago: University of Chicago Press, 1992), pp. 127, 136.

9. James A. Davis, "Changeable Weather in a Cooling Climate," *Public Opinion Quarterly* 56 (Fall 1992): 261–306. In a survey of forty-two items in the General Social Survey from 1972 through 1989, Smith found that crime was the only issue that changed in a conservative direction.

10. William G. Mayer, *The Changing American Mind* (Ann Arbor: University of Michigan Press, 1992), p. 123.

11. Tom W. Smith, "Liberal and Conservative Trends in the United States Since World War II," *Public Opinion Quarterly* 54 (Winter 1990): 479–507. He also found that no general trend to more conservative opinion occurred in 1970s.

12. Martin P. Wattenberg, *The Rise of Candidate-Centered Politics* (Cambridge, MA: Harvard University Press, 1991), chapter 4.

13. Ronald Reagan, *An American Life* (New York: Simon & Schuster, 1990), pp. 471, 479; Richard Sobel, ed., *Public Opinion in U.S. Foreign Policy: The Controversy over Contra Aid* (Lanham, MD: Rowman and Littlefield, 1993); Page and Shapiro, *The Rational Public,* p. 276. See also CBS News/*New York Times* Poll, December 1, 1986, table 5; CBS News/*New York Times* Poll (news release, October 27, 1987), table 17; "Americans on Contra Aid: Broad Opposition," *New York Times,* January 31, 1988, sec. 4, p. 1.

14. Reagan, *An American Life,* p. 479.

15. Memo from Richard Wirthlin to Ronald Reagan, April 10, 1985. My thanks to Lawrence R. Jacobs and Robert Y. Shapiro for sharing a copy of the memo.

16. This may have been the result of the military buildup that did occur, but the point remains that while Reagan wanted to continue to increase defense spending, the public was unresponsive to his wishes. Larry M. Bartels, "The American Public's Defense Spending Preferences in the Post–Cold War Era," *Public Opinion Quarterly* 58 (Winter 1994): 479–508; Seymour Martin Lipset, "Beyond 1984: The Anomalies of American Politics," *PS* 19 (1986): 229; Mayer, *The Changing American Mind,* pp. 51, 62, 133. See also "Defense," *Gallup Report,* May 1987, pp. 2–3; "Opinion Outlook," *National Journal,* June 13, 1987, p. 1550; CBS News/*New York Times* Poll, October 27, 1987, table 15.

17. This view is articulated in Christopher Wlezien, "Dynamics of Representation: The Case of U.S. Spending on Defense," *British Journal of Political Science* 26 (January 1996): 81–103.

18. Michael K. Deaver, *A Different Drummer: My Thirty Years with Ronald Reagan* (New York: HarperCollins, 2001), p. 154.

19. George P. Shultz, *Turmoil and Triumph* (New York: Scribner's, 1993), p. 339.

20. Larry Speakes, *Speaking Out: The Reagan Presidency From Inside the White House* (New York: Avon Books, 1988), p. 198.

21. Edwin Meese III, *With Reagan: The Inside Story* (Washington, DC: Regnery Gateway, 1992), p. 220.

22. Page and Shapiro, *The Rational Public,* pp. 271–281; John E. Reilly, ed., *American Public Opinion and U.S. Foreign Policy 1987* (Chicago: Chicago Council on Foreign Relations, 1987), chapters 5, 6; Mayer, *The Changing American Mind,* chapters 4, 6.

23. Lipset, "Beyond 1984," pp. 228–229; Mayer, *The Changing American Mind,* chapters 5, 6; Page and Shapiro, *The Rational Public,* pp. 133, 136, 159; William Schneider, "The Voters' Mood 1986: The Six-Year Itch," *National Journal,* December 7, 1985, p. 2758. See also "Supporting a Greater Federal Role," *National Journal,* April 18, 1987,

p. 924; "Opinion Outlook," *National Journal,* April 18, 1987, p. 964; "Federal Budget Deficit," *Gallup Report,* August 1987, pp. 25, 27; Davis, "Changeable Weather in a Cooling Climate." See also CBS News/*New York Times* Poll, October 27, 1987, tables 16, 20; Robert Y. Shapiro and John T. Young, "Public Opinion and the Welfare State: The United States in Comparative Perspective," *Political Science Quarterly* 104 (Spring 1989): 59–89.

24. See, for example, Robert F. Durant, *The Administrative Presidency Revisited* (Albany, NY: SUNY Press, 1992); Dan B. Wood, "Principals, Bureaucrats, and Responsiveness in Clean Air Enforcement," *American Political Science Review* 82 (March 1988): 213–234.

25. See, for example, John A. Fleishman, "Trends in Self-identified Ideology from 1972 to 1982: No Support for the Salience Hypothesis," *American Journal of Political Science* 30 (1986); pp. 517–541; Martin P. Wattenberg, "From a Partisan to a Candidate-centered Electorate," in *The New American Political System,* ed. Anthony King (Washington, DC: American Enterprise Institute, 1990), pp. 169–171; Wattenberg, *The Rise of Candidate-Centered Politics,* pp. 95–101.

26. Stimson, *Public Opinion in America*, pp. 64, 126–127.

27. Mayer, *The Changing American Mind,* p. 127.

28. David Gergen, *Eyewitness to Power: The Essence of Leadership* (New York: Simon & Schuster, 2000), p. 220.

29. Memorandum by Richard Wirthlin, May 9, 1985. My thanks to Lawrence R. Jacobs and Robert Y. Shapiro for a copy of the memo.

30. Wirthlin Poll, May 6–8, 1985.

31. CBS News/*New York Times* polls of May 6, 1985, and May 29–June 2, 1985.

32. "Do you feel that President Reagan has told the public everything he knows about the Iran-Contra affair or that he is holding back certain information?" in polls of January 16–19, 1987, and August 24–September 2, 1987.

33. Ivor Crewe, "Values: The Crusade that Failed," in *The Thatcher Effect: A Decade of Change,* ed. Dennis Kavanagh and Anthony Seldon (Oxford: Oxford University Press, 1989), p. 241. See also Ivor Crewe, "Has the Electorate Become Thatcherite?" in *Thatcherism,* ed. Robert Skidelsky (London: Chatto and Windus, 1988); Ivor Crewe and Donald Searing, "Ideological Change in the British Conservative Party," in *American Political Science Review* 82 (June 1988): 361–384.

34. Ivor Crewe and Donald Searing, "Mrs. Thatcher's Crusade: Conservatism in Britain, 1972–1986," in *The Resurgence of Conservatism in Anglo-American Democracies,* ed. B. Cooper, Allan Kornberg, and William Mishler (Durham, NC: Duke University Press, 1988).

35. John Rentoul, *Me and Mine: The Triumph of the New Individualism* (London: Unwin Hyman, 1989), p. 158.

36. John Curtice, "Interim Report: Party Politics," in *British Social Attitudes: The 1987 Report,* ed. Roger Jowell, Sharon Witherspoon, and Lindsay Brook (Aldershot Hants, UK: SCPR/Gower, 1986), chapter 8, 171–182. See also John Curtice, "Political Partisanship," in *British Social Attitudes: The 1986 Report,* ed. Roger Jowell, Sharon Witherspoon, and Lindsay Brook (Aldershot Hants, UK: SCPR/Gower, 1986), chapter 3, 39–53.

37. Robert Y. Shapiro and John T. Young, "Public Opinion and the Welfare State: The United States in Comparative Perspective," *Political Science Quarterly* 104 (Spring 1989): 59–89.

38. Quoted in R. W. Apple, "Bush Sure-Footed on Trail of Money," *New York Times,* September 29, 1990, p. 8. See also Reed L. Welch, "Tuning In or Tuning Out: The Influence of Televised Presidential Addresses on Public Opinion," unpublished Ph.D. dissertation, Texas A&M University, 1997.

39. Wirthlin memo to President Reagan on April 20, 1985.

40. Robert S. Erikson, Michael B. MacKuen, and James A. Stimson, *The Macro Polity* (New York: Cambridge University Press, 2002), pp. 219, 369.

41. Page and Shapiro, *The Rational Public,* chapter 7.

Chapter 4. Charisma and Personality

1. A search of the Lexis-Nexis database identified more than three thousand stories during 1999–2000 in U.S. newspapers in which the adjective "charismatic" was applied to someone.

2. Romans, Chapter 12, and 1 Corinthians, Chapter 12.

3. Rudolf Sohm, *Kirchenrecht,* Vols. 1 and 2 (Leipzig: Duncker and Humboldt, 1892).

4. Max Weber, *Economy and Society,* Vol. 1, ed. Guenther Roth and Claus Wittich (New York: Bedminster Press, 1968), pp. 212–301; Max Weber, *Economy and Society,* Vol. 3, ed. Guenther Roth and Claus Wittich (New York: Bedminster Press, 1968), pp. 1112, 941–1211.

5. Weber, *Economy and Society,* Vol. 1, p. 245. See also Weber, *Economy and Society,* Vol. 3, p. 1117. Weber treated the concept of charisma in an explicitly value-free fashion, emphasizing the nature of the authority relationship rather than the direction in which the charismatic figure led. See, for example, Weber, *Economy and Society,* Vol. 1, pp. 241–242; Weber, *Economy and Society,* Vol. 3, p. 1112. The lack of normative emphasis distressed some later commentators. See Carl J. Friedrich, "Political Leadership and the Problem of Charismatic Power," *Journal of Politics* 23 (February 1961): 3–24.

6. Weber, *Economy and Society,* Vol. 1, p. 242.

7. Weber, *Economy and Society,* Vol. 1, p. 242; Weber, *Economy and Society,* Vol. 3, pp. 1112–1114.

8. Weber, *Economy and Society,* Vol. 3, p. 1113; see also pp. 1111–1112.

9. Weber, *Economy and Society,* Vol. 1, p. 241.

10. Weber, *Economy and Society,* Vol. 1, p. 247.

11. Weber, *Economy and Society,* Vol. 1, pp. 246–254; Weber, *Economy and Society,* Vol. 3, pp. 1121–1148.

12. Ann Ruth Willner, *The Spellbinders: Charismatic Political Leadership* (New Haven: Yale University Press, 1984), pp. 14–15.

13. Willner, *The Spellbinders,* p. 60.

14. James MacGregor Burns, *Leadership* (New York: Harper & Row, 1978), pp. 243–244.

15. Burns, *Leadership*, p. 244.

16. Charles Lindholm, *Charisma* (Cambridge, MA: Basil Blackwell, 1990), p. 7.

17. David Aberbach, *Charisma in Politics, Religion and the Media* (New York: New York University Press, 1996), p. 16. See also p. 7.

18. A point made in Max Weber, *On Charisma and Institution Building*, ed. S. N. Eisenstadt (Chicago: University of Chicago Press, 1968), p. xxii.

19. See, for example, D. L. Cohen, "The Concept of Charisma and the Analysis of Leadership," *Political Studies* 20 (No. 3, 1972): 299–305; and Peter L. Berger, "Charisma and Religious Innovation: The Social Location of Israelite Prophecy," *American Sociological Review* 28 (December 1963): 940–950.

20. This point is nicely made in William Spinrad, "Charisma: A Blighted Concept and an Alternative Formula," *Political Science Quarterly* 106 (Summer 1991): 295–311.

21. See, for example, K. J. Ratnam, "Charisma and Political Leadership," *Political Studies* 12 (No. 3, 1964): 341–354; and Cohen, "The Concept of Charisma and the Analysis of Leadership."

22. Arthur Schweitzer, *The Age of Charisma* (Chicago: Nelson Hall, 1984), pp. 6, 8.

23. David E. Apter, "Nkrumah, Charisma, and the Coup," *Daedalus* 97 (Summer 1968): 763. Moreover, Nkrumah's charisma applied only to a small band of followers who accepted his hortatory language.

24. Richard R. Fagen, "Charismatic Authority and the Leadership of Fidel Castro," *Western Political Quarterly* 18 (June 1965): 275–284.

25. Aberbach, *Charisma in Politics, Religion and the Media*, pp. 2–3.

26. Robert C. Tucker, "The Theory of Charismatic Leadership," *Daedalus* 97 (Summer 1968): 744; Robert C. Tucker, *Politics as Leadership* (Columbia: University of Missouri Press, 1981), pp. 95–96.

27. Douglas Madsen and Peter G. Snow, *The Charismatic Bond: Political Behavior in Time of Crisis* (Cambridge, MA: Harvard University Press, 1991), pp. 21–23.

28. Aberbach, *Charisma in Politics, Religion and the Media*, pp. 4, 7.

29. Willner, *The Spellbinders*, chapter 2.

30. Willner, *The Spellbinders*, p. 8.

31. Ernest R. House, *Jesse Jackson and the Politics of Charisma* (Boulder, CO: Westview, 1988), pp. 118–119, chapters 10–11.

32. Bernard M. Bass, *Handbook of Leadership*, 3d ed. (New York: Free Press, 1990), chapter 12.

33. See, for example, Bass, *Handbook of Leadership*, pp. 198–201; Jay A. Conger, Rabindra N. Kanungo, and associates *Charismatic Leadership* (San Francisco: Jossey-Bass, 1988); Jay A. Conger, *The Charismatic Leader: Behind the Mystique of Exceptional Leadership* (San Francisco: Jossey-Bass, 1989); Jay A. Conger and Rabindra N. Kanungo, "Toward a Behavioral Theory of Charismatic Leadership in Organizational Settings," *Academy of Management Review* 12 (No. 4, 1987): 637–647.

34. Lindholm, *Charisma*, p. 6.

35. Edward B. Portis, "Charismatic Leadership and Cultural Democracy," *The Review of Politics* 49 (Spring 1987), p. 241.

36. Schweitzer, *The Age of Charisma*.

37. Edward A. Shils, "Charisma, Order, and Status," *American Sociological Review* 30 (April 1965): 199–213; Edward A. Shils, *The Constitution of Society* (Chicago: University of Chicago Press, 1982), chapter 5.

38. Clifford Geertz, "Centers, Kings, and Charisma: Reflections on the Symbolics of Power," in *Culture and Its Creators,* ed. Joseph Ben-David and Terry Nichols Clark (Chicago: University of Chicago Press, 1977).

39. Amitai Etzioni, *A Comparative Analysis of Complex Organizations* (New York: Free Press, 1961), chapters 9–10.

40. Barbara Kellerman, "Leadership as a Political Act," in *Leadership: Multidisciplinary Perspectives,* ed. Barbara Kellerman (Englewood Cliffs, NJ: Prentice-Hall, 1984), p. 83.

41. Peter Dennis Bathory, "Leadership in the Twentieth Century: Private Language and Public Power," in *Leadership in America: Consensus, Corruption, and Charisma,* ed. Peter Dennis Bathory (New York: Longman, 1978), p. 47.

42. Aberbach, *Charisma in Politics, Religion and the Media.*

43. James G. Hunt, "Organizational Leadership: The Contingency Paradigm and Its Challenges," in *Leadership: Multidisciplinary Perspectives,* ed. Barbara Kellerman (Englewood Cliffs, NJ: Prentice-Hall, 1984), pp. 113–138, especially pp. 132–134.

44. Peter F. Drucker, *The New Realities* (New York: Harper & Row, 1989), p. 108.

45. Madsen and Snow, *The Charismatic Bond.*

46. Madsen and Snow, *The Charismatic Bond,* p. 54.

47. Madsen and Snow, *The Charismatic Bond,* pp. 76–77.

48. Madsen and Snow, *The Charismatic Bond,* chapter 3.

49. Madsen and Snow, *The Charismatic Bond,* chapter 4.

50. For one effort at this, see Willner, *The Spellbinders,* p. 61.

51. Tucker, "The Theory of Charismatic Leadership," p. 737.

52. Arthur H. Miller, Martin P. Wattenberg, and Oksana Malanchuk, "Schematic Assessments of Presidential Candidates," *American Political Science Review* 80 (June 1986): 521–540.

53. Miller, Wattenberg, and Malanchuk, "Schematic Assessments of Presidential Candidates."

54. Martin P. Wattenberg, "Why Clinton Won and Dukakis Lost," *Party Politics* 1 (No. 2, 1995): 248.

55. Burns, *Leadership,* p. 54.

56. Charles P. Cell, "Charismatic Heads of State: The Social Context," *Behavior Science Research* 9 (No. 4, 1974): 255–305.

57. Tom Wicker, *One of Us* (New York: Random House, 1991), p. 251.

58. Bruce Miroff, "John F. Kennedy: The Claim of Excellence," in *Leadership in America: Consensus, Corruption, and Charisma,* ed. Peter Dennis Bathory (New York: Longman, 1978), pp. 163–175.

59. Arthur M. Schlesinger, Jr., *The Politics of Hope* (Cambridge, MA: Houghton Mifflin, 1963), pp. 10–11.

60. National Election Studies.

61. Matthew A. Baum and Samuel Kernell, "From 'Dr. New Deal' to 'Dr. Win-the-War': Assessing the Constituency Foundations of Franklin Roosevelt's Popular Support,"

paper presented at the annual meeting of the Midwest Political Science Association, Chicago, April 15–17, 1999, pp. 17–18.

62. Quoted in Samuel Kernell, *Going Public,* 3d ed. (Washington, DC: Congressional Quarterly Press, 1997), p. 145.

63. Kernell, *Going Public,* p. 146.

64. Kernell, *Going Public,* p. 146.

65. Kernell, *Going Public,* p. 147.

66. Quoted in "Tax Cut Passed by Solid Margin in House, Senate," *Congressional Quarterly Weekly Report,* August 1, 1981, p. 1374. See also Kernell, *Going Public,* pp. 150–151.

67. Kernell, *Going Public,* p. 169–170. See also p. 146.

68. Kernell, *Going Public,* p. 149.

69. Quoted in William Greider, "The Education of David Stockman," *Atlantic,* December 1981, p. 51.

70. David Stockman, *The Triumph of Politics* (New York: Harper & Row, 1986), pp. 208–209, 214–215, 251, 253, 260–261, 264–265. See also "White House's Lobbying Apparatus . . . Produces Impressive Tax Vote Victory," *Congressional Quarterly Weekly Report,* August 1, 1981, pp. 1372–1373.

71. Laurence I. Barrett, *Gambling with History* (New York: Penguin, 1984), pp. 160–161; Greider, "The Education of David Stockman," p. 50.

72. Marc A. Bodnick, "'Going Public' Reconsidered: Reagan's 1981 Tax and Budget Cuts, and Revisionist Theories of Presidential Power," *Congress and the Presidency* 17 (Spring 1990): 13–28.

73. See "Reagan's Legislative Strategy Team Keeps His Record of Victories Intact," *National Journal,* June 26, 1982, p. 1130.

74. *Gallup Report,* November 1981, No. 194, pp. 3–8.

75. Kernell, *Going Public,* p. 152.

76. *Gallup Report,* November 1981, No. 194, p. 9.

77. ABC News/*Washington Post* Poll, August 12, 1987.

78. Kernell, *Going Public,* p. 169.

79. Doris Kearns Goodwin, "FDR's Fireside Chats," *Media Studies Journal* 14 (Winter 2000), p. 76.

80. Richard Hofstadter, *The American Political Tradition* (New York: Vintage, 1954), p. 316.

81. Matthew A. Baum and Samuel Kernell, "Economic Class and Popular Support for Franklin Roosevelt in War and Peace," *Public Opinion Quarterly* 65 (Summer 2001): 198–229.

82. See Elmer E. Cornwell, Jr., *Presidential Leadership of Public Opinion* (Bloomington: Indiana University Press, 1965), pp. 262–263. Cornwell reports the other instances of FDR pointedly discussing pending legislation as social security, holding company legislation, and some other items on April 28, 1935; a program he had just sent to Congress to cope with the then-current recession on April 14, 1938; and wartime economic stabilization legislation on April 28, 1942. The president never obtained majority support for his court-packing bill. See Gregory A. Caldeira, "Public Opinion and the U.S. Supreme Court: FDR's Court-Packing Plan," *American Political Science Review* 81 (December 1987): 81–82.

83. John C. Donovan, "Congressional Isolationists and Roosevelt Foreign Policy," *World Politics* 3 (April 1951): 316.

84. *Gallup Opinion Index,* November 1978, pp. 8–9.

85. Interview with Richard Wirthlin, Princeton, NJ, April 4, 1987.

86. William C. Adams, "Recent Fables about Ronald Reagan," *Public Opinion,* October/November 1984, pp. 7–8; Austin Ranney, "Reagan's First Term," in *The American Elections of 1984,* ed. Austin Ranney (Washington, DC: American Enterprise Institute, 1985), pp. 33–34. See also Barry Sussman, "Reagan's Policies are the Key—Not His Personality," *Washington Post Weekly Edition,* February 13, 1984, p. 37.

87. Everett Carll Ladd, "Is Election '84 Really a Class Struggle?" *Public Opinion,* April/May 1984, pp. 42–43.

88. George C. Edwards III, "Comparing Chief Executives," *Public Opinion,* June/July 1985, p. 51. There were no data on Richard Nixon during the Watergate period.

89. Martin P. Wattenberg, *The Rise of Candidate-Centered Politics* (Cambridge, MA: Harvard University Press, 1991), p. 90.

90. Richard E. Neustadt, *Presidential Power and the Modern Presidents* (New York: Free Press, 1990), p. 79.

91. For example, see "Reagan and the Contras," CBS News/*New York Times* Poll, news release, August 25, 1987, table 8.

92. George C. Edwards III, *The Public Presidency* (New York: St. Martin's Press, 1983), pp. 239, 243.

93. Gallup News Service, *Poll Release,* October 21, 1999.

94. Dick Morris, *The New Prince* (Los Angeles: Renaissance Books, 1999), p. 211.

Chapter 5. The Politics of Veneration

1. Forrest McDonald, *The American Presidency: An Intellectual History* (Lawrence: University Press of Kansas, 1994), pp. 209, 253.

2. Joseph J. Ellis, *Founding Brothers* (New York: Knopf, 2001), p. 121.

3. Barry Schwartz, *George Washington: The Making of an American Symbol* (New York: Free Press, 1987), p. 14.

4. Schwartz, *George Washington,* pp. 6, 13, 17.

5. Schwartz, *George Washington,* pp. 18–20.

6. James Thomas Flexner, *George Washington and the New Nation, 1783–1793* (Boston: Little, Brown, 1969), pp. 422–423.

7. Schwartz, *George Washington,* pp. 18, 20.

8. Schwartz, *George Washington,* p. 32.

9. Paul K. Longmore, *The Invention of George Washington* (Berkeley: University of California Press, 1988), pp. 184, 200, 203–204, 208–210, 294; Schwartz, *George Washington,* pp. 81–89.

10. Longmore, *The Invention of George Washington,* p. 207.

11. Schwartz, *George Washington,* pp. 115–117.

12. Schwartz, *George Washington,* especially pp. 17, 20, 73–89, 97, 192–193.

13. Schwartz, *George Washington,* pp. 16, 18.

14. Schwartz, *George Washington,* p. 191.

15. Forrest McDonald, *The Presidency of George Washington* (Lawrence: University Press of Kansas, 1974), p. 25; James Thomas Flexner, *George Washington in the American Revolution, 1775–1783* (Boston: Little, Brown, 1967), p. 550.

16. Longmore, *The Invention of George Washington,* pp. 181–183.

17. Schwartz, *George Washington,* pp. 24–28, 44; Garry Wills, *Cincinnatus: George Washington and the Enlightenment* (Garden City, NY: Doubleday, 1984).

18. Flexner, *George Washington and the New Nation,* pp. 161–196; Michael P. Riccards, *A Republic, If You Can Keep It: The Foundation of the American Presidency, 1700–1800* (New York: Greenwood Press, 1987), pp. 65–75.

19. Marvin Kitman, *George Washington's Expense Account* (New York: Harper & Row, 1988).

20. See Schwartz, *George Washington,* chapter 7; Flexner, *George Washington in the American Revolution,* p. 550.

21. James Hart, *The American Presidency in Action, 1789* (New York: Macmillan, 1948), chapter 3, especially pp. 57, 66–67.

22. Flexner, *George Washington and the New Nation,* pp. 221–222, 248, 251, 398–399; McDonald, *The Presidency of George Washington,* pp. 78, 186; James Thomas Flexner, *George Washington: Anguish and Farewell, 1793–1799* (Boston: Little, Brown, 1969), pp. 133–135, 138, 142, 152; Glenn A. Phelps, "George Washington: Precedent Setter," in *Inventing the American Presidency,* ed. Thomas E. Cronin (Lawrence: University Press of Kansas, 1989), pp. 265, 268.

23. McDonald, *The Presidency of George Washington,* p. 24. McDonald suggests that Washington did not really understand the funding issue.

24. McDonald, *The Presidency of George Washington,* chapter 2; Riccards, *A Republic, If You Can Keep It,* p. 86.

25. McDonald, *The Presidency of George Washington,* pp. 64–65, 185. See also Flexner, *George Washington and the New Nation,* pp. 240, 248, 251, 278–283, 308–309; and Riccards, *A Republic, If You Can Keep It,* p. 97.

26. Flexner, *George Washington: Anguish and Farewell,* pp. 207–209, 229; and McDonald, *The Presidency of George Washington,* pp. 165, 185–186.

27. Schwartz, *George Washington,* p. 45.

28. McDonald, *The Presidency of George Washington,* p. 114.

29. Flexner, *George Washington and the New Nation,* p. 295.

30. Riccards, *A Republic, If You Can Keep It,* pp. 112–113, 115, 166, 169, 173.

31. Phelps, "George Washington," p. 278; Riccards, *A Republic, If You Can Keep It,* p. 116.

32. Riccards, *A Republic, If You Can Keep It,* p. 119.

33. Flexner, *George Washington: Anguish and Farewell,* pp. 199–201.

34. Forrest McDonald, *Alexander Hamilton* (New York: Norton, 1979), p. 203.

35. McDonald, *The Presidency of George Washington,* p. 24; Flexner, *George Washington and the New Nation,* p. 164; Phelps, "George Washington," p. 266.

36. Flexner, *George Washington and the New Nation,* p. 168. The term *pivot* is from Washington's undelivered address he prepared for his first inauguration. In it he wrote

that the election of Congress was the "pivot on which turns the first Wheel of government; a Wheel which communicates motion to all the rest." See John C. Fitzpatrick, ed., *The Writings of George Washington From the Original Manuscript Sources, 1745–1799,* Vol. 30 (Westport, CT: Greenwood Press, 1970), pp. 299–300.

37. See, for example, Phelps, "George Washington," p. 65.

38. Stephen Decatur, Jr., *Private Affairs of George Washington from the Records and Accounts of Tobias Lear, Esquire, His Secretary* (Boston: Houghton-Mifflin 1933), p. 134; Riccards, *A Republic, If You Can Keep It,* p. 106.

39. Hart, *The American Presidency in Action,* p. 77.

40. Flexner, *George Washington and the New Nation,* p. 221. His citations are composed of a short reference to the delicacy of introducing specific legislation in Congress in a memo that is otherwise not concerned with the separation of powers and an ambiguous sentence in Washington's diary entry of May 7, 1790. See John C. Fitzpatrick, ed., *The Writings of George Washington From the Original Manuscript Sources, 1745–1799,* Vol. 31 (Westport, CT: Greenwood Press, 1970), p. 493; and John C. Fitzpatrick, ed., *The Diaries of George Washington, 1748–1799,* Vol. 4 (Boston: Houghton-Mifflin, 1925), p. 128.

41. Wilbourn E. Benton, ed., *1787: Drafting the U.S. Constitution,* Vol. II (College Station: Texas A&M Press, 1986), pp. 1094–1309.

42. Max Farrand, ed., *The Records of the Federal Convention of 1787,* Vol. II (New Haven, CT: Yale University Press, 1966), p. 587.

43. See Fitzpatrick, ed., *The Writings of George Washington,* Vol. 29, p. 410; Fitzpatrick, ed., *The Writings of George Washington,* Vol. 30, pp. 300–301; and Fitzpatrick, ed., *The Writings of George Washington,* Vol. 35, pp. 228–229. See also Fitzpatrick, ed., *The Writings of George Washington,* Vol. 31, p. 493; and Fitzpatrick, ed., The *Diaries of George Washington,* p. 128.

44. See, for example, Ralph L. Ketcham, *Presidents Above Party: The First American Presidency, 1789–1829* (Chapel Hill: University of North Carolina Press, 1984), p. 90.

45. Phelps, "George Washington," pp. 261, 263–265, 269–273, 275–278; Riccards, *A Republic, If You Can Keep It,* p. 104; Hart, *The American Presidency in Action,* chapter 4.

46. See, for example, Riccards, *A Republic, If You Can Keep It,* pp. 190–191.

47. See, for example, Robert Scigliano, *The Supreme Court and the Presidency* (New York: Free Press, 1971), pp. 63–64, 67, 70–71; Phelps, "George Washington," p. 272; Flexner, *George Washington and the New Nation,* p. 399.

48. See, for example, Flexner, *George Washington and the New Nation,* pp. 215–218; Hart, *The American Presidency in Action,* pp. 87–96.

49. Decatur, *Private Affairs of George Washington,* pp. 58–60. Flexner doubts that Washington actually went to the Senate. See Flexner, *George Washington and the New Nation,* p. 224.

50. Edmund S. Morgan, *The Genius of George Washington* (New York: Norton, 1980), p. 6.

51. Flexner, *George Washington and the New Nation,* p. 403.

52. Flexner, *George Washington and the New Nation,* pp. 215–218.

53. Decatur, *Private Affairs of George Washington,* pp. 58–60.

54. John F. Hoadley, *Origins of American Political Parties, 1789–1803* (Lexington: University Press of Kentucky, 1986).

55. Hoadley, *Origins of American Political Parties,* pp. 140, 176. See also Riccards, *A Republic, If You Can Keep It,* p. 131.

56. Hoadley, *Origins of American Political Parties,* p. 137.

57. Flexner, *George Washington: Anguish and Farewell,* pp. 277–278; and McDonald, *The Presidency of George Washington,* p. 164.

58. Ketcham discusses in *Presidents Above Party* the ideal of the patriot leader above faction that was widely held in the late-eighteenth century.

59. Flexner, *George Washington and the New Nation,* p. 382; McDonald, *The Presidency of George Washington,* p. 78. See also Flexner, *George Washington: Anguish and Farewell,* p. 328.

60. McDonald, *The Presidency of George Washington,* p. 65.

61. Riccards, *A Republic, If You Can Keep It,* pp. 119, 143.

62. Flexner, *George Washington: Anguish and Farewell,* pp. 255, 276.

63. Phelps, "George Washington," pp. 277–278.

64. Quoted in P. Bradley Nutting, "'Tobias Lear, S.P.U.S.': First Secretary to the President," *Presidential Studies Quarterly* 34 (Fall 1994): 715–716.

65. Wills, *Cincinnatus,* pp. 102–105.

66. Decatur, *Private Affairs of George Washington,* pp. 78–79, 201, 212; Riccards, *A Republic, If You Can Keep It,* p. 102.

67. Decatur, *Private Affairs of George Washington,* pp. 47, 67, 298.

68. Riccards, *A Republic, If You Can Keep It,* pp. 130–131.

69. Riccards, *A Republic, If You Can Keep It,* p. 158.

70. Riccards, *A Republic, If You Can Keep It,* p. 107.

71. Schwartz, *George Washington,* pp. 54, 69–73. See also Riccards, *A Republic, If You Can Keep It,* pp. 176–177, 186–187.

72. Graham G. Dodds, "George Washington: The Origins of Presidential–Press Relations," in *George Washington and the Origins of the American Presidency,* ed. Mark J. Rozell, William D. Pederson, and Frank J. Williams (Westport, CT: Praeger, 2000), pp. 189–191; Flexner, *George Washington and the New Nation,* p. 251; and Carol Sue Humphrey, "George Washington and the Press," in *George Washington and the Origins of the American Presidency,* ed. Mark J. Rozell, William D. Pederson, and Frank J. Williams (Westport, CT: Praeger, 2000), p. 162.

73. Quoted in McDonald, *The Presidency of George Washington,* pp. 132–133. The quotation from the *National Gazette* is from March 2, 1792, and the quotation from the *New-York Journal* is from December 7, 1792.

74. Graham G. Dodds, "George Washington: The Origins of Presidential–Press Relations," p. 189

75. McDonald, *The Presidency of George Washington,* p. 132. See also McDonald, *The American Presidency,* p. 212.

76. Flexner, *George Washington: Anguish and Farewell,* pp. 217, 245–247. See also Humphrey, "George Washington and the Press," pp. 164–165; and Dodds, "George Washington: The Origins of Presidential–Press Relations," p. 192.

77. Flexner, *George Washington: Anguish and Farewell,* pp. 280–281.

78. Schwartz, *George Washington,* pp. 39, 190–191.

79. See Jeffrey K. Tulis, *The Rhetorical Presidency* (Princeton, NJ: Princeton University Press, 1987).

80. Flexner, *George Washington: Anguish and Farewell,* p. 291.

81. See, for example, McDonald, *The Presidency of George Washington,* pp. 169–174.

82. Hoadley, *Origins of American Political Parties,* pp. 137–138; Riccards, *A Republic, If You Can Keep It,* pp. 178–179. There was some concern in the House that it would be worse to defeat the treaty than accept unpopular provisions.

83. See McDonald, *The Presidency of George Washington,* p. 38.

84. See Riccards, *A Republic, If You Can Keep It,* pp. 110–111; Hart, *The American Presidency in Action,* pp. 131–133; Charles A. Beard, *The Economic Origins of Jeffersonian Democracy* (New York: Macmillan, 1915), chapter 3.

85. Riccards, *A Republic, If You Can Keep It,* pp. 177, 181. The representative who broke the tie in Washington's favor, Frederick Muhlenberg, a previously vocal opponent of the treaty, was stabbed by his own brother-in-law, a rabid Democratic-Republican, a few days later, and was defeated in the next election.

86. Decatur, *Private Affairs of George Washington,* pp. 52, 258; Flexner, *George Washington and the New Nation,* pp. 196, 313

87. See Hart, *The American Presidency in Action,* p. 130.

88. Flexner, *George Washington and the New Nation,* pp. 196–197, 201–202, 283–284, 313; Flexner, *George Washington: Anguish and Farewell,* pp. 15, 70, 330.

89. Phelps, "George Washington," pp. 273–275. See also Riccards, *A Republic, If You Can Keep It,* pp. 121–123, 159.

90. Riccards, *A Republic, If You Can Keep It,* pp. 98, 134, 161.

91. McDonald, *The Presidency of George Washington,* p. 186.

92. McDonald, *The Presidency of George Washington,* p. 28.

93. Wills, *Cincinnatus,* p. 130.

94. McDonald, *The Presidency of George Washington,* p. 107.

Chapter 6. Disseminating the Message

1. James E. Anderson, *Public Policy and Politics in America* (North Scituate, MA: Duxbury, 1978); Frank Baumgartner and Bryan D. Jones, *Agendas and Instability in American Politics* (Chicago: University of Chicago Press, 1993); Roger W. Cobb and Charles D. Elder, *Participation in American Politics: The Dynamics of Agenda-Building* (Boston: Allyn and Bacon, 1972); Anthony Downs, "Up and Down with Ecology: The Issue Attention Cycle" *Public Interest* 28 (1972): 38–50; Roy B. Flemming, John Bohte, and B. Dan Wood, "One Voice Among Many: The Supreme Court's Influence on Attentiveness to Issues in the United States, 1947–1990," *American Journal of Political Science* 41 (October 1997): 1224–1250; Charles O. Jones, *The Presidency in a Separated System* (Washington, DC: Brookings Institution, 1994); John Kingdon, *Agendas, Alternatives, and Public Policies,* 2d ed. (Boston: Little, Brown, 1995); Paul C. Light, *The President's Agenda,* 3d ed. (Baltimore, MD: Johns Hopkins University Press, 1999); B. Guy Peters and Brian W. Hogwood, "In Search of the Issue-Attention Cycle," *Journal of Politics* 47 (Feb-

ruary 1985): 238–253; Jack L. Walker, "Setting the Agenda in the U.S. Senate: A Theory of Problem Selection," *British Journal of Political Science* 7 (October 1977): 433–445.

2. See, for example, Samuel P. Huntington, "Congressional Responses to the Twentieth Century," in *The Congress and America's Future,* 2d ed., ed. David B. Truman (Englewood Cliffs, NJ: Prentice-Hall, 1965); Ronald C. Moe and Steven C. Teel, "Congress as a Policymaker: A Necessary Reappraisal," *Political Science Quarterly* 85 (September 1970): 443–470.

3. Kingdon, *Agendas, Alternatives, and Public Policies,* p. 23.

4. Baumgartner and Jones, *Agendas and Instability in American Politics,* p. 241.

5. An exception is Jeffrey E. Cohen, "Presidential Rhetoric and Agenda Setting," *American Journal of Political Science* 39 (February 1995): 87–107, who found that the president was able to influence the *public's* agenda through State of the Union messages.

6. "U.S. Dependence on Foreign Oil," *Gallup Poll Monthly,* February 1991, p. 35.

7. CBS News/*New York Times* Poll, June 24, 1986, table 9.

8. CBS News/*New York Times* Poll, October 22–24, 1995.

9. Philip E. Converse, "The Nature of Belief Systems in Mass Publics," in *Ideology and Discontent,* ed. David Apter (New York: Free Press, 1964), pp. 206–261.

10. Charles W. Ostrom, Jr., and Dennis M. Simon, "The President's Public," *American Journal of Political Science* 32 (November 1988): 1096–1119.

11. David Gergen, *Eyewitness to Power: The Essence of Leadership* (New York: Simon & Schuster, 2000), pp. 54, 186.

12. Gergen, *Eyewitness to Power,* p. 54.

13. Gergen, *Eyewitness to Power,* p. 54

14. Lee Sigelman and Cynthia Whissell, " 'The Great Communicator' and 'The Great Talker' on the Radio: Projecting Presidential Personas," *Presidential Studies Quarterly* 32 (March 2002): 137–146.

15. Sigelman and Whissell, " 'The Great Communicator' and 'The Great Talker' on the Radio."

16. See Jones, *The Presidency in a Separated System,* chapter 5.

17. On continuity in foreign policy despite changes in the occupant of the presidency, see William J. Dixon and Stephen M. Gardner, "Presidential Succession and the Cold War: An Analysis of Soviet-American Relations, 1948–1988," *Journal of Politics* 54 (February 1992): 156–175.

18. Quoted in John C. Donovan, *The Politics of Poverty,* 2d ed. (Indianapolis, IN: Pegasus, 1973), p. 111.

19. Baumgartner and Jones, *Agendas and Instability in American Politics.*

20. Kingdon, *Agendas, Alternatives, and Public Policies,* pp. 34–42.

21. Flemming, Bohte, and Wood, "One Voice Among Many."

22. See, for example, Adam Clymer, "Majority in Poll Expect Congress to Cut Spending," *New York Times,* November 17, 1985, sec. 1, p. 1.

23. Quoted in Paul C. Light, *The President's Agenda: Domestic Policy Choice from Kennedy to Carter* (Baltimore, MD: Johns Hopkins University Press, 1982), p. 54. See also Robert Shogan, *Promises to Keep* (New York: Thomas Y. Crowell, 1977), p. 205.

24. See, for example, Jacqueline Calmes, "The 99th Congress: A Mixed Record of Success," *Congressional Quarterly Weekly Report* 44 (October 25, 1986): 2647.

25. Tim Groeling and Samuel Kernell, "Congress, the President, and Party Competition via Network News," in *Polarized Politics,* ed. Jon R. Bond and Richard Fleisher (Washington, DC: Congressional Quarterly Press, 2000), pp. 85–93.

26. Benjamin I. Page and Robert Y. Shapiro, *The Rational Public* (Chicago: University of Chicago Press, 1992), pp. 12–13.

27. Fay Lomax Cook, Tom R. Tyler, E. G. Goetz, M. T. Gordon, D. Protess, D. Leff, and H. L. Molotch, "Media and Agenda-Setting: Effects on the Public, Interest Group Leaders, Policy Makers, and Policy," *Public Opinion Quarterly* 47 (Spring 1983): 16–35; James W. Dearing and Everett M. Rogers, *Agenda Setting* (Thousand Oaks, CA: Sage, 1996); William Gonzenbach, *The Media, the President, and Public Opinion: A Longitudinal Analysis of the Drug Issue, 1984–1991* (Mahwah, NJ: Lawrence Erlbaum, 1996); Shanto Iyengar, Mark D. Peters, and Donald R. Kinder, "Experimental Demonstrations of the 'Not-So-Minimal' Consequences of Television News Programs," *American Political Science Review* 76 (December 1982): 848–858; Michael Bruce MacKuen and Steven Lane Coombs, *More than News* (Beverly Hills, CA: Sage, 1981), chapters 3–4; Maxwell McCombs and George Estrada, "The News Media and the Pictures in Our Heads," in *Do the Media Govern? Politicians, Voters, and Reporters in America,* ed. Shanto Iyengar and Richard Reeves (Thousand Oaks, CA: Sage, 1997); Maxwell McCombs and Donald Shaw, "The Evolution of Agenda Setting Research: Twenty-five Years in the Marketplace of Ideas," *Journal of Communication* 43 (Spring 1993): 58–67; David L. Protess and Maxwell McCombs, eds., *Agenda Setting: Readings on Media, Public Opinion, and Policymaking* (Hillsdale, NJ: Lawrence Erlbaum, 1991); James P. Winter and Chaim H. Eyal, "Agenda-Setting for the Civil Rights Issue," *Public Opinion Quarterly* 45 (Fall 1981): 376–383; Doris A. Graber, "Agenda-Setting: Are there Women's Perspectives?" in *Women and the News,* ed. Laurily Epstein (New York: Hastings House, 1978), pp. 15–37; Lawrence R. Jacobs and Robert Y. Shapiro, *Politicians Don't Pander* (Chicago: University of Chicago Press, 2000), pp. 232–233.

28. Doris A. Graber, *Mass Media and American Politics,* 6th ed. (Washington, DC: Congressional Quarterly Press, 2002), p. 207.

29. Martin Linsky, *Impact: How the President Affects Federal Policymaking* (New York: W. W. Norton, 1986), p. 87.

30. See George C. Edwards III and Stephen J. Wayne, *Presidential Leadership,* 6th ed. (New York: St. Martin's, 2002), chapter 5.

31. Michael B. Grossman and Martha J. Kumar, *Portraying the President* (Baltimore, MD: Johns Hopkins University Press, 1981); John A. Maltese, *Spin Control: The White House Office of Communications and the Management of Presidential News* (Chapel Hill: University of North Carolina Press, 1992); Mark J. Rozell, *The Press and the Ford Presidency* (Ann Arbor: University of Michigan Press, 1992); Mark J. Rozell, *The Press and the Bush Presidency* (Westport, CT: Praeger, 1996).

32. Sheldon Gilberg, Chaim Eyal, Maxwell McCombs, and David Nicholas, "The State of the Union Address and the Press Agenda," *Journalism Quarterly* 57 (Winter 1980): 584–588.

33. Wayne Wanta, Mary Ann Stephenson, Judy VanSlyke Turk, and Maxwell E. McCombs, "How President's State of Union Talk Influenced News Media Agendas," *Journalism Quarterly* 66 (Autumn 1989): 537–541.

34. B. Dan Wood and Jeffrey S. Peake, "The Dynamics of Foreign Policy Agenda Setting," *American Political Science Review* 92 (March 1998): 173–184.

35. George C. Edwards III and B. Dan Wood, "Who Influences Whom? The President, Congress, and the Media," *American Political Science Review* 93 (June 1999): 327–344. See also Jacobs and Shapiro, *Politicians Don't Pander,* pp. 201–202.

36. Mark Hertsgaard, *On Bended Knee: The Press and the Reagan Presidency* (New York: Farrar, Straus, and Giroux, 1988), pp. 107–108; Larry Speakes, *Speaking Out* (New York: Scribner's, 1988), p. 301.

37. Jacobs and Shapiro, *Politicians Don't Pander,* p. 140, agree with this point.

38. Grossman and Kumar, *Portraying the President,* pp. 99–100; see also p. 314.

39. Jason DeParle, "Moynihan Says Clinton Isn't Serious About Welfare Reform," *New York Times,* January 8, 1994, p. 8.

40. The president seemed to recognize this in an interview during the summer of 1993. See Jack Nelson and Robert J. Donovan, "The Education of a President," *Los Angeles Times Magazine,* August 1, 1993, p. 39.

41. Quoted in Thomas L. Friedman and Maureen Dowd, "Amid Setbacks, Clinton Team Seeks to Shake Off the Blues," *New York Times,* April 25, 1993, sec. 1, p. 12.

42. Quoted in Gerald M. Boyd, "Rethinking a Tax Plan Strategy," *New York Times,* June 12, 1985, sec. A, p. 14.

43. Quoted in Dick Kirschten, "For Reagan Communication Team . . . It's Strictly One Week at a Time," *National Journal,* March 8, 1986, p. 594.

44. See, for example, Michael Waldman, *POTUS Speaks* (New York: Simon & Schuster, 2000), pp. 42–43.

45. Quoted in Jann S. Wenner and William Greider, "President Clinton," *Rolling Stone,* December 9, 1993, p. 80.

46. Bob Woodward, *The Agenda: Inside the Clinton White House* (New York: Simon & Schuster, 1994) p. 241; comments by Clinton White House chiefs of staff Leon Panetta and Erskine Bowles on the importance of focusing the president's message at the *Forum on the Role of the White House Chief of Staff,* Washington, DC, June 15, 2000.

47. Thomas L. Friedman, "Scholars' Advice and New Campaign Help the President Hit His Old Stride," *New York Times,* November 17, 1993, p. A10; Nelson and Donovan, "The Education of a President," p. 14.

48. "Excerpts from Clinton's Question and Answer Session in the Rose Garden," *New York Times,* May 28, 1993, p. A10. See also David S. Broder and Dan Balz, "Clinton Finds Change Harder than Expected," *Washington Post,* May 14, 1993, p. A11.

49. Nelson and Donovan, "The Education of a President," p. 14.

50. See, for example, Jacobs and Shapiro, *Politicians Don't Pander,* pp. 286–287.

51. Waldman, *POTUS Speaks,* p. 224.

52. Waldman, *POTUS Speaks,* p. 219.

53. Waldman, *POTUS Speaks,* p. 268.

54. John H. Kessel, *Presidents, the Presidency, and the Political Environment* (Washington, DC: Congressional Quarterly Press, 2001), p. 64.

55. Waldman, *POTUS Speaks,* p. 268.

56. See, for example, Project for Excellence in Journalism, *The First 100 Days: How*

Bush Versus Clinton Fared in the Press (Washington, DC: Project for Excellence in Journalism, 2001).

57. Quoted in Jann S. Wenner, "Bill Clinton: The Rolling Stone Interview," *Rolling Stone,* December 28, 2000–January 4, 2001, p. 91.

58. Gallup Poll of September 24–26, 1993.

59. Gallup Poll of October 28–30, 1993.

60. Quoted in "For Health Care, Time Was a Killer," *New York Times,* August 29, 1994, p. A8.

61. Jacobs and Shapiro, *Politicians Don't Pander,* pp. 114, 142.

62. Jacobs and Shapiro, *Politicians Don't Pander,* p. 112–152.

63. Quoted in Wenner, "Bill Clinton," p. 102.

64. Jacobs and Shapiro, *Politicians Don't Pander,* p. 124, chapter 4.

Chapter 7. Framing the Message

1. Quoted in "MX Debate: It's Not Over," *New York Times,* March 30, 1985, pp. 1, 8. See also "Senate Hands Reagan Victory on MX Missile," *Congressional Quarterly Weekly Report,* March 23, 1985, pp. 515–523.

2. Quoted in Gerald M. Boyd, " 'General Contractor' of the White House Staff," *New York Times,* March 4, 1986, sec. A, p. 22.

3. See, for example, Daniel Kahneman, Paul Slovic, and Amos Tversky, *Judgment Under Uncertainty: Heuristics and Biases* (New York: Cambridge University Press, 1982); Arthur Lupia, "Shortcuts versus Encyclopedias: Information and Voting Behavior in California Insurance Reform Elections," *American Political Science Review* 88 (March 1994): 63–76; Herbert A. Simon, "A Behavioral Model of Rational Choice," *Quarterly Journal of Economics* 69 (February 1955): 99–118; Samuel L. Popkin, *The Reasoning Voter* (Chicago: University of Chicago Press, 1991); Paul M. Sniderman, Richard Brody, and Philip E. Tetlock, *Reasoning and Choice* (New York: Cambridge University Press, 1991).

4. E. Tory Higgins and Gary A. King, "Accessibility of Social Constructs: Information-Processing Consequences of Individual and Contextual Variation," in *Personality, Cognition, and Social Interaction,* ed. N. Cantor and J. F. Kihlstrom (Hillsdale, NJ: Erlbaum, 1981); Robert S. Wyer, Jr., and Jon Hartwick, "The Recall and Use of Belief Statements as Bases for Judgments," *Journal of Experimental Social Psychology* 20 (January 1984): 65–85; Thomas K. Srull and Robert S. Wyer, Jr., *Memory and Cognition in Their Social Context* (Hillsdale, NJ: Erlbaum, 1989); Thomas K. Srull and Robert S. Wyer, Jr., "The Role of Category Accessibility in the Interpretation of Information about Persons: Some Determinants and Implications," *Journal of Personality and Social Psychology* 37 (No. 10, 1979): 1660–1672; Thomas K. Srull and Robert S. Wyer, Jr., "Category Accessibility and Social Perception: Some Implications for the Study of Person Memory and Interpersonal Judgments," *Journal of Personality and Social Psychology* 38 (No. 6, 1980): 841–856; Richard R. Lau, "Construct Accessibility and Electoral Choice," *Political Behavior* 11 (March 1989): 5–32.

5. Philip E. Converse, "The Nature of Belief Systems in Mass Publics," in *Ideology and Discontent,* ed. David E. Apter (New York: Free Press, 1964).

6. John R. Zaller, *The Nature and Origins of Mass Opinion* (New York: Cambridge University Press, 1992), pp. 42–48; James H. Kuklinski and Norman Hurley, "On Hearing and Interpreting Messages: A Cautionary Tale of Citizen Cue-Taking," *Journal of Politics* 56 (August 1994): 729–751; Jeffrey Mondak, "Source Cues and Policy Approval: The Cognitive Dynamics of Public Support for the Reagan Agenda," *American Journal of Political Science* 37 (February 1993): 186–212.

7. See, for example, William A. Gamson and Andre Modigliani, "The Changing Culture of Affirmative Action," in *Research in Political Sociology,* Vol. 3, ed. Richard D. Braungart (Greenwich, CT: JAI Press, 1987), p. 143; William A. Gamson and Andre Modigliani, "Media Discourse and Public Opinion on Nuclear Power: A Constructionist Approach," *American Journal of Sociology* 95 (July 1989): 1–37; William A. Gamson, *Talking Politics* (Cambridge, UK: Cambridge University Press, 1992); Donald R. Kinder and Lynn M. Sanders, *Divided by Color: Racial Politics and Democratic Ideals* (Chicago: University of Chicago Press, 1996); and Zhongdang Pan and Gerald M. Kosicki, "Framing Analysis: An Approach to News Discourse," *Political Communication* 10 (No. 1, 1993): 55–75.

8. For the latter view that framing does not work by altering the accessibility to different considerations, see James N. Druckman, "On the Limits of Framing Effects: Who Can Frame?" *Journal of Politics* 63 (November 2001): 1041–1066. See also Thomas E. Nelson, Rosalee A. Clawson, and Zoe M. Oxley, "Media Framing of a Civil Liberties Conflict and Its Effect on Tolerance," *American Political Science Review* 91 (September 1997): 567–584; and Joanne M. Miller and Jon A. Krosnick, "News Media Impact on the Ingredients of Presidential Evaluations: Politically Knowledgeable Citizens Are Guided by a Trusted Source," *American Journal of Political Science* 44 (April 2000): 301–315.

9. Over the past generation, the research on public opinion has produced a large number of studies showing the effect of framing on people's opinions. For evidence of the impact of framing effects, see Stanley Feldman and John Zaller, "The Political Culture of Ambivalence: Ideological Responses to the Welfare State," *American Journal of Political Science* 36 (February 1992): 268–307; Donald R. Kinder and Lynn M. Sanders, "Mimicking Political Debate with Survey Questions: The Case of White Opinion on Affirmative Action for Blacks," *Social Cognition* 8 (No. 1, 1990): 73–103; Donald R. Kinder and Lynn M. Sanders, *Divided by Color: Racial Politics and Democratic Ideals* (Chicago: University of Chicago Press, 1996); Thomas E. Nelson and Donald R. Kinder, "Issue Frames and Group-Centrism in American Public Opinion," *Journal of Politics* 58 (November 1996): 1055–1078; Nelson, Clawson, and Oxley, "Media Framing of a Civil Liberties Conflict and Its Effect on Tolerance"; Thomas E. Nelson, Rosalee A. Clawson, and Zoe M. Oxley, "Toward a Psychology of Framing Effects," *Political Behavior* 19 (September 1997): 221–246; Thomas E. Nelson and Zoe M. Oxley, "Issue Framing Effects on Belief Importance and Opinion," *Journal of Politics* 61 (November 1999): 1040–1067; John Zaller and Stanley Feldman, "A Simple Theory of the Survey Response: Answering Questions versus Revealing Preferences," *American Journal of Political Science* 36 (August 1992): 579–616; Amos Tversky and Daniel Kahneman, "The Framing of Decisions and the Psychology of Choice," *Science* 211 (30 January 1981): 453–458; Dennis Chong, "How People Think, Reason, and Feel about Rights and Liber-

ties," *American Journal of Political Science* 37 (August 1993): 867–899; William G. Jacoby, "Issue Framing and Public Opinion on Government Spending," *American Journal of Political Science* 44 (October 2000): 750–767; Daniel Kahneman and Amos Tversky, "Choices, Values, and Frames," *American Psychologist* 39 (April 1984): 341–350; Daniel Kahneman and Amos Tversky, "Rational Choice and the Framing of Decisions," in *Rational Choice: The Contrast between Economics and Psychology,* ed. Hillel J. Einhorn and Robin M. Hogarth (Chicago: University of Chicago Press, 1987); Jon A. Krosnick and Donald R. Kinder, "Altering the Foundations of Support for the President through Priming," *American Political Science Review* 84 (June 1990): 497–512; Joseph N. Cappella and Kathleen Hall Jamieson, *Spiral of Cynicism: The Press and the Public Good* (New York: Oxford University Press, 1997); John H. Aldrich, John Sullivan, and Eugene Borgida, "Foreign Affairs and Issue Voting: Do Presidential Candidates Waltz Before a Blind Audience?" *American Political Science Review* 83 (March 1989): 123–141; W. Russell Neuman, Marion K. Just, and Ann N. Crigler, *Common Knowledge: News and the Construction of Political Meaning* (Chicago: University of Chicago Press, 1992); Nicholas A. Valentino, Vincent L. Hutchings, and Ismail K. White, "Cues that Matter: How Political Ads Prime Racial Attitudes During Campaigns," *American Political Science Review* 96 (March 2002): 75–90.

10. For a good discussion of this point, see Lawrence R. Jacobs and Robert Y. Shapiro, *Politicians Don't Pander* (Chicago: University of Chicago Press, 2000), pp. 49–52.

11. See, for example, William B. Riker, *The Art of Political Manipulation* (New Haven, CT: Yale University Press, 1986); William B. Riker, "The Heresthetics of Constitution Making: The Presidency in 1787, with Comments on Determinism and Rational Choice," *American Political Science Review* 78 (March 1984): 1–16.

12. Byron E. Shafer and William J. M. Claggett, *The Two Majorities: The Issue Context of Modern American Politics* (Baltimore, MD: Johns Hopkins University Press, 1995).

13. John R. Petrocik, "Divided Government: Is It All in the Campaigns?" in *The Politics of Divided Government,* ed. Gary W. Cox and Samuel Kernell (Boulder, CO: Westview Press, 1991); John R. Petrocik, "Issue Ownership in Presidential Elections, with a 1980 Case Study," *American Journal of Political Science* (August 1996): 825–850.

14. Andrew Gelman and Gary King, "Why Are American Presidential Elections Campaign Polls So Variable When Votes Are So Predictable?" *British Journal of Political Science* 23 (Part 4, 1993): 409–451.

15. See, for example, Carl Albert, interview by Dorothy Pierce McSweeny, April 13, 1969, interview 3, transcript, pp. 8–9, Lyndon Johnson Library, Austin, TX.

16. See, for example, Richard P. Nathan, Charles F. Adams, Jr., and associates, *Revenue Sharing: The Second Round* (Washington: Brookings Institution, 1977).

17. These examples are discussed by Kathleen Hall Jamieson, *Eloquence in an Electronic Age* (New York: Oxford University Press, 1988), pp. 127–133.

18. For discussions of attempts at framing, see Murray Edelman, *The Symbolic Uses of Politics* (Urbana: University of Illinois Press, 1964); Murray Edelman, *Politics as Symbolic Action* (Chicago: Markham, 1971); Murray Edelman, *Political Language: Words that Succeed and Policies that Fail* (New York: Academic Press, 1977); Gamson and Modigliani, "The Changing Culture of Affirmative Action"; Gamson and Modigliani,

"Media Discourse and Public Opinion on Nuclear Power"; Gamson, *Talking Politics;* William A. Gamson and Katherine E. Lasch, "The Political Culture of Social Welfare Policy," in *Evaluating the Welfare State,* ed. Shimon E. Spiro and Ephraim Yuchtman-Yaar (New York: Academic Press, 1983).

19. See, for example, Dan Quayle, *Standing Firm* (New York: HarperCollins, 1994), p. 94; Charles Kolb, *White House Daze* (New York: Free Press, 1994).

20. David Gergen, *Eyewitness to Power: The Essence of Leadership* (New York: Simon & Schuster, 2000), p. 348.

21. Quoted in Steven V. Roberts, "Return to the Land of the Gipper," *New York Times,* March 9, 1988, p. A28.

22. Ronald Reagan, *Where's the Rest of Me? The Autobiography of Ronald Reagan* (New York: Karz, 1965), p. 138.

23. "Democrats Look to Salvage Part of Stimulus Plan," *Congressional Quarterly Weekly Report,* April 24, 1993, p. 1002.

24. Bob Woodward, *The Agenda: Inside the Clinton White House* (New York: Simon & Schuster, 1994), pp. 243, 247–248.

25. "Pollster: Mistakes Made," *Bryan–College Station Eagle,* May 23, 1993, p. A8.

26. Woodward, *The Agenda,* pp. 226–227. See also p. 241, 247–248, 250.

27. Jann S. Wenner and William Greider, "President Clinton," *Rolling Stone,* December 9, 1993, p. 43.

28. Woodward, *The Agenda,* p. 313.

29. An exception to the experimental nature of framing studies is Jacoby, "Issue Framing and Public Opinion on Government Spending." He employed National Election Studies data to present both frames to the same sample. Even here, however, the framing occurred in the context of an interview in which different frames were presented at different times.

30. Zaller, *The Nature and Origins of Mass Opinion,* p. 99, chapter 9.

31. See Paul M. Sniderman and Sean M. Theriault, "The Dynamics of Political Argument and the Logic of Issue Framing," paper presented at the annual meeting of the Midwest Political Science Association, Chicago, 1999. See also Paul M. Sniderman, "Taking Sides: A Fixed Choice Theory of Political Reasoning," in *Elements of Reason: Understanding and Expanding the Limits of Political Rationality,* ed. Arthur Lupia, Mathew D. McCubbins, and Samuel L. Popkin (New York: Cambridge University Press, 2000).

32. Donald P. Haider-Markel and Mark R. Joslyn, "Gun Policy, Opinion, Tragedy, and Blame Attribution: The Conditional Influence of Issue Frames," *Journal of Politics* 63 (May 2001): 520–543.

33. John Zaller, "Elite Leadership of Mass Opinion: New Evidence from the Gulf War," in *Taken by Storm: The Media, Public Opinion, and U.S. Foreign Policy in the Gulf War,* ed. W. Lance Bennett and David L. Paletz (Chicago: University of Chicago Press, 1994), pp. 186–209.

34. W. Russell Neuman, *The Paradox of Mass Politics; Knowledge and Opinion in the American Electorate* (Cambridge, MA: Harvard University Press, 1986), pp. 170, 172, 177–178, 186.

35. Converse, "The Nature of Belief Systems in Mass Publics"; William G. Jacoby,

"The Sources of Liberal-Conservative Thinking: Education and Conceptualization," *Political Behavior* 10 (No. 4, 1988): 316–332; Robert C. Luskin, "Measuring Political Sophistication," *American Journal of Political Science* 31 (November 1987): 856–899; Neuman, *The Paradox of Mass Politics;* Edward G. Carmines and James A. Stimson, "The Two Faces of Issue Voting," *American Political Science Review* 74 (March 1980): 78–91; Zaller, *The Nature and Origins of Mass Opinion,* p. 48.

36. James H. Kuklinski, Paul J. Quirk, Jennifer Jerit, David Schwieder, and Robert F. Rich, "Misinformation and the Currency of Democratic Citizenship," *Journal of Politics* 62 (August 2000): 790–816.

37. Zaller, *The Nature and Origins of Mass Opinion,* pp. 102–113.

38. Zaller, "Elite Leadership of Mass Opinion"; Zaller, *The Nature and Origins of Mass Opinion.*

39. See, for example, James H. Kuklinski and Norman L. Hurley, "On Hearing and Interpreting Political Messages: A Cautionary Tale of Citizen Cue-Taking," *Journal of Politics* 56 (August 1994): 729–751.

40. Druckman, "On the Limits of Framing Effects: Who Can Frame?" See also Miller and Krosnick, "News Media Impact on the Ingredients of Presidential Evaluations."

41. "Reagan Loses Ground on 'Contra' Aid Program," *Congressional Quarterly Weekly Report,* March 8, 1986, pp. 535–536.

42. Steven V. Roberts, "Senate Upholds Arms for Saudis, Backing Reagan," *New York Times,* June 6, 1986, sec. A, pp. 1, 10. The thirty-four votes did sustain the president's veto, however.

43. Kuklinski, et al., "Misinformation and the Currency of Democratic Citizenship"; Robert C. Luskin, James S. Fishkin, and Roger Jowell, "Considered Opinions: Deliberative Polling in the UK," unpublished manuscript, University of Texas at Austin.

44. Woodward, *The Agenda,* pp. 110–111, 171–172, 235, 245, 314–315, 325.

45. Woodward, *The Agenda,* p. 171.

46. Woodward, *The Agenda,* p. 165.

47. Gallup Poll of September 24–26, 1993.

48. For a discussion of the administration's efforts to employ priming, see Jacobs and Shapiro, *Politicians Don't Pander,* pp. 76, 102–116, 284.

49. Darrell M. West and Diane J. Heith, "Harry and Louise Go to Washington: Political Advertising and Health Care Reform," paper presented at the annual meeting of the American Political Science Association, New York, September 1–4, 1994, p. 10.

50. Gallup Polls of August 8–9, 1994, and August 15–16, 1994.

51. Quoted in Adam Clymer, "Poll Finds Public Is Still Doubtful Over Costs of Clinton Health Plan," *New York Times,* March 15, 1994, p. A1.

52. "Health Care Reform: The Lost Chance," *Newsweek,* September 19, 1994, pp. 28–32. The *Newsweek* Poll of September 8–9, 1994, found that 28 percent of the public wanted health care reform passed in 1994, while 66 percent preferred to start over again the next year. See also "Will Reform Bankrupt Us?" *Newsweek,* August 15, 1994, p. 51.

53. This was a finding in a poll taken by White House pollster Stanley Greenberg for the Democratic Leadership Council. Discussed in Richard L. Berke, "Centrist Democrats' Poll Warns Clinton of Unrest," *New York Times,* November 18, 1994, p. A10.

54. "As NAFTA Countdown Begins, Wheeling, Dealing Intensifies," *Congressional Quarterly Weekly Report,* November 13, 1993, p. 3104.

55. David E. Rosenbaum, "Both Sides Emphasize Stakes of the Trade Vote," *New York Times,* November 15, 1993, p. C16.

56. Quoted in R. W. Apple, Jr., "A High Stakes Gamble That Paid Off," *New York Times,* November 18, 1993, p. A14.

57. Woodrow Wilson quoted in William Small, *To Kill a Messenger: Television News and the Real World* (New York: Hastings, 1970), p. 221.

58. President Carter, quoted in Michael Baruch Grossman and Martha Joynt Kumar, "Carter, Reagan, and the Media: Have the Rules Really Changed or the Poles of the Spectrum of Success?," paper presented at the Annual Meeting of the American Political Science Association, New York, September 3–6, 1981, p. 8.

59. "Campaign 2000 Final: How TV News Covered the General Election Campaign," *Media Monitor* 14 (November/December 2000); Stephen J. Farnsworth and S. Robert Lichter, *The Nightly News Nightmare* (Lanham, MD: Rowman and Littlefield, 2003), pp. 80–82.

60. Farnsworth and Lichter, *The Nightly News Nightmare,* p. 172.

61. Project for Excellence in Journalism, *The First 100 Days: How Bush Versus Clinton Fared in the Press* (Washington, DC: 2001).

62. Thomas E. Patterson, *Doing Well and Doing Good* (Cambridge, MA: Shorenstein Center, 2000), pp. 2–5.

63. Sam Donaldson, quoted in "Washington Press Corps," *Newsweek,* May 25, 1981, p. 90.

64. Quoted in Michael B. Grossman and Martha J. Kumar, *Portraying the President* (Baltimore, MD: Johns Hopkins University Press, 1981), p. 26.

65. Kathleen Hall Jamieson and Joseph N. Capella, "The Role of the Press in the Health Care Reform Debate of 1993–1994," in Doris Graber, Denis McQuail, and Pippa Norris, eds., *The Politics of News, The News of Politics* (Washington, DC: Congressional Quarterly Press, 1998), pp. 118–119.

66. Quoted in Grossman and Kumar, *Portraying the President,* p. 43.

67. See *Media Monitor,* May/June 1998 and June/July 1998.

68. Farnsworth and Lichter, *The Nightly News Nightmare,* p. 51.

69. Sam Donaldson, *Hold On, Mr. President* (New York: Random House, 1987), pp. 196–197.

70. Thomas E. Patterson, *Out of Order* (New York: Knopf, 1993), pp. 16–21, 113–115; Matthew R. Kerbel, *Edited for Television* (Boulder, CO: Westview, 1994), pp. 111–112; Kevin G. Barnhurst and Catherine A. Steele, "Image-Bite News: The Visual Coverage of Elections on U.S. Television, 1968–1992," *Press/Politics* 2, (No. 1, 1997): 40–58, S. Robert Lichter and Richard E. Noyes, *Good Intentions Make Bad News,* rev. ed. (Lanham, MD: Roman and Littlefield, 1997), pp. 116–126; Richard Nadeau, Richard G. Niemi, David P. Fan, and Timothy Amato, "Elite Economic Forecasts, Economic News, Mass Economic Judgments, and Presidential Approval," *Journal of Politics* 61 (February 1999): 109–135.

71. "Campaign 2000 Final"; Farnsworth and Lichter, *The Nightly News Nightmare,* p. 88.

72. Dwight F. Davis, Lynda Lee Kaid, and Donald L. Singleton, "Information Effects of Political Commentary," *Experimental Study of Politics* 6 (June 1977): 45–68; Lynda Lee Kaid, Donald L. Singleton, and Dwight F. Davis, "Instant Analysis of Televised Political

Addresses: The Speaker versus the Commentator," in *Communication Yearbook I,* ed. Brent D. Ruben (New Brunswick, NJ: Transaction Books, 1977), pp. 453–464; John Havick, "The Impact of a Televised State of the Union Message and the Instant Analysis: An Experiment," unpublished paper, Georgia Institute of Technology, 1980.

73. David L. Paletz and Robert M. Entman, *Media-Power-Politics* (New York: Free Press, 1981), p. 70.

74. Katherine Graham, *Personal History* (New York: Vintage, 1998).

75. See, for example, *Media Monitor,* June/July 1998.

76. Patterson, *Doing Well and Doing Good,* p. 10; Patterson, *Out of Order,* p. 20; Lichter and Noyes, *Good Intentions Make Bad News.*

77. Patterson, *Out of Order,* pp. 3–27; "Clinton's the One," *Media Monitor* 6 (November, 1992): 3–5; Lichter and Noyes, *Good Intentions Make Bad News,* chapters 6–7, especially pp. 288–299; Patterson, *Doing Well and Doing Good,* p. 10; Farnsworth and Lichter, *The Nightly News Nightmare,* pp. 114–116, 119, 130, 165, 168–169.

78. Patterson, *Doing Well and Doing Good,* pp. 10, 12.

79. *Media Monitor,* May/June 1995, pp. 2–5; Thomas E. Patterson, "Legitimate Beef: The Presidency and a Carnivorous Press," *Media Studies Journal* 8 (Spring 1994): 21–26. However, compare Andras Szanto, "In Our Opinion . . . Editorial Page Views of Clinton's First Year," *Media Studies Journal* 8 (Spring 1994): 97–105; Lichter and Noyes, *Good Intentions Make Bad News,* p. 214.

80. Patterson, *Out of Order,* p. 22, chapter 2; Cappella and Jamieson, *Spiral of Cynicism;* Jacobs and Shapiro, *Politicians Don't Pander,* p. 231.

81. Shanto Iyengar, *Is Anyone Responsible?* (Chicago: University of Chicago Press, 1991), p. 2. See also Shanto Iyengar, Mark D. Peters, and Donald R. Kinder, "Experimental Demonstrations of the 'Not-So-Minimal' Consequences of Television News Programs," *American Political Science Review* 76 (December 1982): 848–858;; Larry M. Bartels, "Messages Received: The Political Impact of Media Exposure," *American Political Science Review* 87 (June 1993): 267–285; and Dhavan V. Shah, Mark D. Watts, David Domke, David P. Fan, and Michael Fibison, "News Coverage, Economic Cues, and the Public's Presidential Preferences, 1984–1996," *Journal of Politics* 61 (November 1999): 914–943. There is also evidence that presidential approval is influenced by elite opinion, as brought to the public's attention in the mass media., See Richard A. Brody, *Assessing the President* (Stanford, CA: Stanford University Press, 1991).

82. Jon A. Krosnick and Donald R. Kinder, "Altering the Foundations of Support for the President through Priming," *American Political Science Review* 84 (June 1990): 497–512; Iyengar, *Is Anyone Responsible?* chapter 8.

83. Jon A. Krosnick and Laura A. Brannon, "The Impact of the Gulf War on the Ingredients of Presidential Evaluations: Multidimensional Effects of Political Involvement," *American Political Science Review* 87 (December 1993): 963–975. See also Shanto Iyengar and Adam Simon, "News Coverage of the Gulf Crisis and Public Opinion," in *Taken by Storm,* ed. W. Lance Bennett and David L. Paletz, (Chicago: University of Chicago Press, 1994).

84. George C. Edwards III, Andrew Barrett, and Reed Welch, "Explaining Presidential Approval: The Significance of Issue Salience," *American Journal of Political Science* 39 (February 1995): 108–134.

85. Shanto Iyengar and Donald R. Kinder, *News That Matters* (Chicago: University of Chicago Press, 1987).

86. Iyengar, Peters, and Kinder, "Experimental Demonstrations of the 'Not-So-Minimal' Consequences of Television News Programs." See also Bartels, "Messages Received."

87. Frederick T. Steeper, "Public Response to Gerald Ford's Statements on Eastern Europe in the Second Debate," in *The Presidential Debates: Media, Electoral, and Public Perspectives,* ed. George F. Bishop, Robert G. Meadow, and Marilyn Jackson-Beeck (New York: Praeger, 1978), pp. 81–101.

88. Michael J. Robinson, "News Media Myths and Realities," in *Elections in America,* ed. Kay Lehman Schlozman (Boston: Allen and Unwin, 1987), p. 149.

89. Kathleen Hall Jamieson and Paul Waldman, eds., *Electing the President 2000: The Insiders' View* (Philadelphia: University of Pennsylvania Press, 2001), pp. 5–6.

90. Thomas E. Patterson, *The Mass Media Election: How Americans Choose Their President* (New York: Praeger, 1980), pp. 84–86, 98–100, 105, chapter 2; Doris A. Graber, "Personal Qualities in Presidential Images: The Contribution of the Press," *Midwest Journal of Political Science* 16 (February 1972): 295; Doris A. Graber, *Mass Media and American Politics,* 6th ed. (Washington, DC: Congressional Quarterly Press, 2002), pp. 260–263.

91. Gerald R. Ford, *A Time to Heal: The Autobiography of Gerald R. Ford* (New York: Harper & Row, 1979), p. 289; see also pp. 343–344.

92. See Mark J. Rozell, *The Press and the Ford Presidency* (Ann Arbor: University of Michigan Press, 1992).

93. Patterson, *Out of Order,* chapter 3; Kerbel, *Edited for Television,* pp. 60–64, 88; Lichter and Noyes, *Good Intentions Make Bad News,* chapters 6–7.

94. Jacobs and Shapiro, *Politicians Don't Pander,* pp. 176–182, 214–215; Jamieson and Cappella, "The Role of the Press in the Health Care Reform Debate of 1993–1994."

95. Jacobs and Shapiro, *Politicians Don't Pander,* pp. 232–255.

96. Capella and Jamieson, *Spiral of Cynicism.*

97. Dhavan V. Shah, Mark D. Watts, David Domke, and David P. Fan, "News Framing and Cueing of Issue Regimes: Explaining Clinton's Public Approval in Spite of Scandal," *Public Opinion Quarterly* 66 (Fall 2002): 339–370.

98. Miller and Krosnick, "News Media Impact on the Ingredients of Presidential Evaluations."

99. The Pew Research Center for the People and the Press Poll, July 19–23, 2000.

100. Quoted in Bob Woodward, *The Choice* (New York: Simon & Schuster, 1996), p. 315.

Chapter 8. Receiving the Message

1. John E. Mueller, *War, Presidents, and Public Opinion* (New York: Wiley, 1973); Lyn Ragsdale, "The Politics of Presidential Speechmaking, 1949–1980," *American Political Science Review* 78 (December 1984): 971–984; Roy L. Behr and Shanto Iyengar, "Television News, Real World Cues, and Changes in the Public Agenda," *Public Opinion Quarterly* 49 (Spring 1985): 38–57; Lyn Ragsdale, "Presidential Speechmaking and the

Public Audience," *Journal of Politics* 49 (August 1987): 704–736; Dennis M. Simon and Charles W. Ostrom, "The Impact of Televised Speeches and Foreign Travel on Presidential Approval," *Public Opinion Quarterly* 53 (Spring 1989): 58–82; Paul Brace and Barbara Hinckley, "Presidential Activities from Truman through Reagan: Timing and Impact," *Journal of Politics* 55 (May 1993): 382–398; Jeffrey E. Cohen, *Presidential Responsiveness and Public Policy-Making* (Ann Arbor: University of Michigan Press, 1997).

2. Joe S. Foote, "Ratings Decline of Presidential Television," *Journal of Broadcasting and Electronic Media* 32 (Spring 1988): 225.

3. A. C. Nielsen, *Nielsen Newscast* (Northbrook, IL: Nielson, 1975).

4. Foote, "Ratings Decline of Presidential Television," pp. 227–229.

5. Gallup Poll of August 3, 1993.

6. Gallup Poll of September 3, 1993.

7. Gallup/CNN/*USA Today* Poll question, "About how much of the President's (Bill Clinton) speech on Bosnia did you happen to watch tonight—all of it, most of it, only part of it, or none of it?" (November 27, 1995). All of it: 18 percent; most of it: 8 percent; only part of it: 19 percent; none of it: 55 percent.

8. Samuel Kernell, *Going Public,* 3d ed. (Washington, DC: Congressional Quarterly Press, 1997), pp. 131–132.

9. Joe S. Foote, *Television Access and Political Power* (New York: Praeger, 1990), p. 153.

10. Nielsen Media Research, *2000 Report on Television: The First Fifty Years* (New York, 2000), pp. 12–13.

11. My thanks to Samuel Kernell for making this data available.

12. Matthew A. Baum and Samuel Kernell, "Has Cable Ended the Golden Age of Presidential Television?" *American Political Science Review* 93 (March 1999): 99–114.

13. Nielsen Media Research, *2000 Report on Television,* pp. 12–13.

14. Foote, "Ratings Decline of Presidential Television," pp. 228–229.

15. Remarks made at a forum of chiefs of staff held on June 15, 2000, at the Woodrow Wilson Center in Washington, DC.

16. Vincent Price and John Zaller, "Who Gets the News? Alternative Measures of News Reception and Their Implications for Research," *Public Opinion Quarterly* 57 (Summer 1993): 136; and Vincent Price and John Zaller, "Evaluations of Media Exposure Items in the 1989 NES Pilot Study," in *Technical Report to the National Election Studies Board of Overseers* (Ann Arbor, MI: Institute for Social Research, 1990).

17. Lisa de Moraes, "President Bush Has America Tuning In," *Washington Post,* January 21, 2002, p. C7.

18. Alex Kuczynski, "TV Viewers Want $1 Million, Not a Million Clinton Words," *New York Times,* January 29, 2000, p. A10.

19. *Washington Post,* March 1, 2001, p. C1.

20. Moraes, "President Bush Has America Tuning In."

21. Jim Rutenberg, "Speech Had Big Audience Despite Networks' Action," *New York Times,* October 9, 2002, p. A13.

22. Foote, "Ratings Decline of Presidential Television," p. 225.

23. ABC and a few CBS and NBC affiliates did not air this address. This was also the

only address in Table 7.3 that was not delivered during prime time, having begun the address at 7:30 P.M. Eastern Standard Time.

24. Reed Lynn Welch, "Tuning In or Tuning Out: The Influence of Televised Presidential Addresses on Public Opinion," unpublished Ph.D. dissertation, Texas A&M University, 1997, pp. 91–97.

25. See, for example, M. Margaret Conway, *Political Participation in the United States,* 3d ed. (Washington, DC: Congressional Quarterly Press, 2000); Melvin L. DeFleur and Sandra J. Ball-Rokeach, *Theories of Mass Communication* (New York: Longman, 1989).

26. Susan T. Fiske and Shelley E. Taylor, *Social Cognition,* 2d ed. (New York: McGraw Hill, 1991), pp. 149–152.

27. Doris A. Graber, *Processing the News,* 2d ed. (New York: Longman, 1988), p. 105.

28. See Doris A. Graber, *Mass Media and American Politics,* 6th ed. (Washington, DC: Congressional Quarterly Press, 2002), pp. 203–205, and sources cited therein.

29. Roberta Glaros and Bruce Miroff, "Watching Ronald Reagan: Viewers' Reaction to the President on Television," *Congress and the Presidency* 10 (Spring 1983): 25–46.

30. Jonathan L. Freedman and David O. Sears, "Selective Exposure," in *Advances in Experimental Social Psychology,* ed. Leonard Berkowitz (New York: Academic Press, 1965); David O. Sears and Jonathan L. Freedman, "Selective Exposure to Information: A Critical Review," *Public Opinion Quarterly* 23 (Summer 1967): 194–213; John L. Cotton, "Cognitive Dissonance in Selective Exposure," in *Selective Exposure to Communication,* ed. Dolf Zillman and Jennings Bryant (Hillsdale, NJ: Lawrence Erlbaum Associates, 1985); Lewis Donohew and Philip Palmgreen, "A Reappraisal of Dissonance and the Selective Exposure Hypothesis," *Journalism Quarterly* 48 (Autumn 1971): 412–420; William J. McGuire, "Personality and Susceptibility to Social Influence," in *Handbook of Personality Theory and Research,* ed. Edgar F. Borgatta and W. W. Lambert (Chicago: Rand-McNally, 1968); Robert A. Wicklund and Jack Brehm, *Perspectives on Cognitive Dissonance* (Hillsdale, NJ: Erlbaum, 1976); Diana C. Mutz and Paul S. Martin, "Facilitating Communication across Lines of Political Difference: The Role of Mass Media," *American Political Science Review* 95 (March 2001): 97–114.

31. Daniel J. O'Keefe, *Persuasion: Theory and Research* (Newbury Park, CA: Sage Publications, 1990).

32. Graber, *Mass Media and American Politics,* p. 206.

33. The speeches for which we lack the relevant data are April 29, 1982, and September 14, 1986.

34. See, for example, John Condry, *The Psychology of Television* (Hillsdale, NJ: Lawrence Erlbaum Associates, 1989), pp. 38–39.

35. Doris A. Graber, *Mass Media and American Politics,* 5th ed. (Washington, DC: Congressional Quarterly Press, 1997), p. 195.

36. Reed L. Welch, "Is Anybody Watching?: The Audience for Televised Presidential Addresses," *Congress and the Presidency* 27 (Spring 2000): 41–58.

37. Alexis S. Tan, "Media Use, Issue Knowledge and Political Involvement," *Public Opinion Quarterly* 44 (Summer 1980): 241–248; and Jan Leighley, "Participation as a Stimulus of Political Conceptualization," *Journal of Politics* 53 (February 1991): 198–211.

38. Welch, "Is Anybody Watching?"

39. James G. Webster and Jacob Wakshlag, "Measuring Exposure to Television," in *Selective Exposure to Communication,* ed. Dolf Zillman and Jennings Bryant (Hillsdale, NJ: Lawrence Erlbaum Associates, 1985).

40. See also Vincent Price and John Zaller, "Who Gets the News?," pp. 133–164.

41. Reid Hastie and Bernadette Park, "The Relationship between Memory and Judgments Depends on Whether the Task Is Memory-Based or On-Line," *Psychological Review* 93 (July 1986): 258–268; Reid Hastie and Nancy Pennington, "Notes on the Distinction between Memory-Based Versus On-Line Judgments," in *On-Line Cognition in Person Perception,* ed. John N. Bassili (Hillsdale, NJ: Lawrence Erlbaum Associates, 1989); Milton Lodge, Marco R. Steenbergen, and Shawn Brau, "The Responsive Voter: Campaign Information and the Dynamics of Candidate Evaluation," *American Political Science Review* 89 (June 1995): 309–326; Meryl Lichtenstein and Thomas Srull, "Processing Objectives as a Determinant of the Relationship Between Recall and Judgment," *Journal of Experimental Social Psychology* 23 (March 1987): 93–118; Kathleen M. McGraw and Neil Pinney, "The Effects of General and Domain-Specific Expertise on Political Memory and Judgment," *Social Cognition* 8 (Spring 1990): 9–30.

42. Lodge, Steenbergen, and Brau, "The Responsive Voter."

43. Michael X. Delli Carpini and Scott Keeter, *What Americans Know About Politics and Why it Matters* (New Haven, CT: Yale University Press, 1996); Alan I. Abramowitz, "Name Familiarity, Reputation, and the Incumbency Effect in a Congressional Election," *Western Political Quarterly* 28 (December 1975): 668–684; W. Russell Neuman, *The Paradox of Mass Politics: Knowledge and Opinion in the American Electorate* (Cambridge, MA: Harvard University Press, 1986).

44. Jon K. Dalager, "Voters, Issues, and Elections: Are the Candidates' Messages Getting Through?" *Journal of Politics* 58 (May 1996): 486–515.

45. Welch, "Tuning In or Tuning Out," chapters 7–8.

46. Frank Biocca, "Viewers' Mental Models of Political Messages: Toward a Theory of the Semantic Processing of Television," in *Television and Political Advertising,* ed. Frank Biocca (Hillsdale, NJ: Lawrence Erlbaum Associates, 1991), p. 29.

47. See, for example, John P. Robinson and Mark R. Levy, *The Main Source: Learning from Television News* (Beverly Hills, CA: Sage, 1986); Phillip J. Tichenor, George A. Donohue, and Clarice N. Olien, "Mass Media Flow and Differential Growth in Knowledge," *Public Opinion Quarterly* 34 (Summer 1970): 159–170; Dalager, "Voters, Issues, and Elections."

48. Price and Zaller, "Who Gets the News?"; Stephen E. Bennett, "Know-nothings Revisited: The Meaning of Political Ignorance Today," *Social Science Quarterly* 69 (June 1988): 476–490; Robinson and Levy, *The Main Source.*

49. Philip E. Converse, "Public Opinion and Voting Behavior," in *The Handbook of Political Science,* Vol. 1, ed. Fred I. Greenstein and Nelson Polsby (Reading, MA: Addison-Wesley, 1975), p. 97.

50. Milton Lodge, Kathleen M. McGraw, Pamela Johnston Conover, Stanley Feldman, and Arthur H. Miller, "Where is the Schema? Critiques," *American Political Science Review* 85 (December 1991): 1357–1380; Susan T. Fiske and Donald R. Kinder, "Involvement, Expertise, and Schema Use: Evidence from Political Cognition," in *Person-*

ality, Cognition, and Social Interaction, ed. Nancy Cantor and John F. Kihlstrom (Hillsdale, NJ: Lawrence Erlbaum Associates, 1981); Hazel Markus and Robert B. Zajonc, "The Cognitive Perspective in Social Psychology," in *Theory and Method,* 3d ed., ed. Gardner Lindzey and Elliot Aronson (New York: Random House, 1985); Susan T. Fiske, Donald R. Kinder, and W. Michael Larter, "The Novice and the Expert: Knowledge-Based Strategies in Political Cognition," *Journal of Experimental and Social Psychology* 19 (July 1983): 381–400.

51. Gregory S. Andriate and Michael J. Beatty, "Cognitive Complexity and Cognitive Backlog in Human Information Processing," in *Information and Behavior,* ed. Brent Ruben (New Brunswick, NJ: Transaction, 1988); Victor C. Ottati and Robert S. Wyer, "The Cognitive Mediators of Political Choice: Toward a Comprehensive Model of Political Information Processing," in *Information and Democratic Processes,* ed. John A. Ferejohn and James H. Kuklinski (Chicago: University of Illinois Press, 1990), p. 209. See also Fiske, Kinder, and Larter, "The Novice and the Expert."

52. Richard T. Petty and John E. Cacioppo, *Communication and Persuasion* (New York: Springer, 1986); Thomas E. Nelson, Rosalee A. Clawson, and Zoë M. Oxley, "Toward a Psychology of Framing Effects," *Political Behavior* 19 (September 1997): 221–246.

53. Larry M. Bartels, "Post-Cold War Defense Spending Preferences," *Public Opinion Quarterly* 58 (Winter 1994): 479–508; Philip E. Converse, "Information Flows and the Stability of Partisan Attitudes," *Public Opinion Quarterly* 26 (Winter 1962): 578–599; John A. Krosnick and Laura A. Brannon, "The Impact of the Gulf War on the Ingredients of Presidential Evaluation: Multidimensional Effects of Political Involvement," *American Political Science Review* 87 (December 1993): 963–975; John R. Zaller, *The Nature of Mass Opinion* (Cambridge: Cambridge University Press, 1992); John Zaller, "Elite Leadership of Mass Opinion: New Evidence from the Gulf War," in *Taken by Storm: The Media, Public Opinion, and U.S. Foreign Policy in the Gulf War,* ed. W. Lance Bennett and David L. Paletz (Chicago: University of Chicago Press, 1994), pp. 186–209.

54. Jeffrey W. Koch, "Political Rhetoric and Political Persuasion: The Changing Structure of Citizens' Preferences on Health Insurance During Policy Debate," *Public Opinion Quarterly* 62 (Summer 1998): 209–229.

55. Foote, *Television Access and Political Power,* pp. 60, 67–68.

56. Foote, *Television Access and Political Power,* pp. 67–68.

57. Foote, *Television Access and Political Power,* pp. 65–66, 68, 86–90.

58. Foote, *Television Access and Political Power,* pp. 87–88.

59. Foote, *Television Access and Political Power,* pp. 68, 86–90.

60. Interview with Marlin Fitzwater, March 5, 2001.

61. Ann Devroy and Eric Pianin, "Clinton Offers Balanced Budget Plan; Preserving Education, Controlling Medicare Are Priorities in 10-Year Program," *Washington Post,* June 14, 1995, p. A1.

62. Michael Waldman, *POTUS Speaks* (New York: Simon & Schuster, 2000), p. 267.

63. The Project for Excellence in Journalism, *The First 100 Days: How Bush Versus Clinton Fared In the Press* (2001).

64. Waldman, *POTUS Speaks,* p. 268.

Chapter 9. Accepting the Message

1. See, for example, James A. Stimson, *Public Opinion in America: Moods, Cycles, and Swings* (Boulder, CO: Westview, 1991); Benjamin I. Page and Robert Y. Shapiro, *The Rational Public* (Chicago: University of Chicago Press, 1992); William G. Mayer, *The Changing American Mind* (Ann Arbor: University of Michigan Press, 1992); Tom W. Smith, "Liberal and Conservative Trends in the United States Since World War II," *Public Opinion Quarterly* 54 (Winter 1990): 479–507; James H. Kuklinski and Gary Segura, "Of Endogeneity, Exogeneity, Time, and Space: Public Opinion and Political Representation," *Legislative Studies Quarterly* 20 (January 1995): 3–22; Christopher H. Achen, "Mass Political Attitudes and the Survey Response," *American Political Science Review* 69 (December 1975): 1218–1231; Robert S. Erikson, "The SRC Panel Data and Mass Political Attitudes," *British Journal of Political Science* 9 (January 1979): 89–114.

2. David O. Sears and Carolyn L. Funk, "Evidence of the Long-Term Persistence of Adults' Political Predispositions," *Journal of Politics* 61 (February 1999): 1–28.

3. John R. Zaller, *The Nature and Origins of Mass Opinion* (New York: Cambridge University Press, 1992), p. 44.

4. Richard R. Lau, Richard A. Smith, and Susan T. Fiske, "Political Beliefs, Policy Interpretations, and Political Persuasion," *Journal of Politics* 53 (August 1991): 644–675.

5. See, for example, Sidney Kraus and Dennis Davis, *The Effects of Mass Communication on Political Behavior* (University Park: Pennsylvania State University Press, 1976); Leon Festinger, *A Theory of Cognitive Dissonance* (Evanston, IL: Row, Peterson, 1957); Jack W. Brehm and Arthur C. Cohen, *Explorations in Cognitive Dissonance* (New York: Wiley, 1962); John S. Steinbruner, *The Cybernetic Theory of Decision* (Princeton, NJ: Princeton University Press, 1974), chapter 4.

6. Susan T. Fiske and Shelley E. Taylor, *Social Cognition*, 2d ed. (New York: McGraw Hill, 1991), pp. 149–152.

7. See Zaller, *The Nature and Origins of Mass Opinion*, p. 59, for a broader version of this argument.

8. The seminal work on perceptual screening is Bernard R. Berelson, Paul F. Lazerfeld, and William N. McPhee, *Voting: A Study of Opinion Formation in a Presidential Campaign* (Chicago: University of Chicago Press, 1954). See also Benjamin I. Page, *Choices and Echoes in Presidential Elections: Rational Man and Electoral Democracy* (Chicago: University of Chicago Press, 1978), pp. 184–186.

9. See Morris P. Fiorina, *Retrospective Voting in American National Elections* (New Haven, CT: Yale University Press, 1981), for a discussion of party identification being at least partly a result of retrospective evaluations of party performance. Research has not focused directly on this question, but there is also some support for the argument that party identification is at least partially a response to evaluations of public policy. See, for example, Fiorina, *Retrospective Voting in American National Elections;* Benjamin I. Page and Calvin C. Jones, "Reciprocal Effects of Policy Preferences, Party Loyalty, and the Vote," *American Political Science Review* 73 (December 1980), 1071–1089; Gregory B. Markus, "Political Attitudes During an Election Year: A Report on the 1980 NES Panel," *American Political Science Review* 76 (September 1982): 538–560; Charles H. Franklin

and John E. Jackson, "The Dynamics of Party Identification," *American Political Science Review* 77 (December 1983): 957–973.

10. Philip E. Converse and George Dupeux, "De Gaulle and Eisenhower: The Public Image of the Victorious General," in *Elections in the Political Order,* Angus Campbell, Philip E. Converse, Warren E. Miller, and Donald E. Stokes (New York: Wiley, 1966), pp. 324–325.

11. The averages may be influenced by the number of polls taken during a given period. For example, if more polls were taken during a portion of the year when the president was high in the polls than when he was lower, his average for the year might be inflated. I have controlled for this problem by averaging the polls for each month before computing a yearly average.

12. Martin P. Wattenberg, *The Decline of American Political Parties, 1952–1996* (Cambridge, MA: Harvard University Press, 1998); Thomas M. Konda and Lee Sigelman, "Public Evaluations of the American Parties, 1952–1984," *Journal of Politics* 49 (August 1987): 814–829.

13. Marc J. Hetherington, "Resurgent Mass Partisanship: The Role of Elite Polarization," *American Political Science Review* 95 (September 2001): 619–631; Larry M. Bartels, "Partisanship and Voting Behavior, 1952–1996," *American Journal of Political Science* 44 (January 2000): 35–50; Stephen C. Craig, "The Decline of Partisanship in the United States: A Reexamination of the Neutrality Hypothesis," *Political Behavior* 7 (No. 1, 1985): 57–78; John E. Stanga and James F. Sheffield, "The Myth of Zero Partisanship: Attitudes toward American Political Parties, 1964–84," *American Journal of Political Science* 31 (November 1987): 829–855; and Raymond E. Wolfinger, "Dealignment, Realignment, and Mandates in the 1984 Election," in *The American Election of 1984,* ed. Austin Ranney (Durham, NC: Duke University Press, 1985). Other research finding an important effect of party identification on candidate evaluation includes Charles W. Ostrom, Jr., and Dennis M. Simon, "The President's Public," *American Journal of Political Science* 32 (November 1988): 1096–1119. See also Angus Campbell, Philip E. Converse, Warren E. Miller, and Donald E. Stokes, *The American Voter* (New York: Wiley, 1964), chapter 5; and Roberta S. Sigel, "Effect of Partisanship on the Perception of Political Candidates," *Public Opinion Quarterly* 28 (Fall 1964): 483–496.

14. Bruce E. Keith, David B. Magleby, Candice Nelson, Elizabeth Orr, Mark C. Westlye, and Raymond E. Wolfinger, *The Myth of the Independent Voter* (Berkeley: University of California Press, 1992).

15. See Mark Peffley, Stanley Feldman, and Lee Sigelman, "Economic Conditions and Party Competence: Processes of Belief and Revision," *Journal of Politics* 49 (February 1987): 100–121, for evidence that prior beliefs and partisanship minimize the effects of new information on views of party competence in handling the economy.

16. Robert S. Erikson, Michael B. MacKuen, and James A. Stimson, *The Macro Polity* (New York: Cambridge University Press, 2002), chapter 9.

17. Erikson, MacKuen, and Stimson, *The Macro Polity,* pp. 344, 374.

18. Christopher Wlezien, "The Public as a Thermostat: Dynamics of Preferences for Spending," *American Journal of Political Science* 39 (November 1995): 981–1000; Christopher Wlezien, "Dynamics of Representation: The Case of U.S. Spending on Defense," *British Journal of Political Science* 26 (January 1996): 81–103.

19. David Kahneman and Amos Tversky, "Prospect Theory: An Analysis of Decision Under Risk," *Econometrica* 47 (March 1979): 263–292; David Kahneman and Amos Tversky, "Choices, Values, and Frames," *American Psychologist* 39 (April 1984): 341–350.

20. David L. Hamilton and Mark P. Zanna, "Differential Weighting of Favorable and Unfavorable Attributes in Impressions of Personality," *Journal of Experimental Research in Personality* 6 (Nos. 2–3, 1972): 204–212; Susan T. Fiske, "Attention and Weight in Person Perception: The Impact of Negative and Extreme Behavior," *Journal of Personality and Social Psychology* 38 (No. 6, 1980): 889–906.

21. Richard Lau, "Two Explanations for Negativity Effects in Political Behavior," *American Journal of Political Science* 29 (February 1985): 119–138.

22. Joseph N. Cappella and Kathleen Hall Jamieson, *Spiral of Cynicism: The Press and the Public Good* (New York: Oxford University Press, 1997).

23. Michael D. Cobb and James H. Kuklinski, "Changing Minds: Political Arguments and Political Persuasion," *American Journal of Political Science* 41 (January 1997): 88–121.

24. Cobb and Kuklinski, "Changing Minds: Political Arguments and Political Persuasion."

25. On the role of emotion in political decision making, see George E. Marcus, W. Russell Neuman, and Michael MacKuen, *Affective Intelligence and Political Judgment* (Chicago: University of Chicago Press, 2000).

26. Page and Shapiro, *The Rational Public,* chapter 7; Erikson, MacKuen, and Stimson, *The Macro Polity,* pp. 219, 369.

27. See George C. Edwards III and Tami Swenson, "Who Rallies? The Anatomy of a Rally Event," *Journal of Politics* 59 (February 1997): 200–212.

Chapter 10. Going Public in Perspective

1. For example, the author of a recent and important work on the effect of presidential campaigns found that they affect the vote by about 4 percentage points. See James E. Campbell, *The American Campaign: U.S. Presidential Campaigns and the National Vote* (College Station: Texas A&M University Press, 2000).

2. See James David Barber, *The Presidential Character,* 4th ed. (Englewood Cliffs, NJ: Prentice Hall, 1992).

3. Richard Hofstadter, *The American Political Tradition* (New York: Vintage, 1954), p. 316.

4. See, for example, Jeffrey K. Tulis, *The Rhetorical Presidency* (Princeton, NJ: Princeton University Press, 1987), pp. 179–180; David Zarefsky, *President Johnson's War on Poverty* (University: University of Alabama Press, 1986).

5. See George C. Edwards III and Stephen J. Wayne, *Presidential Leadership,* 6th ed. (Boston: Wadsworth, 2002), chapter 5.

6. Michael B. Grossman and Martha J. Kumar, *Portraying the President* (Baltimore, MD: Johns Hopkins University Press, 1981); John A. Maltese, *Spin Control: The White House Office of Communications and the Management of Presidential News* (Chapel Hill: University of North Carolina Press, 1992); Mark J. Rozell, *The Press and the Ford Presidency* (Ann Arbor: University of Michigan Press, 1992); Mark J. Rozell, *The Press and the Bush Presidency* (Westport, CT: Praeger, 1996).

7. George C. Edwards III and B. Dan Wood, "Who Influences Whom? The President, Congress, and the Media," *American Political Science Review* 93 (June 1999): 327–344.

8. George C. Edwards III and Andrew Barrett "Presidential Agenda Setting in Congress," in *Polarized Politics: Congress and the President in a Partisan Era,* ed. Jon R. Bond and Richard Fleisher (Washington, DC: Congressional Quarterly Press, 2000).

9. Jeffrey E. Cohen, *Presidential Responsiveness and Public Policy-Making* (Ann Arbor: University of Michigan Press, 1997).

10. Kim Quaile Hill, "The Policy Agenda of the President and the Mass Public: A Research Validation and Extension," *American Journal of Political Science* 41 (October 1998): 1328–1334.

11. Andrew Barrett, "Gone Public: The Impact of Presidential Rhetoric in Congress," unpublished Ph.D. dissertation, Texas A&M University, 2000.

12. Matthew Eshbaugh-Soha, "Signaling Influence," unpublished Ph.D. dissertation, Texas A&M University, 2002.

13. E. H. Carr, *Conditions of Peace* (New York: Macmillan, 1942), p. 6.

14. Kathryn Dunn Tenpas, "Promoting President Clinton's Policy Agenda: DNC as Presidential Lobbyist," *American Review of Politics* 17 (Fall/Winter 1996): 287–293.

15. Anthony Corrado, "Giving, Spending, and 'Soft Money,'" *Journal of Law and Policy* 6 (No. 1, 1997): 51–52.

16. For more on groups in the permanent campaign, see Burdett Loomis, "The Never Ending Story: Campaigns without Elections," in *The Permanent Campaign and Its Future,* ed. Norman Ornstein and Thomas Mann (Washington, DC: American Enterprise Institute and Brookings Institution, 2000), pp. 162–184.

17. Hugh Heclo, "Campaigning and Governing: A Conspectus" in *The Permanent Campaign and Its Future,* ed. Norman Ornstein and Thomas Mann (Washington, DC: American Enterprise Institute and Brookings Institution, 2000), pp. 11–15, 34.

18. David Brady and Morris Fiorina, "Congress in the Era of the Permanent Campaign," in *The Permanent Campaign and Its Future,* ed. Norman Ornstein and Thomas Mann (Washington, DC: American Enterprise Institute and Brookings Institution, 2000), p. 156.

19. Norman J. Ornstein and Thomas E. Mann, "Conclusion: The Permanent Campaign and the Future of American Democracy," in *The Permanent Campaign and Its Future,* ed. Norman Ornstein and Thomas Mann (Washington, DC: American Enterprise Institute and Brookings Institution, 2000), p. 225.

20. James MacGregor Burns, *Roosevelt: The Lion and the Fox* (New York: Harcourt, Brace and World, 1956), pp. 166–168.

21. Burns, *Roosevelt,* p. 168.

22. Quoted in Jack Valenti, *A Very Human President* (New York: W. W. Norton, 1975), p. 144. See also Doris Kearns, *Lyndon Johnson and the American Dream* (New York: Harper & Row, 1976), pp. 216–217; Eric F. Goldman, *The Tragedy of Lyndon Johnson* (New York: Dell, 1974), pp. 306–307; Harry McPherson, *A Political Education* (Boston: Little, Brown, 1972), pp. 268, 428.

23. Lyndon B. Johnson, *The Vantage Point* (New York: Popular Library, 1971), p. 323. See also Goldman, *The Tragedy of Lyndon Johnson,* pp. 306–307.

24. Quoted in McPherson, *A Political Education,* pp. 267–268.

Index